D0916752

The Online Catalog

The Online Catalog

A CRITICAL EXAMINATION
OF PUBLIC USE

by

Thomas A. Peters

McFarland & Company, Inc., Publishers
Jefferson, North Carolina, and London

British Library Cataloguing-in-Publication data are available

Library of Congress Cataloguing-in-Publication Data

Peters, Thomas A., 1957–
    The online catalog : a critical examination of public use / by
Thomas A. Peters.
        p.   cm.
    Includes bibliographical references (p. 247) and index.
    ISBN 0-89950-600-3 (lib. bdg. : 50# alk. paper) ⊗
    1. Catalogs, On-line—Use studies.   2. On-line bibliographic
searching.   3. Library catalogs and readers.   I. Title.
Z699.35.C38P47   1991
025.3'132—dc20   90-53602
                                                              CIP

©1991 Thomas A. Peters. All rights reserved

Manufactured in the United States of America

McFarland & Company, Inc., Publishers
  Box 611, Jefferson, North Carolina 28640

To my three girlfriends,
Vicki, Maria, and Libby

Acknowledgments

I thank the University of Missouri for granting me a development leave to work on the research presented in this book. My colleagues at the Miller Nichols Library at the University of Missouri–Kansas City supported this project in innumerable ways, especially Martin Kurth, who shared with me many of his concerns about online catalogs, subject access, and transaction log analysis. Discussions with other members of the nascent Remote Users Research Group such as Sally Kalin, Neal Kaske, and Beth Sandore stimulated my thinking about remote users.

The friendly staff of the Interlibrary Loan office at the Miller Nichols Library quickly obtained copies of all the documents I needed. The University of Missouri Office of Library Systems, particularly George Rickerson and Kurt Kopp, have been generous and supportive in providing me with printouts of the transaction log data used in the research project. George Rickerson also provided helpful comments on earlier drafts of this book and the research projects leading up to it. The McFarland editorial staff has been encouraging throughout the project. Finally, I would like to thank my wife for her support and patience. I am responsible for all remaining errors.

Contents

Abbreviations

ARL	Association of Research Libraries
BITNET	Because It's Time Network
BRS	Bibliographic Retrieval Services, a commercial online database vendor
CARL	Colorado Alliance of Research Libraries
CD-ROM	Compact Disk Read-Only Memory
CIP	Cataloging in Publication
CLR	Council on Library Resources
COM	Computer Output Microform
CPU	Central Process Unit
DDC	Dewey Decimal Classification
DIALOG	a commercial online database vendor
EPIC	a commercial online database vendor
ISBN	International Standard Book Number
ISIS	Integrated Scholarly Information Systems
ITC	Information Technology Center
LC	Library of Congress
LCS	Library Computer System at the University of Illinois
LCSH	*Library of Congress Subject Headings*
LUMIN	Libraries of the University of Missouri Information System
MARC	Machine-Readable Cataloging
MARO	Machine-Readable Output
MELVYL	the online catalog system of the University of California
MicroLIAS	personal computer bibliographic software to be used with LIAS (Library Information Access System), the online catalog at Penn State University

MSUS/PALS	Minnesota State Universities System Project for Automated Library Systems
NLM	National Library of Medicine
OCLC	Online Computer Library Center, formerly the Ohio College Library Center, a bibliographic utility
OKAPI	the online catalog of the Polytechnic of Central London
OPAC	Online Public Access Catalog
PACS-L	Public Access Computer Systems List, an electronic conference on BITNET
PCBIS	personal computer bibliographic software to be used with TRLN, the online catalog system of Triangle Research Network Libraries
RLIN	Research Libraries Information Network
SDC	System Development Corporation, a commercial online database vendor
SDI	Selective Dissemination of Information
SSS	Search Session Starts
SULIRS	Syracuse University Libraries Information Retrieval System
TS	Total Searches
UDES	Unique Data-Entry Searches
UTLAS	a bibliographic utility, formerly the University of Toronto Library Automation System
VTLS	Virginia Technical Library System
WLN	Western Library Network, formerly the Washington Library Network

Tables and Graphs

Tables

Graphs

Chapter 1

Introduction and History of Online Catalogs

Introduction

What possibly could be wrong with online catalogs? By most counts, they are a vast improvement over earlier forms of the library catalog, especially the card catalog—the dominant catalog form for the last century. In about two decades they have reached a mature state of reliable functioning. The third generation of online catalog systems approaches. As a technological device, the online catalog has achieved wide user acceptance and approval.

Modern technology always has projected great promise. The development of the online catalog—a particular instance of modern computer and telecommunications technology—has participated in projecting that feeling. With an acceleration of technological development coupled with increasing funding, it seems that the problems of the storage and retrieval of bibliographic information can be solved. In order to gain bibliographic control over the increasing output of scholarly information, computer technology seems to be the best means to that end. Computer technology was developed just in time to harness the power of the information explosion.

The users of online catalogs, however, remain a question and a problem. Early online catalog use studies determined the acceptance of online catalogs by public users, but few studied the dynamics of actual use. It was revealed that most users reportedly liked the new catalog form, but it could not be discovered how they were actually using the online catalog. Because the evolution of user behavior was not traced from the beginning of the development of online catalogs, information professionals now find themselves in the midst of a revolution in online catalog user behavior. Users are expecting the library catalog to do more than it has ever done. User interest seems to be slowly moving away from the type of information normally contained in bibliographic records for books. In one direction they want access to expanded bibliographic information, such as tables of contents, citations within the text, and keywords from book indices. This direction of user interest culminates in the desire to have the full text of all documents available online. The vision of fully automated textual information—libraries on computer chips—has been a controlling image of this technological advance. If full text becomes available online, the need for separate library catalogs would cease. The catalog would become the collection, and the collection would become the catalog. These users want the process of identifying, locating, and retrieving a document to become completely automated.

In another direction, users are becoming more interested in local holdings information, circulation information, and other information not typically found in a library catalog. Many online catalogs offer users the ability to verify the local status of items without having to consult a member of the library staff. The culmination of this area of user demand is a completely self-service library, where checkouts, holds, interlibrary loan requests, reference questions, and similar tasks are managed by the automated library system. These users accept the role of the library in the overall flow of information, and they want the online catalog to include more library services.

The role of users within information storage and retrieval systems has engendered much research and debate. Of course, the user is an important component in the use of online catalogs, but perhaps research has focused too much on the attitudes, skills, and reactions of users. The impact studies undertaken tended to try to determine if most users liked the new catalog format. It became a natural next step to try to discover the demographic characteristics of those users (and nonusers) who liked and disliked the catalog.

One motivating idea of this book is that the use, not the users, needs to be understood first. One vision of online catalog research sees users (especially the demographic characteristics of various user groups) as so much red herring. This book will focus on actual user behavior and the theoretical implications of online catalogs, especially regarding the use of remote access.

It is time to take the online catalog seriously, more seriously than in the past. The online catalog is still searching for a useful context. Professional interest in online catalogs has various sources. Some people study online catalog systems in order to purchase one. They want to learn about online catalog systems so that they can write intelligent, comprehensive requests for proposals. Others see online catalogs as the leading edge of technological innovation in libraries. They follow online catalog developments to keep up with the current technological trends and to anticipate the future.

This book is written with other interests in mind. It is intended for the reader who wants to understand the online catalog in a broad context as a technological device. The online catalog finally is coming into its own as a unique and promising catalog form, but by doing so it has raised questions about the viability of the library catalog and the identity of the library. The troubling questions about online catalogs are not technological and economic, but philosophical, pedagogical, and ethical. Librarians and librarianship perhaps suffer from a certain naiveté about technological tools, devices, and systems. Popular perceptions of technology underlie many professional reports about technology in libraries. Online catalogs often are understood as mere tools. The online catalog has yet to be fully appreciated, both by public users and by professional intermediaries, as a new technological device.

Two observations motivate this book. First, most of the literature that passes for studies of catalog use are, in fact, not that but studies of user attitudes, usually gathered via the method of the self-administered questionnaire. Research into online catalog use finally is broadening its horizons. The possibilities opened up by transaction log analysis will receive much attention in this book.

Second, a new type of online catalog use (other than in-house staff use and in-house public access use) is emerging: remote access. Remote access to online catalogs may be the first stage in a new era in academic librarianship. Remote access will affect the structure, usage, economics, and politics of academic libraries. Until remote access became possible, all public users of libraries had one thing in common. They all had to come to the library to use it.[1] As the ways and means of bringing information to the workplace continue to expand and improve, libraries and other information intermediaries will need to reexamine their essential functions.

Librarianship and Technology

In order to think about online catalogs, their purpose, and their use, we must broaden our horizons a little and think briefly about the place of libraries and technology in our society. Albert Borgmann, a prominent philosopher of technology, has noted that technology becomes most concrete and evident in technological devices (Borgmann, 1984; 3). One purpose of this book is to critically examine online catalogs and their use in the light of these broader concerns. Evidence of the use of online catalogs provides a working lab for testing and exploring some of the main ideas of the philosophy of technology.

There has been a debate going on for some time in the information profession regarding the relationship between libraries and technological innovation. Libraries and society generally find themselves in a double bind when it comes to the implementation of technology and its effects on everything else. Perhaps it is the nature of technological advance that we cannot determine the manner in which the technological innovation will be utilized until it is actually used in real settings. However, once a technological innovation has been used in real situations, it is difficult or impossible, for a combination of reasons, to decide to remove the technology and go back to the old methods. Langdon Winner (1986), another commentator on modern technology, calls this bind "technological determinism." All technological innovation is a Pandora's box, unleashing we know not what until it has been released. Online catalogs are a technological innovation in libraries producing profound effects on many aspects of the profession, from the thoroughly practical to the entirely theoretical and alarmingly ethical.

The adoption of technology by society is generally divided into three stages. The first stage focuses on the mechanization of established procedures to realize greater efficiencies and productivity. During the second stage, procedures change because new tasks can be accomplished through automation. In the final stage, society and its institutions change. Library automation is still in the first stage—mere mechanization (Morris, 1989; 58). Before the novelty of online catalogs as a format for the library catalog wears off, we need to think about what the development and implementation of online catalogs have meant for library and scholarly processes.

Some writers argue that libraries have been exemplary in their implementation of new technologies. Just the right mix of professional enthusiasm and skepticism is evident. Budgetary constraints have been salutary in this respect, because they have kept many libraries from advancing too quickly. Libraries as a whole have followed the prudent middle path between the wild enthusiasm of technology enthusiasts and the reactionary resistance of neo–Luddites.

Other commentators disagree. They argue that librarianship as a whole has missed the whole point and many of the possibilities of the new technologies. In the past, libraries have used the technology mainly to automate the existing workload and to maintain the existing organizational structure. Automation has made things easier but not, as yet, fundamentally different (Molholt, 1985; 285). Some writers, such as Bryan Pfaffenberger (1990), suggest that librarians as a group are akin to the nineteenth-century Luddites, differing from their more violent cousins only regarding methods, not mission. Josie-Marie Griffiths is one of the many writers who think the library profession as a whole tends to view the potential of the new technologies too narrowly (Drabenstott, 1988; 107).

Librarians may have misperceived the importance of technological advances by making the automated tool itself a matter of concern and debate. An online catalog, these arguments frequently state, is in principle no different than a hammer or other simple tool. If the tool helps you complete the task, it is good and worthwhile. If not, it should be changed or abandoned. Libraries should not make technology the issue. Technological devices are tools to be employed for the benefit of users in the attainment of the service and process objectives of the library (Lee Jones, 1984; 152). The tone of nonchalance found in this argument rarely recurs during actual library automation projects. In a later chapter this attitude toward online catalogs as mere tools will be shown to be based on a prereflective notion of the meaning of technology.

What exactly is the relationship between librarianship and technology? What should it be? Is technological innovation the cause and librarianship the effect? Perhaps the automation of the various stages in the flow of information will produce radical changes in the mission of the library. Are the tools of advancing technology the same as the simple tools studied by grade school students—the hammer, the block and tackle, and the inclined plane? Have professional librarians ever decided not to accept a new technology? If not, if we are controlled by "technological determinism" (Winner, 1986; 9), why even bother to think about online catalogs and try to understand them better?

Online Catalogs and the Philosophy of Technology

Online catalogs certainly function in different contexts, and they can also be evaluated in different contexts. The context of the development of the library catalog, of computerization and human adaptation to the new era, and of all modern technological advances and the underlying premises that support modern technology all can provide points of reference during the evaluation process. Most commentators without reflection (or at least in an unexplicit fashion) choose to evaluate online catalogs within the first context. The middle context has increasingly gained attention. For example, Charles Hildreth (1982; 33) states that "online catalogs represent a special application of interactive computer systems, and the searching of an online catalog is a subset of human interaction with computers." Although it is often stated that online catalogs are designed and intended for a variety of users, online catalogs have not been accepted to the extent of the telephone or the television, so scholars and researchers do not consider online catalogs in broader contexts.

The meaning and importance of libraries and technology in general has at least some influence on the meaning of online catalogs for public users and the profession. As some of the tenets and key concerns of the philosophy of technology are reviewed, what is known about online catalogs and users' behavior and attitudes may provide good sounding boards to test the principles of an emerging philosophy of technology.

In the literature on online catalogs published to date, writers tend to take a rather narrow view of online catalogs. Sometimes the impact of online catalogs on users and the organizational structure will be predicted or studied, but rarely is the online catalog placed in a broader category of technological devices that are changing the rules and behavior patterns of modern human communication. Equally rare are investigations of the implications of online catalogs for the structure of information generation, storage, and retrieval—the entire life cycle of recorded scholarly information.

Separation of process and product. Albert Borgmann (1984; 4) suggests that the division between the commodity produced and the productive machinery is the distinctive feature of the modern technological device. The product is provided to the consumer without requiring the consumer to have much knowledge about the necessary processes in obtaining the product. This characteristic of online catalogs was noted fairly early in their development. In 1978 Goldstein and Ford, for example, stated that the new technology allows the bibliographic retrieval operations to be separated from the format (interface) presented to the user (Hildreth, 1982; 70). In essence, with online catalogs the interface presented to the user often has little or nothing to do with the actual processing going on behind the scenes. This fact has important implications for the use of online catalogs. The catalog no longer is required to appear onstage before the user group.

If the online catalog has separated product from process in ways other catalog forms do not, philosophical and psychological (perceptual) issues are involved. Online catalog researchers and developers apparently see nothing wrong with this trend, but philosophers of technology are more cautious. In an extrapolation and inversion of the Marxist sense of alienated labor, users of new technological systems are alienated users. Whereas workers are alienated from the fruit of their labor, users of modern technological devices rarely see and appreciate the labor behind the fruit. Borgmann (1984; 4) suggests that the rule of the device paradigm endangers the focal concerns in our lives. People do not gather around modern furnaces in the same way they used to gather in front of the hearth. Similarly, the online catalog is not a focal point for the institution and the user in the same way card catalogs were. Remote access probably will change how the catalog and the library are perceived by remote public users.

Stumbling Blocks to Getting Started with the Topic

Some formidable stumbling blocks exist when embarking on an examination of the meaning of online catalogs. The situational imperative is such that it seems pointless to begin examining the implications of this new type of catalog.

Online catalogs are book catalogs only. Two very good reasons exist for not even considering the subject of this book. First, even though the rumors of the death of the book have been premature, the book as a vehicle for the transmission of ideas seems to be losing some of its market share. Since online catalogs are closely allied to collections of books, one must wonder if the future costs of further development of online catalogs would be prudent and justifiable. Some critics argue that online catalog systems already sap too much of the institutions' financial resources. Truly good, not just adequate, online catalog systems may be developed about the time the book ceases to be a major factor in the storage and transmission of ideas among scholars and researchers in nearly all disciplines.

This potential stumbling block is rather easily avoided, because many observers have urged designers to expand online catalogs by including other things besides bibliographic records for books. Expanding the scope of online catalogs in this way has been a major focus of attention in the 1980s. The earlier conceptualizations of online catalogs as merely another form of the venerable library catalog have generally been superseded by acknowledgment—based partly on studies of online catalog use and partly on further technological advances, particularly in the area of communications—that the online catalog is somehow qualitatively different from previous catalog forms. It is generally accepted now that the online catalog at least has the potential to advance far beyond the old, formal, conceptual boundaries of a library catalog. These new information storage and retrieval devices are still labeled online catalogs, but the definition of a library catalog needs to be revised if these new devices are to be included under that rubric.

No control over online catalog development. As a second stumbling block to considering the topic, some critics may argue that, because we lack the power of choice in the matter of online catalog development, it is useless to think critically about online catalogs and their use. Research in library and information science tends to be driven by perceived applications, and this way of looking at online catalogs yields no apparent efficacies. More mundane commentators have noted that librarians have little choice now because the burden of online catalog design and development has passed to private sector developers and vendors. Others argue that something in the very nature of technological innovation allows little or no choice in the matter of whether or not to adopt the new technology. Is technological development "an inevitable course of events in which attempts to propose moral and political limits have no place" (Winner, 1986; 17)? Technological and economic imperatives usually carry the day.

This is a much more serious stumbling block that must be addressed before we can proceed. The question boils down to whether it is worthwhile and efficient to think earnestly about something when it appears at first glance that you have little or no power to change what you intend to examine. This stumbling block leads us to the ethics or morality of scholarly inquiry. Is it worthwhile studying something when the applications are not immediately self-evident? It is commonly believed that the only reason for studying online catalogs is to ultimately change and improve the systems. A central thesis of this book is that there are other ways to think about the problems and potential solutions to online catalog use. It is ironic that this question causes despair when it is posed in the area of scholarly, philosophical inquiry, but is accepted as an inevitable given when the activity is technological research and development. This book tries to reveal the openness of the question of what ought to be done once the studies are complete. The anticipated applications are not as closed and self-evident as they seem. Changing the system is just one of several options.

The Role of the Library

The new technologies have led to a reconceptualization of the academic library. It is evolving into an online information utility that provides users with access to local public-access computer systems and acts as a gateway to remote systems (Bailey, 1989; 179). Questions have been raised about the internal structure and activities of libraries as well as the role of libraries in society as a whole, particularly the emerging culture of information. The traditional function of the academic library has been to provide information to scholars in useful forms, but advances in information storage and retrieval technology have made this function difficult to execute (Weiskel, 1988; 17).

Essentially Conservative. For reasons based on the structure of the flow of information, rather than on the psychological traits of librarians as a group, libraries are essentially conservative. Librarians cannot implement revolutionary changes in libraries. Technological change must be introduced in a way and at a pace that is acceptable to the user groups (De Gennaro, 1987; 4). Most users accepted online catalogs, but often they were implemented as secondary, experimental alternatives to the old card catalog. The incompleteness of retrospective conversion projects allowed online catalogs to be phased in.

More than just another information retrieval system. It is commonly heard, often in the context of the futher privatization of the information industry, that the library is just one of many information retrieval systems. Some analysts have warned that this view of the nature of the library could be too narrow. Paul Lacey, for example, suggests we should think about the library not primarily as an information retrieval system but as a social system—a teaching-learning milieu in which retrieval of information is only a part of the goal (Lacey, 1982; 118). When considering future technology-driven changes in library collections and services, it is important to remember that the library has a social role as a provider of no-cost or low-cost information to those who cannot afford to obtain this information directly from publishers and other information vendors (Bailey, 1989; 179). This function usually is more explicit in public library mission statements. Vending information, nevertheless, is just one of many library goals. The function of the library and the online catalog in the teaching mission of academic institutions will be examined in Chapter 7.

Technology and organizational structure. New technologies have affected the organizational structures of libraries, making the existing structures obsolete. Michael Gorman (1984) at Illinois has written on the need to organize library staffs along subject lines, not along functional lines. Through online technologies and decentralized processing, the barriers to access which were created by the division of labor between the reference librarians and the cataloger are beginning to crumble (Herschman, 1987; 346). By and large, the institutional implications of library automation have received much more attention than the implications for users. Chapter 13 will examine the institutional implications of online catalogs.

How Important Are Online Catalogs?

Online catalogs are the most visible form of library automation. Library staff and public users tend to view the library catalog as a fundamental aspect of the library as a whole. Anne Lipow found that most staff members who have been trained to use the online catalog, even if they do not use it as part of the normal duties of their position, associate knowledge about the online catalog and searching techniques with knowledge of the entire library system (Van Pulis, 1985; 3). Frederick Kilgour has commented that online catalogs and photoduplication equipment are the only two technological innovations introduced into libraries in this century that have had an immediate, significant effect on patrons.[2]

The development and implementation of online catalog systems also has encouraged many librarians to think beyond the simple realization of efficiencies within library routines. The introduction and acceptance of online catalogs have forced librarians to reconsider many assumptions about the profession and the present and future role of the library.

Statements about the positive aspects of online catalogs tend to stress the revolutionary nature of online catalog development. They also emphasize the highly visible nature of catalog automation—a form of library automation directly affecting the user and usage patterns. Betsy Baker and Beth Sandore (1987; 196) mention the enduring need for library catalogs. Librarians always will maintain some representation of library holdings, and this information will remain part of the integral function of library service, regardless of its form or scope. The online catalog is the first major development that brings the benefits of library automation directly to the patron (Hildreth, 1985A; 236). The online catalog in the library may provide the most democratic access to computer technology available in our society—reaching patrons of all ages, educational levels, and cultural backgrounds (Judith Adams, 1988; 32). The online catalog will exert the single most powerful influence on library users (Lee Jones, 1984; 152).

Edwin Brownrigg and Clifford Lynch (1983; 105) correctly focus on the access potential of online catalogs as the strongest reason for the existence of catalogs in online form. The advent of information technology has given librarians the opportunity to solve the problem of access to bibliographic information. Online catalogs have allowed libraries to expand access as rapidly as the production of published information has expanded. Access points, both in terms of the standard record structure and in terms of the physical location of terminals, have increased dramatically. Online catalogs have been a truly revolutionary development, with the emphasis on access—perhaps even distributed access.

Other commentators see the online catalog as misdirected, ominous, or limiting. Often a fear is expressed that the proliferation of online access information will shift the academic library away from its traditional mission. Perhaps it is because we lack confidence in our professional selves and the enduring importance of libraries that we have been so easily persuaded that we must become information brokers, and that our libraries must become online databases (Cart, 1987; 40). The development and implementation of online catalogs may be seen as a contributing factor in the value shift away from the notion of a collection of intellectual works to the notion of a database containing information with little or no inherent value. The concept of an electronic database reveals nothing about the potential value of the contents to users, nor about the criteria and work used to create the database. A collection posits a collector, while a database does not.

Historical Development of Online Catalogs

In order to understand how online catalogs arrived where they are today, a brief review of the history of online catalog development is necessary. Interest in the historical development of online catalogs rests primarily in how that development is evident in current systems. The history of the development of catalogs in general has affected how both developers and users view the current online catalogs. In a sense, current systems and usage patterns are historical artifacts of the development of the library catalog. The current interfaces and usage patterns embody a history of assumptions, perhaps even agendas.

Many types of histories of online catalogs are possible. Charles Hildreth, for example, is an excellent historian of the factual historical development of online catalogs. Other types of histories of online catalogs need to be written. A history of online catalog development is needed that emphasizes the political and conceptual origins of these devices. Was there widespread professional enthusiasm for the new catalog format? Was that enthusiasm rooted in a reaction to working prototypes, to the idea and promise of an automated catalog, or to the idea of increased institutional efficiencies? Were the efficiencies of the users of the system ever an integral part of the design and development process? What is the history of the politics of online catalogs?

Historical Conditions

Richard De Gennaro has written eloquently on the history of online catalogs (for example, see De Gennaro, 1983). At the time online catalogs were developed, the library catalog had reached a remarkable degree of standardization and stasis as a device. Online catalogs upset that stasis, and it appears that the standardization enjoyed during the era of the card catalog will not return for some time. The acceptance of the card catalog at the turn of the century marked a trend toward standardization. The widespread acceptance of the online catalog in early 1980s marked a trend toward experimentation in library catalog design (Cochrane and Markey, 1983; 338). As remote access to online catalogs becomes more prevalent, user frustration over the lack of a standardized interface will increase.

Four factors were necessary for the development and acceptance of online library catalogs. First, the technology had to be available, and, secondly, at a cost that was perceived as cost-efficient by potential purchasers of online catalogs. Third, the systems had to be acceptable to users with their specific needs. The major findings of the CLR study confirm this point. Finally, the online catalogs had to mesh with the goals of the libraries which developed or purchased the systems. Questions of cost efficiencies and technological availability, however, should have little interest to researchers of the use of online catalogs. They are largely or completely out of our control. The third and fourth conditions, regarding the needs of users and the theoretical implications of online catalogs vis-à-vis library goals, should command our attention. Most research into online catalogs has focused on users' needs, especially user attitudes and opinions about online catalogs.

Technological development and economics are important, but the other two conditions should not be underemphasized. The requisite technology for the birth of online catalogs (other than the MARC record structure, perhaps) developed outside the profession. Technological development led to a rethinking of the format of the bibliographic records within the library catalog, if not its function. The dominant trends in library automation during three decades have been shaped and driven by the cost and capabilities of the computer and communications technologies that were available at the time (De Gennaro, 1983; 243). Although this may be true, the survival and transformation of user projects and institutional goals during the age of automation warrant our attention.

Precursors: photocopying, microform, databases. Online catalogs did not develop in a vacuum. Other aspects of library automation served as precursors. For example, the growing use of reprographic technology for republication of library materials was an important step in the process of using technology to facilitate and equalize access to library resources (De Gennaro, 1987; 8). The failure of COM catalogs, the attractions of automated circulation systems, and vendor interest led to the creation and growing interest in online catalogs (Beckman, 1982; 2044). Automated library access to monographic holdings developed after automated access to the journal literature in most fields was well established (Lynch and Berger, 1989; 372). Many of the design features of the prototype online catalog systems, however, did not mimic the automated systems for access to journal articles. The card catalog may have been the most important precursor of online catalogs. Computer databases of journal databases, for example, did not emulate printed abstracts and indexing tools to the extent that early online catalogs emulated the printed card catalogs.

No crisis situation/no user demand. Although the limitations of microform library catalogs were clearly evident, online catalogs did not develop during a crisis situation. There was no pressing need to find an alternative to the card catalog. Users were not clamoring for a new catalog format. A study by Carol Walton, Susan Williamson, and Howard White (1986) at Bryn Mawr and Swarthmore Colleges indicated that most users were satisfied with the card catalog. The technological capability was there, so someone decided to attempt applying the new technologies to the existing systems and routines. This tendency to attempt to apply new technology to existing systems and routines is a common response to technological advance. There seemed to be no overwhelming burden under which librarians and users toiled that motivated them to push for the development and implementation of online catalogs. Consequently, the online catalog was not expected to be a great improvement over previous catalog formats. It was simply seen as a better, faster way to realize certain desirable system and cost efficiencies. The historical conditions under which online catalogs developed helped determine the horizon of possibilities for the new device.

The push for library automation in general did have several positive contributing causes. Growing library budgets, the information explosion, the technological advances all contributed to make automated library systems attractive (Power, 1983; 112).

From what group did the push for transition to online catalogs come? Perhaps online catalogs were first developed so that librarians, particularly catalogers, could gain greater bibliographic control over their materials. The real impetus in library automation was not to master the new technology—the machine (as Sherry Turkle [1984] suggests)—but to develop a machine to master something else. In the same manner, most users do not use an online catalog just to master the device. As they approach the online catalog, they are already looking beyond it. A viable historical hypothesis is that increased bibliographic control at a reduced cost was the impetus behind the development of early online catalog systems. Micheline Hancock-Beaulieu (1989; 26) states the situation bluntly: "The online catalogue was a spin-off which did not stem from any desire to serve the user better."

This pursuit of greater bibliographic control, however, has backfired. In many ways we are farther today from the goal of adequate bibliographic control, and the online catalog may have unwittingly contributed to the backslide. The MARC format, offering visions of absolute control based on a highly flexible record structure, has led to a softening of the concepts of a library catalog and an intellectual work, and a revolution in user behavior and expectations.

Historical assumptions. The development of online catalogs has been primarily a response to the problems of production (including maintenance), rather than to the problems and possibilities of use. Efficient production and maintenance was the chief attraction of online catalogs, not enhanced access. To the extent that access was discussed, an increased number of access points to the bibliographic records were stressed, rather than user access possibilities.

Historically the online catalog has been understood as the technological device that replaced the dominant card catalog form. Both Kilgour and Judith Adams (1988) think that the library profession made a grave error when it assumed that online catalogs and other forms of library automation were intended to increase efficiency and productivity, rather than to redefine information generation, storage, and retrieval.

The anticipated obstacles to broad user acceptance were similar to the perceived obstacles to database searching of commercially vended databases. System designers and computer scientists assumed that more people would use the devices if the devices were easier to use. Difficulty of use was seen as the major obstacle to broad public acceptance and use (Pfaffenberger, 1990; 113). This perception of the alleged main deterrent to use is the driving force behind the push to make online catalogs as transparent and user-friendly as possible.

Three decades of development. The development of online catalogs can be characterized by the three decades during which development has occurred. Patricia Culkin (1989; 172) asserts that online catalogs arose out of the library community's fascination with computer technology in early 1960s. It was a fascination with the new technology and the lure of potential increases in efficiency and cost savings that prompted the initial development of online catalogs. The imagined efficiencies, however, were within the library as an institution, not efficiencies to be realized by the users of information systems. Initially, online catalogs were much more attractive to libraries and librarians than they were to users.

Since the beginning of library automation, tensions have existed over the scope and locus of control of online catalog development and implementation. Since the early 1960s, there have been two parallel and sometimes conflicting lines of development; one focused on local systems and the other on network systems (De Gennaro, 1983; 244). Online catalog development has followed along both paths.

Cataloging utilities (e.g., OCLC) and bibliographic database vendors (e.g., SDC and DIALOG) got started in the mid-1960s prior to the development of any online catalogs (Roy Adams, 1986). Online catalogs were not at the forefront of automated access to bibliographic records, yet they did not seem to draw strongly from the achievements of these earlier automation efforts. Online catalogs often are viewed as poor cousins compared to these older, more powerful, and flexible bibliographic storage and retrieval devices. Online catalog development initially was supported by underfunded institutions (e.g., libraries), and the systems needed to be designed for a broad, untrained user population. These two facts may explain why online catalogs often are not on the leading edge technologically of bibliographic storage and retrieval development.

During the 1970s commercial vendors began to replace the large university libraries as the principal developers of computer-based library systems (De Gennaro, 1983; 247). Librarians created and joined computer-based utilities and service networks in the 1970s because they saw them as the only technically and economically feasible way to bring the power of computer technology to their libraries (De Gennaro, 1983; 247). Centralized processing seemed to be the most economical and efficient way to achieve the desired objectives.

The economic and technical realities of the 1980s favored increased autonomy and local library responsibility (De Gennaro, 1983; 251). A reaction to the economies of scale of the online technologies developed. In the 1980s library administrators tried to regain much of the control over their own operations and decisionmaking that they gave up to the networks in the 1970s (De Gennaro, 1983; 255). In the 1980s remarkably few major new integrated systems projects were under development (De Gennaro, 1985; 236). Many institutions of higher education are getting out of the systems design, development, and support business.

Presenting the Online Catalog to the Public

From the vantage point of the public user, automation of the catalog happened abruptly. For them, one stage of a completely manual process suddenly was automated. The online catalog was presented to the public by the library profession as an efficient replacement for the card catalog. Its unique possibilities as a new technology were not used to gain public acceptance. The public was reassured that the new catalog would do all the things the old card catalog did. The automation of the catalog often was defended as an internal cost-savings measure. The historical conditions of the development of the early systems determined how they were first presented and perceived.

Parties Involved: Libraries, Networks, and Vendors

Users of library catalogs have not been significantly involved in the decisions surrounding the design and implementation of online catalog systems.[3] The strongest pressure for the adoption of online catalogs is coming not from users, but from library management (Walton, Williamson, and White, 1986; 391). The design and implementation of any type of computerized technology raises political issues within the organization in which it is installed. The more online catalogs are expected to perform the functions of inventory control, acquisitions, cataloging, and public access to the collection, the less likely it is that public users will have a system well designed for public use (Estabrook, 1983; 71).

The development of online catalogs in the 1970s and 1980s was governed by bibliographic networks, vendors of automated systems, and technical services librarians, not by the needs and expressed wishes of the library patrons (Judith Adams, 1988; 33). The standardization of access points has been largely the domain of catalogers, while the design of the online catalog has been overseen mainly by the systems offices and personnel (Herschman, 1987; 340). Public services librarians seem to have little control over the system. Technical services librarians control and maintain the database, and system personnel control and maintain the hardware and software. Since they function as intermediaries, public services librarians naturally champion and defend the interests of the users.

Timothy Weiskel (1989; 8) notes that faculty contributions to the design and implementation of online catalog systems usually were minimal or nonexistent. The automation of the library, often accomplished by libraries working alone, quite naturally reflects the needs and priorities of the librarians. Both Weiskel and Francis Miksa (1987) argue that the online catalog primarily is a device to aid the total process of conducting scholarly research. Because librarians, systems designers, and vendors often worked from an unclear or antiquated mental model of research, the resulting online catalog systems are not extremely useful for scholarly research. For various reasons, online catalogs sensitive to the context of users' projects are rare.

The bibliographic networks such as OCLC and RLIN helped make large-scale copy cataloging cost efficient, which made the maintenance and updating of bibliographic databases associated with online catalogs possible. Access to their databases was not designed to be particularly user-friendly, however, because designers assumed that users, even more than users of remote online database search services, would be a relatively small group of trained professionals.

Universities played a significant role in the early stages of research and development of online catalogs, but the research and development burden now has largely been assumed by companies. Richard De Gennaro (1983; 253) defends the role of the commercial vendors. They have the investment capital, the technical expertise, and the managerial flexibility to take risks, develop new products, and explore new markets and services. Vendors, however, do not know the needs, attitudes, and behavior patterns of the end-users as well as librarians do. They do not see the provision of information services as having moral and ethical components. Unlike academic libraries, commercial vendors have no formal ties with institutions that have teaching and research missions.

Within the academic institutions themselves, several groups have been involved in the development and implementation of online catalog systems. Systems designers possess much technical expertise, but they face two problems for which they are ill equipped: understanding the needs and behavior of information seekers, and understanding the nature of information itself and its flow (Molholt, 1985; 287). Technical services librarians function as the maintainers of the database. They usually are entrusted with maintaining and expanding the contents of the database. They focus on the record structure, usually in the MARC format, the control of the vocabulary, and the indexing and access points.

Public services librarians were not a driving force behind the development and early implementation of online catalogs. Many commentators see the reference librarian as the natural intermediary between the user and the system. As advocates for user needs, reference librarians have a duty to represent patrons in the design of a tool central to library usage (Herschman, 1987; 342). Are the mediating skills that reference librarians have developed to help users bridge the gap between their needs and the manual bibliographic system and the institutional system easily transferable and applicable to mediate between the user and an automated system? The ability of current reference systems to respond to the needs of a growing remote user population will be discussed in Chapter 13. Reference librarians should not confine themselves to using a particular catalog and its records; they must become more actively involved at the national level in influencing cataloging policy (Herschman, 1987; 346).

Some commentators see the development of online catalogs as a real coup for public services librarians in their tacit struggle with technical services librarians. Online catalogs have freed public services librarians and the public users from the hidebound rules of cataloging and filing. Because the search methods are less rigid, online catalogs favor reference librarians, rather than technical services librarians (Stoksik, 1985). A new technological device has weakened another economy based on guilds. They hope that public services librarians and users will have more influence on the systems designed to facilitate information storage and retrieval.

Rather than apply the older, formal structure of system designers, computer systems personnel, technical services librarians, and public services librarians to the new demands for development and service of online catalogs, perhaps the necessary groups should be identified along functional lines. Thus the functional groups would include systems designers (ranging historically from large universities to blue sky commercial vendors); maintainers of the system (usually personnel in computing centers and systems offices of the parent institution); maintainers of the database (historically, these have been technical services librarians); and facilitators of access to the database (both public services librarians and computing center personnel). The advantage of thinking along functional lines is that it breaks the conceptual ties between the essential function and the group of people who historically have performed that function. For example, there is no logical reason why technical services librarians could not evolve into the primary facilitators of access to the database. Indeed, perhaps many technical services librarians would argue that they already fill that role. It is not illogical to imagine a system where the users themselves are the principal maintainers of the database, particularly the syndetic structure among the individual bibliographic and authority records.

Current online catalog systems have been influenced by the history of libraries, catalogs, institutions of higher education, and technological advance. The main users of online catalogs—public users and public services staff—have not been major consultants during system development. The next chapter places the online catalog within a context of other catalog forms and other automated information storage and retrieval systems.

Notes

1. The long-standing practices of telephone reference and instances where faculty send graduate students to the library to identify, locate, and retrieve materials do not deflate this assertion, because they are users of the library by proxy, where the task of physically coming to the library merely passes to reference librarians or graduate students.

2. Personal communication, May 13, 1989.

3. See, however, Corey, Spalding, and Fraser, 1983, about the implementation of the LUMIN online catalog system at the University of Missouri.

Chapter 2

Purposes and Traits
of Online Catalogs

Purpose of Online Catalogs

The debate over the purpose of the online catalog has continued unabated since online catalogs were first developed. Remote access has accelerated the debate and extended it to include the purpose of libraries in general. Rather than argue about the purpose of online catalogs as if it were abstract, absolute, and immutable, perhaps it would be better to examine how information professionals and public users think about online catalogs. If it is possible to be proactive or normative about a group's perception of an online catalog, how should these people be encouraged to think about online catalogs? A brief examination of the traditional arguments about the purpose and function of a library catalog will illuminate the present situation.

Definitions of Online Catalogs

Definitions of online catalogs abound. Some tend toward abstraction. Walt Crawford (1987; 2), for example, defines an online catalog as any computer-based set of bibliographic data that can be accessed by library users working directly at a terminal. Other definitions are more grounded and practical. Today's online catalogs typically access machine-readable records for books, journal titles, and audiovisual material, and indicate their circulation status (Drabenstott, 1988; 102). Crawford (1987; 3) suggests that a system should be defined by its functionality, not by its internal techniques and architecture. Functionality, however, is not an absolute. It is dependent on the training, imagination, and purposes of the users of the system. The online catalog itself, nevertheless, as a device demands a certain amount of attention and commands a certain allure.

Michael Buckland (1988; 301) sees the library catalog, especially the card catalog, as essentially a compromise technology, forced by technological and economic necessity to synthesize the purer forms of bibliography and accession lists. Library catalogs, as currently conceived, are a synthesis of bibliographic and holdings records, containing both general statements about editions of works and specific statements about individual copies in particular locations. The catalog should be redefined as "the umbrella for the totality of bibliographical records linked to holdings records that a given library makes available" (Buckland, 1988; 309).

An online catalog combines the separate functions of identifying and locating bibliographic items. Although a catalog can be used to both identify and locate intellectual works, locating is its real strength. The unique contribution of the catalog to scholarship is to help locate copies of books and texts than may have been learned about elsewhere (Wilson, 1983; 16). If the library catalog is primarily a locating device for already known items, union catalogs should be much more attractive than local catalogs.

Other critics stress that library catalogs normally contain records only for items that are ready to be used. Bibliographic records are placed in the catalog only after the items have been placed on the shelves. In older forms of library catalogs, items on order or in process were not included. Items that were not at their proper location on the shelf, for whatever reason, probably should not have been in the catalog, because they were not ready to be used. But it was not technically feasible in a paper-based catalog to indicate items that were circulating or believed to be misshelved, lost, or stolen. The notion that an item is ready to be used includes the idea of easy access. A ready item in a distant geographic location is of little use to a ready user. Ease of access determined what was included in the catalog. If an item were not on the shelf, it would be easier to gain access to an item on order, in process, checked out, or not even in the collection. Some reformers of library catalogs have seen improved access to all materials in the local collection as the primary improvement needed. If it is to respond to the stated needs of users, an online catalog must integrate access to all types of materials in one system and at all states of their status in that system (Beckman, 1982; 2046).

A library catalog perforce must be much more terse than the collection of works to which it provides access. The catalog is necessarily selective, both in what it exhibits and what it indicates about the things it exhibits (Wilson, 1983; 9). Computerization has allowed online catalogs to be less constrictive and cryptic than previous catalog forms.

The debate over definition has been raised to a higher plain. Just as the debate continues over whether libraries are essentially warehouses or service organizations, critics argue about whether the online catalog is basically a database or a communications medium. The library catalog may be perceived as a repository of selected information about the library's collection, or as a functional communications system providing direction and access to bibliographic information (Hildreth, 1982; 32). A trend has developed toward seeing online catalogs more as media, providing windows and gateways to a variety of information. Perhaps the library catalog, regardless of the form it takes, should be thought of as a gateway, rather than as a finite database. The catalog, after all, existed as a gateway technology long before the development of computers. The original intention was to provide a gateway to the items, contents, or intellectual works of the collection. As such, the library catalog was a significant improvement over the older form of gateway to the collection—physically passing through the gate or door-way and browsing the shelves. The notion of the catalog as a gateway is still prevalent. As will be examined in more detail later, some users seem to be using the online catalog less as a gateway to the collection and more as a terminal information system containing information of interest and use in itself. Nevertheless, there is a long history of defining library catalogs as gateways to local collections of works.

Purpose of Information Retrieval Systems in General

Online catalogs occupy the common ground between automated information storage and retrieval devices and library automation efforts. The tendency to see online catalogs either as versions of online database searching or as a project within the larger program of library automation reveals much about the conflicting context within which online catalogs are placed. Database search techniques and automated circulation procedures both have affected online catalog development. A brief examination of the purposes of information retrieval systems in general may help clarify the situation. At the very least, information retrieval systems should help users retrieve information. They do this by collecting and maintaining a body of information that probably is of interest to the perceived potential user group.

When an individual user searches the information retrieval system, however, she or he wants to retrieve only a small subset of the entire body of stored information. It has been argued, therefore, that the main purpose of an information retrieval tool is essentially negative—to help the searcher reject unwanted items as fast as possible and to provide maximum assistance in revising each stage of the request (Swanson, 1979; 11). The task of the user is not so much to find potentially pertinent information, but rather to quickly and efficiently pare away obviously unwanted information. The process is more subtractive or extractive than cumulative.

Purpose of Library Automation

De Gennaro makes a sharp distinction between library automation and information automation. He also assumes that economics is the real driving force behind both library automation and information automation. The development of library automation software, including integrated online systems, has been slow because the market is limited. On the other hand, the development of information automation has been quick because it has a large and lucrative market. The goal of library automation in general is to provide better access to the resources within the library (De Gennaro, 1985; 235). The online catalog is qualitatively different from other automated library systems. While the online catalog, like other internal library automation efforts, provides the staff with the means for efficiently managing the catalog, its ultimate purpose is to give users a means of access, not only to the library's collections, but also to a variety of other local and remote information resources (De Gennaro, 1987; 20).

Purpose of Library Catalogs

The purpose of the library catalog no longer is clear. Cutter's principles are still invoked, but the intonation sounds hollow.[1] Conflicting visions of the direction of future online catalog development are vying for preeminence. Some suggest that the library catalog should be subsumed within a larger institutional information network. The organization of information storage, scholarly communication, and information dissemination should be coordinated at least at the campus level. The era of computerization has radically altered the old economies of scale, so the information profession should be thinking in terms of institutional, regional, national, or even international information storage and retrieval systems. The online catalog could function as a bridge to this new era of broad systems. The long-term goal of catalog information systems should be to make information about remote library collections as accessible to the user as information about the local library collection (Bailey, 1989; 180).

Other critics argue that the online catalog should become an integrated library system, with the emphasis on the internal functions of the library, such as acquisitions, cataloging, circulation, and administration. The ties that bind the library catalog to the library should be maintained or increased. Adding commercially produced indexes and providing remote access to users who are not primary clientele may be viewed by this group as dangerous deviations from the central internal purpose of the library catalog. This line of thought recognizes that the catalog is a superficial bibliographical instrument. It should not be made the complete and definitive guide to the bibliographical universe, but rather an essential local supplement to the complex apparatus for discovering texts (Wilson, 1983; 16).

Still others argue that the online catalog is our last great hope for a reconciliation between book catalogs and journal indexes. The schism that developed over a century ago may now be closed. Another group, led by Buckland, wants to see the library catalog return to its rightful parent, the bibliography, with fewer institutional ties and less emphasis on holdings information and local ownership.

Instruction as a secondary purpose. An important distinction to note throughout this debate is that any instruction the online catalog may provide, or any learning it may encourage, clearly falls within the penumbra of its central, overshadowing purpose as an identifying and locating device. The primary purpose of an online catalog is to help users identify and locate items that may contain information pertinent to the users' present projects. Any learning that may occur is icing on the cake, but instruction is not a library catalog's primary purpose. The instructional qualities of online catalogs are difficult to identify and address, so often they are left off the design agenda.

Nevertheless, an online catalog should encourage user learning and intellectual growth. It should work intelligently with the users, engaging in meaningful dialogue, to elicit expressions of the users' information need (which may change during the course of the search), and to improve the results of the users' search activity (Hildreth, 1987; 665). The notion that the catalog teaches users points to the potential for a broader social purpose for the catalog. Kilgour argues that the purpose of the online catalog must be expressed in societal concepts rather than in narrow terms of bibliography and efficiency (Kilgour, 1984; 320).

Robert Taylor (1986; 24) thinks and writes in the broader context of information systems. His definition of the purpose of information systems makes no mention of the devices as teaching tools, intended to make users better people by making them better retrievers and appliers of information. According to Taylor, the only reason for the existence of an information system is to store and provide information and knowledge in usable chunks to those who presently or in the future will live and work in certain environments and who, as a result, have or will have certain problems which information may help in clarifying or even in solving.

Maintain a local focus and local library control. The debate even spills over into the question of whether catalogs are essential to the library's mission. Most critics agree that catalogs are essential to the central mission of the library, but Buckland and Evan Farber take the opposing viewpoint. The major purpose of computerization in libraries—to signifiantly improve information service to the user—remains unrealized (Azubuike, 1988; 276).

Identification and the catalog's ties to a discrete, local collection often are stressed in discussions of the purpose of library catalogs. David Tyckoson (1989; 8) suggests that the primary role of the library catalog is to index the library collection. The purpose of a catalog is to help patrons identify and locate at least some of the items owned by the library. A catalog is a systematic record of the holdings of a collection. Its purpose, according to Kilgour (1979; 34) is to enable a user of the collection to find the physical location of information contained in the collection. Identification and ownership are key components of that purpose. Crawford (1987; 1) states that library catalogs, while providing access to individual items, establish and indicate the state of the collection. A library catalog should indicate something about the totality of the collection in addition to the individual items comprising it.

Richard Boss, for example, argues that a basic premise behind catalogs is that they should be information locating systems, rather than true information retrieval systems (Drabenstott, 1985; 109). A library catalog should provide access to the bibliographic holdings of the library, with subject access, authority control, and a syndetic structure (Hildreth, 1985A). It seems that an online catalog can function as a tool for identification, location, or storage of information in intellectual works. It also can encourage the growth of human knowledge and understanding about topics and the structure of topics.

The development of online catalogs added much fuel to this debate. Many of the economic and logistical constraints of manual catalogs no longer apply. Online catalogs have forced the profession to question the purposes of the library catalog (Hildreth, 1985A; 241). What types of materials should be accessible through the online catalog? How has the book, as the dominant format for items in most collections, affected the structure and users' understanding of the library catalog? Changes in the methods of scholarship and information dissemination away from books and technological advances have led some thinkers to question whether the purpose of a library catalog should be expanded beyond bibliographic confines. Many analysts want to see online catalogs include nonbibliographic information, such as messaging systems and graphic or aural information. The purpose of a catalog is not only to maintain bibliographic control over books—still the dominant format in most collections.

Identifying, locating, and accessing intellectual works. Any library catalog, regardless of format, combines the two distinct processes of identifying intellectual works (or physical carriers of intellectual works) and locating them. Other methods are available for both types of access. Farber (1984), for example, argues that published bibliographies are an underutilized method for identifying intellectual works on a topic. Simply browsing the shelves is another method for locating items that may contain pertinent intellectual works. The library catalog, nevertheless, is an adequate tool for both tasks, and the fact that it combines the two activities makes it particularly attractive to users.

A recent discussion (April 1990) in the PACS-L Forum (a BITNET electronic mail forum) of the value of remote access to academic online catalogs via the Internet reiterated the distinction between intellectual access and physical access to bibliographic items. It cannot be assumed that all users of online catalogs want physical access to the cataloged collection. Intellectual access is available through an online catalog, but it is limited or truncated, because only certain information from the items themselves is available through the online catalog. Identifying an intellectual work is a first step in gaining intellectual access to the work. Intellectual access has many stages, ranging from simply knowing that the work exists to reading the item from cover to cover several times. Furthermore, the user seeking intellectual access to a collection of works may be satisfied at any stage of the process of increasing intellectual access. It cannot be determined whether a given user of an online catalog ultimately wants to know the correct spelling of an author's name, wants to know which subject headings were assigned to an item, or wants to retrieve and read the complete intellectual work. Intellectual access to a text is a continuum from simply knowing that the text exists to memorizing it.

The idea of end-information. If there is an identifiable group of end-users (regardless of how difficult it may be to define and identify end-users), there may be an identifiable set of end-information within an information storage and retrieval system. For example, call numbers could be considered intermediate information, rather than end-information, because people copy down or memorize call numbers only so that they may retrieve documents. End-information could be defined as the information finally sought. It is extremely sensitive to the context within which the information is sought. Many users of information systems want to advance their projects at hand, not simply find information. They use the catalog in order to find information in order to advance a project.[2] The online library catalog is a device for locating items (and perhaps even end-information) contained in the library's collection. Care must be taken, however, when making assumptions about what users want from an online catalog.

Document identification, document retrieval, and information retrieval. The user of the library actually confronts three phases of the search process. Libraries help users solve problems in three stages: first they identify the documents, then they locate them, then they retrieve them (Swanson, 1979; 13, from a Gordon Williams article of 1964). Sometimes users come to the library and the library catalog only after the potentially pertinent items have been identified. Their reason for using the catalog, therefore, is only to verify local holdings. In addition, they may want to confirm the existence of some item they have only a vague notion of. Remote access users of the library catalog, in particular, seem to concentrate on the middle phase of the search process—location. They seem to have already identified many of the items they search for in the online catalog, and retrieval is not an option for them at the time of searching, because they are physically distant from the collection. Library catalogs have treated the problems of identifying and locating documents liable to help solve an information problems as a one-step process (Swanson, 1979; 13).

Hildreth's working definition of the purpose of automated information retrieval systems raises some key questions. He suggests that the aim of an information retrieval system is to identify documents or other sources of information likely to be relevant and useful—with regard to user's information need or problem—for assessment and possible use by the user (Hildreth, 1989A; 44). Hildreth really is describing a document identification system, such as an online catalog, not an information retrieval system.

Distinctions need to be made between automated document identification systems, automated document retrieval systems, and automated information retrieval systems. In most instances and uses the online catalog functions as an automated document identification system. The information most users want is not contained in the online catalog databases proper. The online catalog usually helps users identify and locate documents likely to contain the information they need. An automated document identification system normally is conceived as an intermediary or enabling technological device, but there is some evidence (described in Chapters 10 and 13) suggesting that the information contained in online catalogs actually is the end-information sought by the users. One path of online catalog development would be to turn the current automated document identification system into bona fide information retrieval systems, probably by making full text available online through the catalog.

In other eras there was a strong correlation—verging on a one-to-one relationship—between the documents held by the library and the information available in the library. The catalog was the tool for locating the documents. Vicariously, therefore, the catalog was the tool for locating the information available locally within the library. This strong correlation has gradually weakened over time. Although today the catalog is still a good tool for locating documents held in the local library, no longer is it a good indication of the information available *through* the local library.

The idea of an automated document retrieval system conjures up fantastic images of robots who go into the stacks and pull documents for users, or perhaps an elaborate system of conveyor belts or pneumatic tubes. It is misleading to refer to online catalogs as document retrieval systems, because document retrieval in most instances still is done the old-fashioned way—by the user—on foot. This distinction will become crucial as the significance and implications of remote access to online catalogs are examined. Remote access to online catalogs can be seen as a first venture into a new service offered by libraries—electronic delivery of information to the point of use.

An online catalog normally functions as a device for identifying and locating documents, rather than as an information retrieval system. Sometimes users want only the publication information or holdings information or the height of the book, but usually users want the information within the book, which most online catalogs currently do not supply.

Successful online catalogs. The online catalog succeeds in at least two ways: users seem to prefer this form of the catalog to all previous forms, and the online catalog is easier to maintain and update than earlier forms (Hildreth, 1989B; 20). In other words, the online catalog satisfies most public users and it makes an essential internal library function more efficient. The logical next question, therefore, is whether the online catalog should or could become something more than a pleasing and efficient device. Measures of the success of an online catalog need to be broadened.

Basic Assumptions About Online Catalogs

Several basic assumptions often are made about online catalogs: the catalog is essential to the mission of the library; all users of the library should be able to use the online catalog with a minimal amount of learning and effort; all of the advanced features are desired and used by many of the users; no matter what type of search is performed, the ultimate goal is to have an item in hand.

Most online catalogs are designed on the assumption that the users come to the catalog with questions or needs and the catalog provides the answers. Users want to use the catalog to gain access to information. They have little interest, it is assumed, in the system itself and its structure. Most online catalogs, therefore, provide little or no opportunity for users to fulfill the needs of catalog maintenance and improvement, such as interface improvements, timely or context-specific syndetic connections, and the correction of errors. If this assumption is accepted, it could be argued that the system itself should be as transparent and self-effacing as possible. Many designers and analysts accept this premise.

Most catalog bibliographic records have a strong bias toward the physical entity of the book over the intellectual content contained within the book. The basic unit for the catalog is not the text but the separate, bibliographically independent, publication (Wilson, 1983; 7). Libraries deal with bibliographic items, not intellectual texts. From the vantage point of the library, it is much easier, and ultimately more useful to most users, to provide access to bibliographic items than to intellectual works. The choice of the physical book as the basic cataloging unit has the consequence that enormous numbers of texts cannot be located through the catalog without first using another bibliographical finding aid, to determine which book or serial the desired intellectual work is in (Wilson, 1983; 8).

The traditional library catalog indicates what a library owns. The concept of a library catalog is tied to the notion of ownership and holdings. In the past there has been a strong positive correlation between ownership and accessibility. If the library owned the item, chances were good that the patron could gain easy access to the item. Users always have been interested more in easy access to information than in questions of ownership. Seekers of information who are more interested in ownership frequent bookstores. Users of libraries have a passing interest in what the library owns because ownership has a proven track record (in paper-based information storage and retrieval systems) of indicating easy accessibility.

The concept of owning information is philosophically challenging, as well as a foreign notion to most people. This often leads to basic abuses of the spirit of copyright, but that is a topic beyond the scope of this book. The unique properties of information also have created some professional misconceptions about the struggle for control over the flow of information. We tend to see the stages in the flow of information as a renewable resource, just like the information itself. This topic will be considered in Chapter 3.

When an online catalog is referred to as a system, most people think of a configuration of hardware, software, and communications links. In this book the online catalog is considered more as an event. The experience of interacting with the online catalog will be the focus of attention. The online catalog will be considered as a system of decisions, valuations, purposes, and behaviors, rather than as a system of electronic devices.

Another basic assumption about online catalogs and their use is that most of the time the searcher is also the end-user. Whereas database searching has a relatively long history of mediated searching by professional searchers, online catalogs are designed for individual searcher-users. On this score at least, online catalogs are designed for individual scholars. In the study of dial access use reported in Chapter 10 onward, it appears that mediated online catalog searching forms a significant portion of all dial access use.

Online Catalogs and the Library's Mission

Online catalog research and development has ties to the mission of the library as well as broader institutional goals. The academic library's mission often is conjoined with the mission of the public library—to serve all people, particularly the information oppressed. The development of the online catalog both encourages and discourages this conjunction. Early studies indicated that online catalogs originally were used primarily by the information-disadvantaged in academe—undergraduates and unaffiliated users. With a wider implementation and use of remote access, a gradual shift away from these user groups may occur. The more advanced online catalog systems become, the more they seem to attract high-end-users of libraries. Technological choices cannot be separated from the social matrix in which those choices are made and the social contexts of their implementation (Estabrook, 1983; 69). Bryan Pfaffenberger (1990) also stresses that the development of new technological devices is influenced strongly by political and social factors.

The politics of library technology. When the politics of library technology are discussed, the internal politics of system implementation and funding receive much more attention than the politics of use. Will remote access to online catalogs and other forms of electronically stored and transmitted information work to erase any disparities in access to bibliographic information? Will there be relatively equal access to the bibliographic items themselves? And what about final access to intellectual works? How will remote access to online information change the concept and realities of access to intellectual works?

Some critics argue that automated information systems in general convey a sense of authoritarianism or elitism. The group of library users is being subdivided into smaller groups, with access to some library services denied to some. The lack of compatibility between systems, constrictive system design options, potential invasion of privacy, barriers to database access and manipulation, and the conjunction of the introduction of user fees with computerization all work to convey the subtle message that online catalogs are in league with authoritarianism, not democracy (Judith Adams, 1988; 32). In his recent book, *Democratizing Information*, Pfaffenberger (1990) takes a dim view of the prospects for the democratization of information through online database technology.

Other commentators defend computerized information systems as engines of democracy and equality. New computer and information technologies are increasing the speed and force of the trend toward decentralization (De Gennaro, 1983; 243). New technology is democratizing the availability of research resources (De Gennaro, 1987; 10). One role for libraries is to act as the great leveler—to provide the knowledge and hardware to serve those who cannot buy into the new information age (Molholt, 1988; 101). The prospect of a leveling trend has special concerns in an academic setting, however, where alarm over the declining quality of teaching and research has been expressed. If everyone has equal access to the record of scholarship, the quality of the record may diminish over time, even though the quantity may increase dramatically. In fact, there may be a positive correlation between the increasing automation of information systems and the overall decline in the quality and usefulness of the recorded body of scholarly information.

The last great hope of librarianship? Perhaps the online catalog is the last great hope of academic libraries and universities to maintain or increase their market share of the research activity of society. It is a sad fact of the information revolution that over the last few years universities as a whole have diminished in relative importance as channels through which people seek information for research purposes in our society (Weiskel, 1986; 553). To fulfill this hope, however, the online catalog will need to move beyond being a pointer to local bibliographic collections. The most important issue facing librarians is how to provide access to the growing volume of information in electronic form, while at the same time maintaining traditional book and journal collections and services and providing appropriate links between the two (De Gennaro, 1987; 38). If the online catalog is to become an online library, we need to confront this possibility squarely and try to plan for it. The purpose of a library catalog is not settled, and it probably never was.

Formal Considerations and Distinctions

An understanding or appreciation of a new technological device usually is built on previous knowledge of apparently similar things. When we encounter something new, we attempt to catagorize it based on what we already know. A user migrating to the online catalog from the card catalog may develop a totally different understanding of the new device than a user coming to the online catalog from experience with the commercial database vendors. The first will see it as an automated card catalog, while the second may see it as an electronic database for the local collection of books. Thus comparisons often are made between online catalogs and other things. Many design and development agendas are premised on a belief that the online catalog should become more like another device or system. Noticeable similarities exist between online catalogs and other forms of library catalogs (e.g., book card, microform, and CD-ROM), online distributed cataloging systems (e.g., OCLC, RLIN, UTLAS, and WLN), published bibliographies, and commercially vended electronic databases, such as those distributed by Dialog and BRS.

Other Catalog Forms

All library catalog formats require the user to formulate the need or problem into a verbalized expression. If the user cannot verbalize the need or problem, access is impossible. He or she must possess certain basic skills before successful use of any catalog is possible. Typing (or, more generally, character entry) is a new skill required by most online catalogs.[3] Patrons do not need to type to be able to use the card catalog (Crawford, 1987; 4), they do need to be able to spell and alphabetize.

Early online catalogs were received by many users as automated card catalogs. The new technological device was not perceived as a radical innovation. It merely modernized an older technological device. If online catalogs belong to a larger family of modern technological devices, we must wonder if other new devices were initially perceived in terms of older, established technologies. For example, was television first perceived as "radio visualized"?

Availability differs from one catalog format to another. The online catalog has received much criticism because it periodically goes down, while card, book, and microform catalogs rarely are unavailable. Card catalogs in particular, however, are available to the user only when the user is in the same location as the card catalog. Remote access has the potential to reverse this argument, making the catalog available even when the library is not open. With the advent of remote access to online catalogs, access to the catalog no longer is concurrent with, or dependent upon, access to the collection. This is a major step toward dissociation of the online catalog and the local collection.

The card catalog is popular because of its constant availability and the immediacy of access it provides (Walton, Williamson, and White, 1986; 396). It is an established technology that users claim to understand reasonably well (Walton, Williamson, and White, 1986; 391). The capability of the card catalog to provide a combination of fast browsing and extensive additional information on demand is unmatched by the online catalog, and they work better for known-item searches than online catalogs. (Crawford, 1987; 4, 5). This raises the interesting question of whether the observed increase in subject searching after the implementation of an online catalog is not the result of years of pent-up demand for better subject access, but rather the result of the fact that online catalogs implicitly encourage subject searching while they discourage known-item searching.

Online catalogs are better than card catalogs, from the user's point of view, because most of them provide keyword searching, additional access points, Boolean operations, quick access to specific help information, and information about the status of the item sought (Crawford, 1987; 5). Online catalogs generally are perceived as having more or better access points, flexibility, and display options. They are faster and more convenient than other catalog forms. Advances in access points, access point manipulation, and display formats in most online catalog systems have advanced the user beyond other forms of the library catalog in terms of flexibility and convenience of use (Hildreth, 1982; 25). Online catalogs have made the retrieval of bibliographic records very fluid, mutable, and user-driven, but the content of individual bibliographic records remains very static and traditional.

With card, book, and microform catalogs, display options are not presented to the user. There is only one display option. Wilson thinks that the big difference between traditional catalog forms and online catalogs is found in the access and display of information. The question of unit and scope remains unquestioned (Wilson, 1983; 9–10).

All other catalog forms are precoordinated. Online catalogs have the capacity to allow postcoordination. With the online catalog, the number of possible retrieval sets is nearly infinite, and users, whether or not they are fully cognizant of it, have control over the creation and manipulation of sets. The online catalog is neither a dictionary catalog nor a classed catalog. In fact, the relationship between individual records within the database has become irrelevant and difficult or impossible to visualize. The bibliographic records are not organized in any meaningful way until the user interacts with the system.

Trend toward union catalogs. For public users, the three main differences between online catalogs and other catalog forms are computerization, the potential for distributed access, and the possibility of unification (Estabrook, 1983; 69). Book catalogs and card catalogs tend to indicate local holdings only, while online catalogs tend to be union catalogs. Brownrigg (1983; 112) thinks that online catalogs naturally facilitate a union or regional scope. Because of their differences of scope, he concludes that circulation and online catalog functions do not belong within the same system. Many online catalogs are union catalogs because the development of computer technology made centralized processing feasible and cost efficient. This situation no longer exists to the degree it once did, but union catalogs persist as a residual effect of the historical development of computer technology.

Changing spatial orientation. Users no longer have normal spatial orientation toward the catalog and its parts. An online catalog never can be observed from the middle distance. It cannot be perceived as a complete thing. The array of terminals commonly found in reference rooms are not the catalog itself, but portals into an unfathomable world. The online catalog differs from all other catalog formats in that the user never sees the online catalog. The computing machinery almost always is hidden from view. Online catalogs may provide ample public access, but they rarely, if ever, make public appearances. This is true both for the machinery and for the database in its entirety.

Book and card catalogs provide rough estimates of the size and worth of the collection. When a patron walks into the reference room to use the card catalog, he or she immediately receives an impression of the size of the collection. COM catalogs fail somewhat in this respect, and online catalogs fail almost completely. The online catalog, at least in theory, but currently not in practice, completely abandons the idea of the library catalog as a "locus amoenus" or place of friendship. The academic online catalog, with its theoretical emphasis on remote access, may be threatening to some librarians because it undermines the notion of the library as the central meeting place on campus. Just as the liver was the seat of the emotions for the ancients, the library often functions as the sentimental heart of the campus community. Current trends in remote access and distribution of electronic information may change all that.

Do all catalog forms enable us to locate a book in space? The older catalog forms gave us only the book's theoretical location, identified by a call number. The online catalog has enabled users to identify both the real location of the book, via circulation records, and the theoretical location, via the call number (Wilson, 1983; 6).

Images of the catalog creators and maintainers. In general, any human product projects certain images of those who create and maintain the product. Each catalog format projects the values of the group of people behind it. In the card catalog human imperfections were evident, while in the online catalog human imperfections and flaws in the database and access points are difficult to detect (Lawry, 1986; 126). With online catalogs, the need to understand the system and searching techniques becomes more crucial to successful use. All computerized systems seem to force the user into linear approaches to information seeking (Estabrook, 1983; 69, 71). Some commentators see hypertext and hypermedia as a major departure from the traditional linear search strategy. Linear search strategies have been linked to masculine modes of perceiving. In Chapter 5, the idea and implications of a hyperlibrary will be considered.

Unique aspects of the online catalog era. The era of the card catalog (circa 1875–1975) was a monolithic era, when the card format for library catalogs clearly dominated all other forms. Many commentators assume that the era of the online catalog will become similarly monolithic. But it may prove to be pluralistic, with different libraries with different access needs choosing from the various catalog forms: book, card, COM, CD-ROM, and online. Has there ever been an era in librarianship when more than one catalog format were simultaneously widely accepted and implemented? In the coming era the various formats may achieve some sort of peaceful coexistence, based on economics, technology, mission, and user needs.

The implementation of online catalogs throughout the developed countries of the world clearly has been a move away from a standardized user interface for library catalogs. Marcia Bates (1989) stresses this in her article. Most end-users of commercially vended bibliographic databases, for example, realize that each database differs in its record structure, indexing, and database contents. Because we are on the heels of an era of the nearly monolithic card catalog, many users of online catalogs seem unaware of the subtle and substantial differences between various online catalog systems. A return to at least a standardized user interface seems a long time off.

O. B. Hardison (1989; 208) suggests that a distinctive manner of the grammar of many modern communications systems, such as film and newspapers, is collage. The online catalog also participates in a grammar of collage, because the catalog is experienced by the user as a sequential series of subsets of the databases created by the user herself. Some of the sets intersect and overlap, while others do not. The entire online catalog database cannot be retrieved. It exists merely as an indefinite number of potential subsets. Only the subsets reveal themselves to users.

The limits of the online catalog. It seems as if the development of online catalogs has few limits. Suddenly all of the questions about scope, record structure, and access points are open to discussion and debate. The limits of the online catalog, however vaguely perceived, are nowhere near being reached. The idea of creating, storing, retrieving, interpreting, and applying scholarly texts in electronic or optical form has not been pushed to its limits. We never will achieve finished total integrated library systems, because we never will be satisfied to freeze the systems when we know that further improvements always will be possible (De Gennaro, 1983; 247). This situation is at once both very liberating and destablizing.

It is frequently assumed that, for most patrons, the catalog is no more than a means to an end. With few exceptions, patrons want materials, not bibliographic records (Crawford, 1987; 1). The upcoming analysis of remote access user behavior, however, raises doubts about this premise. Historically, libraries and librarians have done little to help users manage and manipulate the bibliographic information they retrieve from libraries and other information sources. To date this has not been a major goal of online catalog development.

Several writers, such as Farber and Wilson, have called for limitations to the development of online catalogs, but the limitations would be based on conscious human decisions not to proceed with development, rather than the natural limits imposed by technology, economics, and user acceptance or rejection. Perhaps the technological possibilities override conscious human decisions not to proceed; with economics as the main factor inhibiting technological progress. A broader and clearer understanding of the nature of technological development will be needed to answer this question.

In a sense, however, the limitations of current and future online catalog systems are not determined by economics and technology, but by the uses to which the systems are actually put. Many users, and perhaps many information professionals as well, misinterpret the metaphor of the online catalog being like an automated card catalog as a statement of fact. For many users, the potential power of online catalog systems remains unrealized.

Commercially Vended Bibliographic Databases (BRS, DIALOG)

Christine Borgman has studied the similarities between user behavior toward online catalogs and vended automated bibliographic databases. Online catalogs differ in many ways from bibliographic databases that have been made commercially available through vendors. Traditionally, online commercial databases have relied on a structure and society of mediated searching by trained searchers to provide end-users with specialized information. Online catalog development seems to have avoided this system of intermediaries, although it could be argued that the reference librarian often functions as a search intermediary. If this is true, the intermediary is unavailable to most remote users. It is an assumption of online catalog development and implementation that most searchers of the database are also the end-users of the information retrieved, identified, or located. As more information about remote users of online catalogs becomes known, this assumption will need to be questioned and reexamined. Many remote users of online catalogs may be relatively trained search intermediaries, searching for information for other users within remote organizations.

Most online catalogs have broader subject scopes and a more diverse base of potential users than vended online databases. In many cases, an online catalog can meet more information needs, more breadth and depth of subjects, and more format needs than an online database (Rice, 1987; 307). Even so, many online catalog systems are looking to expand the scope of their databases. For example, some online catalog systems are contemplating providing gateways to other databases, but few commercial online database search services intend to offer gateways to online catalogs (Rice, 1987). The maintainers of online catalogs clearly are the leaders of the present rapprochement between bibliographic citations for books and journal articles.

Still, online catalogs are the poor cousins in the family of online bibliographic databases. They have lagged behind the commercially vended bibliographic databases in terms of the sophistication of the searching techniques. This fact can be explained in several ways. Online catalogs have been designed and developed to be used by any educated adult, and the database industry has more resources at its disposal to reinvest into research and development.

Online catalogs, unlike commercially vended databases with their connect charges, do not encourage the user to develop a search strategy prior to going online. Users pay no penalty for fumbling around online or abandoning a search prematurely. The major portion of most online catalog search sessions is online and interactive. There are few incentives to plan a strategy for searching an online catalog prior to the actual search. The design of online catalog systems and the lack of a connect fee do not encourage users to analyze the information they bring to searches and their behavior during the search. Online catalogs are similar to CD-ROM catalogs in this regard. Users pay no penalty for dallying, experimenting, and wasting CPU (central processing unit) time and or the results of a search statement. Yet the evidence from the transaction log analyses reported in Chapter 12 indicates that many searches are brief (measured either in minutes elapsed or in the number of search statements entered). The pressure to produce is on the catalog system, not the searcher. The opposite assumption dominates many database search sessions, where searchers often feel they have failed if the search session produces no pertinent citations or information.

Commercial databases tend to have well-defined subject parameters, while most online catalogs represent the holdings of libraries with diverse subject collections. However, each user of an automated bibliographic storage and retrieval system, regardless of whether it is an online database or an online catalog, creates a specialized subset of the entire database with each search. The problem of false drops becomes acute in the online catalog environment because online catalogs represent knowledge presented from all perspectives and cumulated over hundreds of years (Prabha, 1989; 34). As the size of online catalog databases continue to grow, the value to most users of precision over recall will increase.

Because they were envisioned as replacements for card catalogs, online catalogs always have been intended for a diverse user group. Online catalogs adopted relatively high standards for ease of use by untrained searchers, while commercial database vendors continued to assume that most users of their product would be fairly well trained in the complex, computer-oriented query languages and user interfaces (Lynch and Berger,

1989; 372). Attempts by the commercial database vendors to broaden their user base to include relatively untrained, novice users came well after the initial development phase of these services. It should be noted that Pfaffenberger (1990) disagrees with this interpretation of the history of online database development. He thinks that the original idea of online bibliographic databases was to make search intermediaries unnecessary.

Remote access has been a fact of life throughout the history of commercially vended databases. Many searchers of databases have only a vague notion of where the databases are located and what they look like, because these notions are absolutely irrelevant to effective use of the database. Users of commercially vended databases have always been remote, dial access users. James Rice (1987; 316) argues that, while the online database searching industry has been restricted to a fairly small and well-defined segment of society, many people will soon have remote access to their online catalogs.

Online library catalogs and commercially vended bibliographic databases do have some similarities. They both developed as technologies with well-defined and well-established value-adding activities just waiting to be made more efficient by automation. The need for technological improvements was there long before the arrival of the technological devices that were promised to deliver greater efficiencies.

It is curious that selective dissemination of information (SDI) services never caught on with online catalogs, like they did with batch processing and commercially vended online databases. There seems to be some demand for monthly or quarterly updates of new items added to the collection on a given subject. The ability to limit a search by year was not available in the system studied, so use of that advanced feature remains unknown.

Distributed Cataloging Systems
(OCLC, RLIN, UTLAS, WLN)

Online catalogs also have roots in distributed cataloging databases. The primary reason for the development and growth of distributed cataloging systems such as OCLC, at least in the beginning, was to avoid repetitive cataloging and increase the efficiency of technical services. They never were designed to be used by the public users of libraries. Most of the current revenue of the networks derive directly or indirectly from shared cataloging and the future viability of the network databases depends on the continuation of shared cataloging (De Gennaro, 1987; 24). Shared cataloging remains focused on the realization of internal efficiencies. The impact on the users of the system, compared to the impact of the development of online catalogs, is minimal.

Recent developments at OCLC, however, have revived interest in the OCLC Online Union Catalog as a public access catalog. The interface to the catalog provided through the EPIC service is more versatile and user-friendly than the old interface, but it mimics the interfaces of the commercial database vendors, so the Online Union Catalog probably will be perceived and used as another commercially vended database. The effect of OCLC's new Maximum Catalog on user's conceptualization and utilization of online catalogs will be interesting to note.

Online Catalogs and Bibliographies

Online catalogs also have ties to published bibliographies. Buckland (1988) basically sees the library catalog as a hybridization between traditional bibliographies and the internal library records about holdings, circulation, orders, etc. Pure bibliographies usually bracket the questions of ownership and location of the full text. Bibliographies provide immense help in identifying intellectual works, and annotated bibliographies often help the user evaluate the pertinence and worth of the items, but few bibliographies help with locating intellectual works. A fundamental reconsideration of the relationships between bibliographies, internal library records, and catalogs is overdue (Buckland, 1988; 299).

Subject bibliography (excluding cataloging) has developed during this century largely outside the mainstream of librarianship (Buckland, 1988; 304). The limitations of late nineteenth-century and early twentieth-century library technology prevented an effective and efficient combination of bibliography with library holdings records, thus making the library catalog a necessity (Buckland, 1988; 308). Those technological limitations no longer exist, so the catalog is no longer necessary as an intermediary between bibliography and local library records. The idea of a catalog is tied to the notion of ownership because almost everything in the bibliographical universe is potentially available at any library (Wilson, 1983; 7).

The main difference between a bibliography and a catalog is that a catalog attempts to provide some indication of who holds or owns the items listed. A premise of this book is that a catalog almost always is better than a bibliography. When users search an information system, in effect they are trying to create personalized catalogs.

Types of Online Catalogs

Over the years different forms of online catalogs have developed. Some online catalogs have become quite large, requiring vast networks of mainframe computers and telecommunications systems to provide access. Other online catalogs have taken advantage of the increased processing and storage capabilities of microcomputers. The advent of CD-ROM technology in the 1980s led to the development of another type of online catalog, although the notion of "online" has been severely stretched. Large online catalogs and small online catalogs require different design goals (Lynch, 1989A; 52). Large online catalogs need to be very precise. The emphasis of this book is on large online catalogs in academic libraries. Miriam Drake agrees with Clifford Lynch that CD-ROM is a giant step backward, because CD-ROM workstations are typically dedicated to a single database, and they force users to come to the library, rather than taking the information to the users (Drake, 1989; 113–114). CD-ROM catalogs will not be a major focus of this book.

Conclusion

This chapter has reviewed definitions and conceptions of online catalogs as well as the differences between online catalogs and other similar devices—worthy topics for conceptual thought and professional debate. Research into online catalogs, however, also must aim to discover how online catalogs are perceived and used by people trying to advance projects. The problem in need of investigation is not what computers are but how they are perceived—how they are incorporated into the web of human culture (Hardison, 1989; 323). We need to examine how and to what extent the online catalog has entered the culture of the university, with its distinct missions of teaching, research, and service. Use of online catalogs must be placed in a context. Chapter 3 will examine the online catalog search session as a unique event in the flow of information.

Our understanding of the purposes and traits of online catalogs remains indeterminate. The minimal statement capable of being made about a library catalog is that somehow it is related to a collection of items somehow containing information which may be of interest or use to a possible group of users. All of the qualifiers are necessary because, prior to actual use, the online catalog is pure potentiality. There may be some value, however, in questioning the assumption that the primary purpose of a library catalog is to help users identify and locate texts.

A library catalog is more than just a distillation of the information contained in the full collection of the intellectual items. Much information retrievable through the online catalog will not be found in the collection itself. Some of the information contained in the catalog, such as the title, also is found in the items. Other information in the catalog, such as subject headings and call numbers, is not found in the items as originally produced (except perhaps in the Cataloging in Publication (CIP) information on the verso of the title page). Much information contained in an online catalog is information independent of the collection of items. The information in the online catalog may be of interest to users in its own right. Perhaps there are more bibliographers in the online catalog user population than we imagine—bibliographers in the sense that they have little interest in the full intellectual content of the items themselves. Their primary reason for using the library catalog is not to gain access to the full text of items.

The information profession no longer can reach a consensus about what an online catalog should contain, its primary purpose, how it should be indexed, how it should be accessed, or how it should be presented. In practice, at least since the advent of the online catalog, no a priori theoretical boundaries for the proper library catalog are being respected (Hildreth, 1989B, 23). We seem to be confronting a crisis of the online library catalog.

Notes

1. It should be noted that Cutter's rules were developed for a *dictionary* catalog. There is ample reason to argue that online catalogs are not dictionary catalogs at all. The records in online catalog databases are not stored in alphabetic order, and it is not essential that retrieved sets of records from the database be presented in alphabetic order.

2. The idea of "advancing" a project probably is more accurate than the desire to "complete" a project because some projects are ongoing and open-ended. Not all users of online catalogs are trying to meet a term paper deadline.

3. Touch screens never gained wide user acceptance, and voice recognition is yet to be widely implemented.

Chapter 3

Information Flow and Search Sessions

The Flow of Information

An online catalog search session exists both as an event in a larger project undertaken by the user and as a moment in the life cycle of the recorded information. Use of bibliographic information by an individual online catalog user is just one segment of a long life cycle, from the moment when the information was born as original knowledge to its eventual death as lost, completely forgotten, or superseded knowledge. The individual search session, then, can be perceived as the intersection of the user's and the information's separate careers. In the terminology of Martin Heidegger's (1977) understanding of modern technology, the search session is the clearing in which the user and the information reveal themselves.

Information seems to flow outward from its sources, but the implied liquid metaphor belies the complex nature of the flow of information, because information is capable of flowing in all directions, including backward to its source. It is capable of rapid growth or replication as it flows, as witnessed in the rapid dissemination of a rumor. Each replication of the original bit of information undergoes a separate life cycle of its own. Accurate mental models of the flow of information are difficult to visualize.

Nevertheless, the flow of information in the world of academic scholarship and academic libraries seems to follow identifiable directions. An examination of the logical stages into which the flow of information can be divided, and what has been the traditional role of the library in that flow, would place online catalog use in a context different from either that of the design of technological devices or of the internal workflow of library systems.

Producers: Traditional Creator and Producer Functions

In the world of scholarly information, producers are the authors who create intellectual works and the publishers who prepare the intellectual works for dissemination by choosing an appropriate medium for effective distribution of the work. The creation of an intellectual work by an author serves as the spring or headwaters in the model of the flow of information. Of course, most new intellectual works are in part syntheses of previously known knowledge, but the knowledge has been interpreted and presented in a new way, hopefully with new knowledge intermingled. Librarians have little control over the process of creating new intellectual works. When authors give titles to their newly created works, rarely do librarians try to influence or control the vocabulary of the title keywords. The creation of intellectual works remains a diversified, dispersed cottage industry.

Publishers begin the process of disseminating the newly created intellectual works. The individual publisher decides in what format an intellectual work would be best distributed. A paperback may be more efficient and effective (in terms of market saturation) than a hardbound book. Perhaps the intellectual work lends itself to distribution on a magnetic or optical disk. As librarians and other intermediaries know, the options for the distribution of intellectual works continue to proliferate. The content of the intellectual work can be a factor in determining the medium and distribution method. It would be inefficient, for example, to publish a directory of online catalog dial access instructions in book format, because the nature of the intellectual work is too mutable to be best contained in the relatively static book medium. The choice of medium should be dependent somewhat on the characteristics of the message.

Middlemen: Traditional Information Service Functions

Libraries and librarians function as intermediaries (a term with slightly positive connotations) or middlemen (a similar term with slightly negative connotations) in the total flow or dissemination of information.[1] Traditionally libraries have been seen as a centralizing midpoint between the multitudes of creators and producers and the multitudes of users. In the past there have been far fewer places where academic information is stored and accessed than where it is created and produced, or evaluated and applied.

If the flow of items carrying intellectual works is likened to the flow of grains of sand in an hourglass, the library comprises the constricting curve in the hourglass. It is a paradox of academic libraries that they simultaneously facilitate and restrict access to recorded scholarly textual information. If the hourglass did not contain a constricting middle curve, it would change into a useless secondglass. Libraries facilitate access by purchasing and centralizing documents of interest to scholars and students. In the past it has not been economically feasible for individual users of libraries to acquire and centralize these documents for each personal project. Academic libraries naturally restrict access in that the multitude of users of the collection must come to the collection to retrieve information.

Document delivery of the physical items is just one way to deliver the intellectual works to the end-users.

Now, however, the number of storage and access points is increasing rapidly. This concerns many librarians. They are reluctant to compete in the marketplace of information services, just like hack writers, lowly students, users, and other producer and consumer groups in the flow of information have been competing in their separate spheres for years.

Information middlemen tend to perceive themselves as disinterested facilitators. Part of the ethics of librarianship assumes a hands-off attitude toward the other two major groups in this outline of the flow of information—the creators/producers and the users. The grumblings of middlemen about the cost of information products is a notable exception to this general observation, but librarians take professional pride in purposefully not trying to control what gets published. Occasionally there are calls to make concerted efforts to influence producer and consumer activities, but generally middlemen assume that it is most prudent to leave both groups alone and try to respond to their behavior and needs.

The first step in the functioning of a middleman is to select and acquire items to be added to the collection. Normally the library develops some notion of its primary clientele, usually based on political affiliations and geographic proximity, and their primary needs vis-à-vis the collection.

The next middleman process is to organize the acquired items. The process of cataloging and classifying a collection of items carrying intellectual works is a value-adding process. Some information is extracted from the items themselves. The title and its verso page normally are the primary sources of information about the item. Some information, such as a call number, is added to the cataloging record from outside the item. Middlemen create internal systems for efficiently monitoring the progress of these activities.

The economics and efficiences of shared, contributed cataloging have meant that little original cataloging is done at the local level anymore. The CIP program has tried to shift some of the burden and cost of cataloging to the producers. Periodical indexing serves as a precedent. Libraries abdicated their control over periodical indexing early in this century to producers and commercial interests. When libraries began purchasing indexing for journals from outside producers, they lost control over the quality and type of indexing (Tyckoson, 1989; 10). Something similar may be happening to the cataloging of monographic items.

Storage and preservation are two more essential middleman functions. This schematic of the flow of information is not watertight. For example, the storage of information also occurs at the stages where the information is published and finally consumed. All information must be stored somewhere—in the brain, in a book, or on a magnetic tape. Often it is stored in multiple locations. Libraries traditionally assumed the function of storing published information of potential interest to the library's defined primary clientele. This has led some people to think of libraries as warehouses of information. In the past, preservation has involved the task of maintaining the carrier of the intellectual text, such as the paper comprising the book. In the future, assuming that many intellectual texts are available in an easily mutable electronic form, a major preservation effort will be needed to preserve the text as originally published, before the consumers alter the text to suit their projects.

In most libraries the burden of retrieval rests on the end-user, but the various public services divisions within the library organization exist to facilitate the end-user's retrieval activities. An online catalog system, for example, facilitates the identification and location of items carrying intellectual works.

Relations between middlemen and producers. Middlemen have a natural urge to establish independence from producers, and consumers naturally want to gain as much control and independence as they can over the bibliographic records and the texts. That is what they are aiming to accomplish as they interact with the information. Conflicts between the three main groups are inevitable, because each depends on the other two. Complaints voiced by middlemen, for example, often resemble concerns and complaints of downstream municipalities about what upstream communities do to the water supply.

The philosopher José Ortega y Gasset proposed the opposite agenda for librarians. He thought librarians should prevent the production of superfluous items and encourage productive work that would fill gaps in the written record of scholarship (Wilson, 1983; 192). A refereed, coordinated production effort would make the need for evaluative online catalogs diminish.

Consumers: Traditional User Functions

In the past, libraries have done little to help users manipulate, manage, and assimilate information. It has been the responsibility of the end-user to analyze the information retrieved—to interpret, evaluate, and apply it. As the amount of available information increases, these functions within the overall flow of information will be increasingly valued by consumers. Whether or not they are performed by librarians, the activities of analysis, evaluation, and interpretation of information will become unique and critical in future information systems (Taylor, 1986; 78). One pressing question for online catalog designers and librarians is whether to become overtly involved in the processes of information analysis. To what extent should the middlemen assist the end-users with their tasks?

In a traditional library setting the burden of retrieving documents and transporting the information back to the workplace was and still is squarely on the shoulders of users. Libraries do quite a bit to facilitate retrieval and transportation of documents to points of end-use (witness the photocopier and the existence of interlibrary loan departments), but the final leg of the journey from creator to user is made by the end-user.

Evaluating potentially pertinent items in the context of the present project is an essential user task. The user must decide if the items retrieved will help advance the information project. Patrick Wilson (1983; 165–171) examines the methods commonly used to establish the cognitive authority of texts.

Finally, the user wants to apply the retrieved and evaluated information to the task at hand—the final cause for beginning the information-seeking process in the first place. Electronic media have made the application of information much more facile. It is inefficient to require the user to rekey all of the information retrieved, evaluated, and assimilated.

The Double Squeeze on Libraries

If this brief schematic of the flow of information is correct, libraries and other middlemen are threatened in two ways. First, they stand to lose a significant market share in the provision of their traditional function—information storage and retrieval. Private sector information middlemen are becoming popular. Second, they are threatened by invasion from the other two main groups, the creators/producers and the users. There are forces in both groups that want to cut out the middleman and assume the functions of storage and retrieval for themselves. Recent technological and economic developments seem to support their cause. Cataloging in Publication and large hard disks on personal computers are the tips of two icebergs converging on middlemen. Libraries may become obsolete—like icemen—their essential functions assumed by the end-user and the producer. The advent of electronic workstations will change the focus of attention from the library to the user (Buckland, 1989B; 392). Electronic workstations will not be used just by scholars. Perhaps scholars will be one of the last groups to adopt them. Libraries, if they continue to exist, will become more transparent.

Online catalog development, on the other hand, seems to be invading the traditional domain of the user. The push is on to give online catalogs a greater role in screening, evaluating, and assessing the information retrieved. A major issue of all research and development concerning intelligent information retrieval is the issue of the control and delegation of roles and task accomplishment between the system and the user (Hildreth, 1989A; 51). It is a policy issue, verging on an educational or ethical issue, over the extent to which the online catalog as a middleman's device should intrude on the traditional end-user functions. It should not be simply or primarily an issue governed by technological and economic feasibility. The combined force of the technological imperative and economic efficiences, however, hides the ethical and educational implications of online catalog design.

The library catalog is a product of middlemen. Producer and consumer groups have little impact on the design of online catalog systems. All of the assimilative work by users on the intellectual content of both the catalog and the collection has little effect on the structure and content of the catalog. As currently conceived and implemented, the online catalog will flourish or decline along with the middleman.

Automatic Flow of Information

All stages in the flow of information are being automated. The effects of the automation on the processes and activities at each stage, human understanding and valuation of each process, and the outcomes of each stage remain unknown. The effects probably will emerge slowly over a long term, longer than the life cycle of many of the technological devices and systems themselves. Michael Zimmerman (1990; 206), for example, wonders about the long-term effects of wordprocessing on language and writing. In the same manner, but at a different stage in the flow of information, we can wonder about the long-term effects of online catalogs and other automated information storage and retrieval devices on formal scholarship and bibliographic learning. How will these devices change the users' perceptions of the universe of recorded scholarly information?

Aspects of the Search Session

Within the context of the flow of information, an online catalog search session is the sequence of events whereby the consumer uses a device designed and maintained by middlemen to gain access to the products of the producers. It is just one stage in a much larger phenomenon of the flow of information. Search sessions should be the fundamental units of study of online catalog use. A smaller unit, such as individual search statements, strays too far from the user's sense of a search. A larger unit, such as a notion of a search that includes several search sessions and several bibliographic storage and retrieval systems, is too difficult to identify for research purposes.

The online catalog search session is a set of cognitive and behavioral activities undertaken by the user, motivated by some need, with anticipated outcomes. Thus the session falls within a broader context of user behavior. Portions of this broader context, such as the user's educational goals and learning style, would be of interest to researchers of search sessions. Other aspects of the broader context of the user's behavior, such as the fact that he or she ate lunch fifteen minutes before beginning a search session, probably is of little interest to researchers. From the user's perspective, however, the developing sense of an information need and the subsequent search session probably are not clearly perceived and entirely self-conscious. From the researcher's point of view, when the growth of the information need reaches the point where user actions begin, the search session begins.

The primary interest in this book is with the search session—an identifiable set of user behavior activities. The meaning of a search session, from the perspective of both the user and the system, needs to be articulated, as do the various aspects of an online catalog search session.

Other commentators have analyzed and categorized the search session. Fidel (1983) identifies eight catagories of variables in the retrieval of information: setting, user, request, database, search system, searcher, search process, and outcome. Cochrane and Markey (1983; 342) also provide a diagram of the major variables affecting online information retrieval, such as the command language, the database, the environment, and the personal characteristics of the searcher. For Walt Crawford (1987; 7) every use of an online system involves presentation, process, and protection. Presentation is how the system and the user interact and communicate. A process is an action that changes the state of the database or the state of the library. Protection involves shields between the system and the user, plus privacy among users. The remainder of this chapter presents a few of the characteristics of online catalog search sessions.

The Searcher

A confusion in library terminology is the frequent utilization of the word "user" to include those people at whom the service is aimed, but who may not actually use the service at all (Blagden, 1988; 126). The intended and actual users of an automated system may be quite disparate. The development of online catalogs probably was motivated by a notion of what types of groups would likely use the devices. Some critics have suggested that online catalogs were developed primarily for librarians, not for users. An actual user population exists, but it may be difficult to identify and describe.

The main areas of concern and interest regarding the searcher are behavior, attitudes, and sense of success when searching the online catalog. Under the category of behavior, the searcher's information retrieval skills, especially while interacting with the online catalog, are of major interest. These skills include data entry skills, such as typing and spelling skills, subject knowledge, knowledge about the system, and conceptualization skills, particularly conceptual flexibility as a means for resolving problems and roadblocks.

Without use, any system is just pure potential. Users decide when and how to use the system. Libraries are open systems to a great degree. The purposes for using an online catalog system come from outside the system, from the individual users. A basic professional tenet is that librarians (and, by extension, designers of automated library systems) should not dictate how information should be sought or used. System designers and librarians may try to guess how users will use they system, or intermediaries may try to instruct users in fruitful, efficient, and proper ways to use the system, or designers may try to design a system that accommodates most or all potential users; but the moment of actual use of the system is in the user's control.

An assumption behind the analysis presented in this book is that the user is not part of the computerized information system. Although others have perceived the user as an essential part of any automated system, the assumption here is that the user comes to the system to retrieve information contained in it. The user actualizes the system, which is external to the user's lived experience until it is realized.

The Automated Search System

The automated search system is the command language and total grammar used to search the various databases and indexes. The primary areas of research interest and concern include the speed of system response, the availability of the system (both geographically and temporally), the intelligibility of system responses, and documentation and help provided in all forms, both on-screen and off. Both its internal consistency and its compatibility with other systems would be of interest. The state of online catalog research has reached a point where questions about internal consistency can expand beyond questions about consistent screen designs and command syntax. An online catalog system also should be internally consistent in the values it projects about both the world of recorded scholarly information and the value of the user's intelligence. An automated search system projects an entire world, not just the quickest, easiest route to achieve the desired outcome.

The Database Being Searched

In online catalogs the database is separate from the search syntax and general user interface. For example, the same database of MARC bibliographic records can be loaded into different online catalog systems and produce remarkably different search results. Regarding the database being searched, middlemen and users are interested in the scope of the database and its overall quality. The record structure employed and both the potential and actual indexes and access points extracted from that record structure are of more interest to middlemen and producers. Users would be interested in who decides (and on what criteria) additions to the database, as well as who actually maintains the database. Middlemen are extremely interested in ownership issues, but consumers are interested only to the extent that ownership provides clues about the scope and probable contents of the database.

The Items Sought; or The Lurking Collection

By its very nature (at least in the past) a library catalog by definition was a catalog to a collection, and most users searched the catalog in order to gain access to specific documents within the collection. The bibliographic records within the database functioned as surrogates for the bibliographic items themselves. To reapply E. M. Forster's lament that the novel must tell a story: Yes, oh dear yes, a catalog must provide access to a collection.[2]

A database of bibliographic records, however, usually is more than just a slice or distillation of the items in the collection. It is more than just, say, the title and its verso page of every item in the collection. A bibliographic database has had value added to it by intermediaries. Records of bibliographic items have two types of attributes: inherent attributes, which are controlled by the authors and producers, and assigned attributes, which are controlled by information intermediaries such as librarians (Swanson, 1979; 10). Both producers and middlemen contribute to the content of standard bibliographic records. Current online catalog systems rely heavily on assigned attributes, such as subject headings assigned by catalogers, for information retrieval. Of the three major groups in the flow of information, only the consumers are not allowed to contribute to the contents of the database.

The product or outcome of an online catalog search session is not self-evident or straightforward. The product may be a retrieved set of bibliographic records, or the potentially retrievable set of bibliographic items, or the insights into the structure of recorded knowledge on a topic, depending on what the user intends. If bibliographic items are the desired product from online catalog searching, after the search the items are still not in hand. The items have been identified (if they were not known prior to the beginning of the search session), and their official status within the local collection has been confirmed, but the items remain unretrieved.

The Information Need (Advancing Projects)

It is difficult to identify and define information needs and information uses. Line, for example, defines "needs" as what an individual ought to have, "wants" as what an individual would like to have, "demand" as what an individual asks for, and "use" as what an individual actually uses (Blagden, 1988; 125). To be faithful to experience, however, it must be noted that projects are more fundamental than information needs. Users need information in order to advance projects. Users want to advance their current projects. Only in that context do they need information. To isolate and focus on the information need is to focus on an intermediate step.

An information need precipitates the actual search session, bringing the user to the online catalog. There is some hurdle the user wants to get over. The user has a project that he or she wants to complete or advance. Some perceived impediment to a continuation of the project has been detected by the user, and she or he has decided that information may be useful in overcoming the hurdle, and that the online catalog may be a good place to locate information. The impediment may be an unresolved mental dilemma (e.g., what is the meaning of life), or bibliographic (e.g., did publisher X or publisher Y publish that book), or mercenary (e.g., I need to find some information so my boss will be pleased with me).

The sense of an information need developing prior to the search session (it could be labeled the a priori information need) certainly influences the subsequent search session, but its influence may be overrated and overemphasized by system designers and intermediaries. It certainly is worthwhile to study more closely the nature of a priori information needs, of the desire for information prior to any major interaction with a particular information storage and retrieval system. Another fruitful area of research, however, would be to study what happens to a user's a priori information need as she or he actually interacts with a specific information system. Some sort of negotiation and alteration occurs during the search session. The dynamics of this "negotiation of need" would be a fruitful research topic. Does the information system help the user clarify and refine the a priori information need?

Part of the user's a priori information need involves an active projection of an anticipated outcome of the search session. This involves not only the information retrieved but also the state of the user's current project. If the information retrieved enables the user to continue toward the completion of the project, the information could be termed pertinent.

The user's intentions surrounding the information have several parameters, including: the intended use of the information in advancing the project; the amount of time and effort involved in retrieving and interpreting the information; the desirable characteristics of the information to be retrieved (such as completeness, precision, reliability, and timeliness); the formal characteristics of the desired information; and the perceived economic value of the information (including the perceived economic and or emotional value of solving the problem or completing the project) (Saracevic, Kantor, Chamis, and Trivison, 1988; 165).

It may be erroneous, nevertheless, to assume that every user of an online catalog is motivated by a pressing problem or need. Perhaps a large percentage of dial access online catalog use is motivated by simple curiosity. The current project may be an ongoing interest in the user and the desire to play and explore may be a significant part of dial access use. A study of the characteristics of playful behavior may be useful in understanding the recorded behavior of online catalog users.

It is commonly argued that current online catalogs by themselves do not satisfy information needs. The catalog merely facilitates the process of identifying and locating documents that may satisfy the need. Bibliographic records are once removed from the intellectual works themselves, and twice removed from the user's actual project activities. Thus an undergraduate student finds a bibliographic record (twice removed) for a book about Shakespeare (once removed) in order to write a term paper on Shakespeare (the current project). It is not difficult to surmise why most undergraduates are not overly interested in the bibliographic records themselves and methods for retrieving them. The possibility must be entertained, however, that the online catalog may be used as a terminal information source more often than is suspected. Nevertheless, there is a growing sense that defining information needs strictly in terms of document identification and retrieval will be inadequate for the design and future development of online catalogs (Hancock-Beaulieu, 1989; 36). Some researchers are focusing on the anomalous states of knowledge within users, and others are thinking about the reformation of intellectual works in the new technological environment. Placing the search session in the context of the user's project may be a useful way to move beyond the notion of information needs.

The Search Process

The use of library catalogs has few observable behaviors associated with it. Most of the activity (e.g., reading, thinking, evaluating, deciding) is not easily studied (Markey, 1984; 17). The use of an online catalog to retrieve information is a complex, furtive process. Charles Hildreth (1982; 34–35) suggests that a sensible model of the information retrieval process should incorporate both the actions of the user and the various components of the system. This assumes, however, that how a new technological device will be used can be known prior to its use. It assumes that designers can imagine how the system will be used without making the design little more than a self-fulfilling prophecy. Many philosophers of technology, however, have suggested that a unique characteristic of the new age of technology is our inability to foretell how a new technology device will be used, or what effects the new system will have on a whole range of other systems that fall within the penumbra of the new system. Chapter 4 will examine these issues in more depth.

Distinctions need to be made between an individual search statement, types of search statements, a search state, a search session, and the total search process as executed by the user, which probably (and should) extends far beyond the online catalog system. Individual search statements are any string of characters sent to the online catalog computer for a response. These search statements fall into different categories. In the study explained in Chapters 10, 11, and 12, search statements identified as unique data-entry searches were isolated and studied. A group of search statements combine to form a search state. Most search sessions comprise more than one search state. For example, an error-correction state within a search session is different from an expansive, risk-taking state. Search states can be defined along the lines of the architecture of the system or across them.

Transaction log analysis began by studying individual search statements. Much transaction logging software records each statement sent from the user to the CPU, line by line.[3] John Tolle (1983A) advanced transaction log analysis by working on the definition and analysis of search states. Thomas Peters and Martin Kurth (1990) are trying to study entire subject search sessions. The ultimate goal is to understand how information seekers identify, locate, and retrieve information, and, specifically, how and where use of the online catalog fits into that process.

The concept of a complete search can be very elusive. Again, analysts must be careful not to let the librarians' penchant for exhaustive searches bias the analysis of searches that appear incomplete. On the other hand, what appears to be a complete online catalog search session may be just one small part of the user's overall search session. The transaction logs analyzed in this study reveal that often the user will search for the same information over a long period of time (days, weeks, or sometimes months), often altering the search queries slightly, sometimes repeating the same sequence of search statements.

The outcome of each online catalog search session is at least one personalized subset of the database.[4] The subset may be a null set, but it is a set the user has created from the entire set of bibliographic, authority, piece, and other records.

As conceived by the designers. System designers, middlemen, and users all develop conceptions about the search process that affect actual observed behavior. The underlying thinking behind the early online catalog designs was to replicate the card catalog (Culkin, 1989; 172). Initial designs of online catalogs, many of which are still being used today in modified form, attempted to serve the same functions as other catalog forms, only faster, more efficiently, and at a lower cost. Visions of lower costs kept library administrators interested, while the perception of increased speed pleased users.

In order to begin and complete a design project, the designers of any automated information system must have a working mental model of how they intend the system to be searched. Most designers want to respond to needs they perceive in users prior to the design of a new device. The functional features and command structures of the user-system interfaces of online catalogs are responses to the user's functional needs as perceived by system designers (Hildreth, 1982; i). Design of online catalogs usually proceeded from some model or conceptualization of the problem-solving process in the real, current world of bibliographic storage and retrieval. Empirical knowledge of real end-user searching behavior normally was not sought and considered (Hildreth, 1982; 34). The designers based their perceptions on hunches rather than systematic research prior to design and development. This is not necessarily a bad design decision to make, but historically it was the method used in the early design of online catalog systems.

The efficient use of system processing capabilities is a prime concern to system designers. Often they try to design the system so that what probably would appear to be the most efficient search for the user also will be an efficient search for the processing system. A design principle could be formulated that purposefully tried to avoid having a single mental model of how to use the system being developed—to encourage users to overcome functional fixity. Some noncommittal principles like this have led to a smorgasbord of search options that only serve to confuse the average user.

As conceived by the intermediary (librarian). The teachers of the use of the online system, who in the case of online catalogs usually are reference librarians, also have an ideal search process to convey to users. Reference librarians mediate between the search process as made possible by the system design and the search process as conceived by the user approaching the system. If, for example, the online catalog is designed to make the passage through an authority file a conspicuous intermediate step in the search process, and if the user appears to have little or no conception of authority files, the reference librarian must mediate between the conflicting conceptions of the search process. Intermediaries also develop their own ideas about the search process. They may want the search process to teach bibliographic concepts as it retrieves a set of bibliographic records. They may want the search process to stress recall over precision. They may agree with many users that speedy response time is an important characteristic of the search process.

As conceived by the user. Finally, the end user of the system must have an intended search process. Often this search process is couched in broader terms, such as how to use the library, where the intended search process of the online catalog is just part of a larger agenda. Ultimately, all of these intentional search processes get realized somehow in an actual search session. Transaction logs record only that—the actual search session realized by an individual user—but sometimes analyzers of transaction logs can make inferences back to one or more of the intentional searches.

Thomas Moran (1981) argues that the user's process of creating a mental model of the online catalog system largely is a process of reconstructing the designer's mental model of the information retrieval process. The designer's mental model, with all its attendant valuations about the purpose and methods of information retrieval, is revealed to the user through the system portion of the human-computer interface. Inherent in the design of an interactive online catalog system is a model of the information seeking and processing tasks of the intended users. As the user interacts with and learns the system, he or she constructs a mental model of the system as a problem-solving tool. The user intuitively reconstructs the designer's a priori mental model of the information retrieval process using this new technological device (see Hildreth, 1982; 40). In essence, the user, with the actual system as the only clue, tries to decipher the designer's mental model of the search process. Hildreth (1982; 41) suspects that the user employs different models of the information retrieval process, depending on the kind of information database or retrieval device being used. The conditions established by the automated information retrieval device determine the mental model formed by the user. This argument assumes that the user's mental model is complete only after he or she actually has used the system, not before. This model-forming process may continue over the sum total of the user's search sessions on the system. If the system changes, the user's mental model (and valuation) of the system gradually changes as well.

The user interface. Hildreth (1982; 33) has studied extensively the interface between the user and the information storage and retrieval system. The user interface is the locus of the interaction undertaken in the use of interactive computer systems. It is curious that Hildreth refers to the user interface as a location. In Chapter 4 comparisons will be made between the sense of space developed during an online catalog search session and Martin Heidegger's idea of the clearing in which Being happens. Is this a new sense of spatial orientation—a new type of clearing—unique to the age of computer technology? Later in the book the strains put on the user's normal spatial orientation by remote access to online catalogs will be examined. Perhaps this is a new type of spatial orientation that is replacing older forms.

Somehow users of online catalogs develop a conceptual model of the system in its totality. Often the user's conceptual model is radically different from the real scope of the database and the system. For example, the user may think that the online catalog is a periodical index.

Hildreth seems to assume that the user comes to the system as a "tabula rasa." He states that the features of the system are encountered by the user at the interface (Hildreth, 1982; 34). If we can assume that the understanding of the features of the system is the major portion of the user's working notion of the system, Hildreth seems to imply that actual use of the system is the main source (perhaps the only source) of information and feedback from which the user constructs the mental model. The opposite hypothesis should be tested—that the major source of material for the user's mental model of the online catalog system comes from nonuse experiences and information, such as advice and tutorials from other people, attitudes about modern technology (and the computer age in particular) formulated prior to the actual interaction with the online catalog system, and documentation provided beyond the horizon of the system's user interface.

An important and neglected interface is not between the user and the online catalog, but rather between the user and the system of recorded scholarly information. The online catalog functions as an intermediary in that ultimate interface. The interface the user wants to establish is not to the online catalog system, but to the system of recorded scholarly information in a given area of interest.

The idea of use: fess-up screens and payoff screens. At some point during a search of most online catalog systems, the user is required to enter some information brought to the search. It may be a title, an author, a topic, a call number, or some other bit of information about the items sought. Although it is conceivable to design an online catalog where the search process consists entirely of option selection steps, never requiring the use to enter data not prompted by the system, this research project did not discover any such existing system. At some point during the search the user is required to "fess-up" and provide some information brought to the search session. In the study to follow in later chapters, the fess-up portion of the search process is called a unique data-entry search. This study suggests that unique data-entry search statements are qualitatively different from other search statements. They have more value as statements, to both users and those who study users, and they reveal more about usage and the users.

The logical complement to the fess-up step of the search is the payoff step, where the information of primary interest to the user within the context of a specific need finally is retrieved from the system. If the process of searching an online catalog involves a series of steps, which step is the primary payoff for the user? Perhaps the profession should not assume without question the display of the bibliographic information as being of most interest to the user. Perhaps piece records, circulation information, and authority file information about subjects, authors, and series are gaining user appreciation and interest. It cannot be assumed that all users of an online catalog want immediate access to the lurking collection. If this were true, demand for remote access to online catalogs probably would not be as strong as it is. Perhaps users are interested only in bibliographic citation information, regardless of whether a particular library holds the item or not. Qualitative information gleaned from the present study indicates that aggregate user interest seems to be shifting away from information about the bibliographic items to other types of information found in online catalogs. When conducting research in the use of online catalogs, researchers must be careful not to make assumptions about what users really want out of the system. The payoff screen is not self-evident. It probably is heavily dependent on situational characteristics, in terms of both the current project and the current search session.

Decision making during the search process. During the course of a search session, users make decisions about both the process of searching and the subject or intent of the search. They came to the device looking for some information (e.g., holdings information, bibliographic information, or books by an author), so they must make decisions as they go not only about whether they have found it, but also about whether their search methods will find what they are seeking. One source of user frustration when using online catalogs is either an obliviousness to the process of searching or a conscious unwillingness to focus on the process over the subject. The user must concentrate simultaneously both on the content of the message and the methods of finding the message. In Chapter 7 the thesis is made and defended that the dichotomy between method and content is not conducive to instructive online catalog search sessions. Decisions searchers make about the search process are the primary concern in this book. As the search session evolves, in addition to interpreting and evaluating the information retrieved, the searcher must always decide whether to continue and, if so, how to continue.

In addition, decisions searchers make about the search process itself can be divided into types. Searchers make decisions about the overall ease and effectiveness of the device they have chosen. This type of decision could be called a summative evaluation. Questionnaire surveys of online catalog users measure users' ability to articulate these types of decisions. Searchers also make decisions during every search session about when to quit searching with a particular device. These could be called decisions regarding continuance. The analysis of transaction logs may help reseachers learn more about the parameters of decisions about continuance.

Types of learning during the search process. Not much research into online catalog systems has studied what learning, if any, occurs during the course of the individual search session and how it occurs. Although it was argued in Chapter 2 that the primary intent of an online library catalog is not computer-assisted instruction, designers and intermediaries should recognize that some form of learning occurs, and researchers should try to determine how and when that learning occurs. Perhaps trial and error is a fundamental way users learn how to use the online catalog. The online catalog search session probably is largely a trial-and-error process, without an a priori end or outcome. During trial-and-error searching, the information need or topic of interest is not stable (Hildreth, 1989A; 22).

Somehow most users do learn how to use the online catalog. Learning probably occurs during the search session. Calls for online catalog development to pursue the goal where the system would conduct a form of reference interview—determining the user's level of expertise and information need—may ignore or retard any learning that occurs during individual search sessions, especially if significant learning occurs through trial and error, as well as shifts in information needs during the course of the search session.

Ideas of a successful search session. How well can the concepts of success and failure regarding online catalog use be defined? Is there a strict dependent relationship between successful search sessions and a successful system? Perhaps a distinction can be made between error and failure, where errors are problems that do not substantially affect results, while failures are problems that lead to unsatisfactory results (see Richard Jones, 1986).

There is a time element in the notion of failure. Some failures are corrected in a matter of seconds, while others go on indefinitely. User frustration is difficult to measure, but it probably is not directly proportional to the length of time required to correct the error. For example, a short time required to correct an error does not imply low user frustration.

There are at least three ways to define and measure the success of a search session. A successful search may be very precise, where the user has achieved efficient use of the system, from the user's point of view. The user found what he or she wanted, only what was wanted, and quickly. A successful search also may be a search that was very satisfying to the user. Many survey studies assume that a satisfied user is a good indication of, if not identical to, a successful search. This book assumes that user satisfaction is dependent on too many variables to serve as a meaningful measure of the success of a search. Finally, recall may be used as a measure of a successful search.

Robert Taylor (1986; 31) identifies four ways to consider the success of a search. Success can be measured in terms of accomplishment, performance, attitude, or cost. Cost and system performance are not primary concerns to most users of most online catalogs. Satisfaction is a type of user attitude after the search session is complete, and precision and recall both fall within the category of desired accomplishments.

Brian Nielsen (1986; 31) also discusses the difficulties inherent in the concept of successful use of an online catalog. The standard idea of a successful search session is where either the user examines all or most of the retrieved bibliographic records, or the user narrows the results in some manner (Crawford, 1990; 48). An assumption here seems to be that exhaustive, persistent search sessions are more successful than brief, precise search sessions.

Perhaps we need to make a distinction between the success of a search session and the value or worth of the session. Taylor (1986; 153) argues that value is strictly in the eye of the user. "The value-added approach [to the assessment of information systems] based on the user-driven model is a behavioral approach, for it assumes that value is in the eye of the beholder, the user of that information." Saracevic, Kantor, Chamis, and Trivison (1988; 169) also make a distinction between the relevance of a retrieved item and its utility, with relevance being more objective and utility more subjective. Relevance is the degree of fit between the question and the retrieved item. Utility is the degree of actual usefulness of answers to an information seeker. Perhaps the concept of user satisfaction is used most frequently as a measure of the utility of search results.

Is the use of an online catalog in any way aesthetic? When users report through surveys and questionnaires that they are satisfied with these new technological devices, is there an aesthetic component to that sense of satisfaction? Does the online catalog teach and delight?

Most questionnaire surveys seem to assume that user expressions of summative evaluation have a strong positive correlation, if not absolute identification, with the success of the search. If the user is happy, the search was a success. Questionnaires and surveys reveal, however, that many users report that they leave an online catalog very happy and satisfied with their search sessions, but the professional judgment of reference librarians and other intermediaries indicates that the search was not a success, if measured in terms over which the user does not have absolute control, such as precision, recall, and efficiency (either in terms of system efficiency or user efficiency). The value of a search session may be the decision solely of the user, but its success can be evaluated on criteria not completely controlled by the user's attitudes and opinions.

The determination of the success of a search session must be kept distinct from the task of assigning responsibility or blame for unsuccessful searches. The searcher, the online catalog system, the collection developer, the search intermediary, or the system designer all may be partially or completely responsible for unsuccessful searches, but assigning blame should not be confused with determining the success or failure of a search session.

A branch of online catalog research needs to focus on the lived experience of interacting with a catalog from the user's point of view. But to go so far as to equate user satisfaction with the success of the search would be misguided. A search session is a series of events with a common purpose. Perhaps research should concentrate more on the events themselves and less on the user response to the events. The users' responses to the same type of event, such as a search that yielded zero hits, will vary greatly, ranging from mild frustration to a halo condemnation (e.g., this system stinks) to a pleasant surprise; but the event remains the same.

Rather than attempt to define, measure, and assess the success or failure of a search session, perhaps we should think in terms of useful frustration. An information need could be defined as a debilitating frustration. Users come to a library because they want something, they know not what. Their current project has reached an impasse. Perhaps the goal should be to make online catalogs challenging, so that some learning can occur, without making them inordinately frustrating.

The mild frustration of a user during the course of an online catalog search session may not be entirely detrimental, nor even avoidable. The notion of a satisfied information need involves a reduction in the frustrating sense of unacquired information that motivates the action as a response to the need.

The shortcoming of thinking in terms of a successful search session or a failed search session is that it focuses on the summative evaluation, downplaying questions and problems experienced by the user during the search. It may be natural and acceptable for the user to make a summative evaluation of the search session, but perhaps the research effort should turn its attention to other concerns.

A user's notion of a search session probably extends far beyond a single session with an online catalog. The intent of most online catalog search sessions may not be to achieve the highest recall possible. The accepted notion of the effectiveness of a retrieved set of bibliographic citations reveals a preference for comprehensive retrieval (i.e., high recall) over the identification of a select set of pertinent sources (i.e., high precision) in a larger context of the user's information project (Pfaffenberger, 1990; 169).

Setting

The setting in which the online catalog is used also demands attention. Questions about ease of access, comfort, and privacy need to be examined. The provision of peripherals, such as seating, printers, and microcomputer workstations affects the search session. The ambient environment probably has an influence on the user's decision to continue or terminate the search session. For example, if most users are forced to stand while they use the online catalog, average search session length probably will not exceed ten minutes.

The setting also is a component of the discussion regarding the right to privacy and confidentiality. The setting of a remote access session with an online catalog may have a profound influence on the user's attitudes toward the catalog, the database, and the session.

Intended and Actual Uses of Retrieved Information

Online catalogs, like most information storage and retrieval systems, are fairly open systems, influenced by factors external to the system itself. Very little is known about the problems motivating users to approach online catalogs, nor about the users' intended uses for the information derived from the system (Saracevic, Kantor, Chamis, and Trivison, 1988; 164). The intended uses of the retrieved information and the actual, observable uses of the information probably differ. Of course, the vital, cognitive uses of information cannot be studied directly. Since most online catalog users are young, the effects of the retrieved information and the structure of that information may have a significant impact on the scholarly development of a young user.

It is a common assumption in the profession that most or all users of online catalogs want to retrieve at least one of the documents cataloged. The hope of finding at least one document containing information that may help to solve the perceived problem motivated the user to attempt to use the online catalog. There may be a tendency, however, to use online catalogs as final information sources, not as a gateway to a nearby collection of bibliographic items.

Discussion

What variables should researchers study to determine the correct use of a system? Are correct uses instances where the system was used as designed, or is correct use more a matter of using the system as efficiently as possible? If we concentrate on efficiency, however, we need to determine from what vantage point efficiency will be defined and measured. Efficiency, like efficacy, is in the eyes of the beholder. What seems efficient to systems personnel may not seem efficient to users. The middlemen and the consumers, as discussed above, are not always at cross purposes, but it is the responsibility of the middlemen to know the needs of the consumers.

There is a fundamental tension or conflict during most or all search sessions. The user of an online catalog is intent on finding enough information to fulfill the task at hand. Once she or he determines that enough has been found, the information need recedes below the threshold of user action. The online catalog system, however, requires users to learn another set of information—about the concepts and mechanics of searching the database—before the user will be able to find any information. The system requires the learning of a separate topic before information on the user's topic at hand can be located. Most users at online catalog terminals want to find information, not learn about how to find information. The recognition of the fundamental tension has caused many designers to devalue the process of learning how to use the online catalog. They strive to make the online catalog and its use as transparent as possible.

Key Questions

A set of unanswered questions remain. What is the purpose of an online catalog? What is the scope of an online catalog? What do we know about users of online catalogs? What do we expect from users of online catalogs? Who should pay for the development of an online catalog? To what extent should future information systems be personalized? The main factors driving the development and evolution of online catalogs are: technology, economics, the library's mission, the history of library catalogs, and user attitudes and needs. Should the observed behavior and expressed needs of users be the ultimate factor in future development of online catalogs and other public access automated library systems?

Even if we decide that the users are (or should be) the dominant factor, we still need to make some fundamental decisions on how to help them. Should we stress user education on many fronts, and try to improve the user as the final actor of the triumvirate in the flow of information? Or should we try to develop systems that take control of many user tasks?

Brownrigg's Hierarchy of Automated Library Systems

Edwin Brownrigg identifies five conceptual stages or plateaus in the hierarchy of automated public access library systems. Most current systems indicate to users places where the answers to their information need are likely to be found. The next step would be to add the evaluative component of the information search process. Thirdly, the material containing the answer could be provided online. Fourthly, the answers themselves could be culled from pertinent documents and presented online. Finally, the most developed automated library systems, according to Brownrigg and Lynch (1983; 114), would provide the answers online to even ill-formed questions and ill-conceived information needs. We should not forget, however, that we are asking the automated system to take over responsibilities traditionally relegated to the user, rather than to help the user do a better job at those tasks.

Struggle for Control

Normally when librarians and information scientists discuss the struggle for bibliographic control, they refer to the struggle to gain control over the expanding universe of bibliographic items. There is a concurrent struggle for bibliographic control amongst the three main groups involved in the flow of information.

Libraries deal with information. Information has the unique property of being a usable commodity that is not depleted by such use (although use does affect the value of the information). Because librarians work with information, often they make the mistake of assuming that this unique property of information transfer applies to all aspects of the profession. They fail to realize that the struggle for market shares of the processing of information (producer, distributor, organizer, retriever, and user) is a struggle for control of the old-fashioned sort—the struggle for a piece of a pie of finite size. There are only so many things that can be done to information, and the struggle for control is for control of that finite set of processes.

Fundamental shifts in control of the essential functions of information flow are under way. When an institution assumes more of the essential function in the flow of information, it should anticipate increased costs. For example, if academic libraries want to shift their interest and allegiance from the antecedent producer sector to the successive consumer sector, they will need more funding coupled with an internal redistribution of funding criteria and priorities.

Notes

1. In William Potter's article (1986) in *Wilson Library Bulletin*, he refers to librarians as middlemen.

2. E. M. Forster, *Aspects of the Novel* (New York: Harcourt, Brace & World, 1927), 25–26.

3. Some transaction logs also record some or all responses sent back from the central processing unit of the computer.

4. A trend in online catalog design seems to be to allow users to browse through indexes to the database. Although browsing through an index technically is not set creation, an implied set is created, bounded by the point where the user enters the index and the point where the user exits.

Chapter 4
Philosophy of Technology and Online Catalogs

Introduction

All too often in the past the idea of a philosophy of the online catalog has been intertwined together with an analysis of the design principles behind online catalogs. Although design principles may be an important part of a philosophy of online catalogs, they do not comprehend the entire subject. A philosophy of the online catalog has important ties to the broader subject of the philosophy of technology, particularly computer technology. This chapter will briefly examine some possible ties.

Technological change has a way of forcing philosophical questions to the forefront. Some philosophical questions, although never completely resolved, remain dormant for years or decades until technological change rasies a whole new set of possibilities. The technological changes currently underway will lead to a fundamental rethinking of the purpose of the library catalog, and perhaps of the library itself. Complex social issues such as copyright, ownership of bibliographic records, and secondary use of machine-readable records will have to be addressed (Drabenstott, 1988; 103).

Our primary interest should be with how users think about and react to the online catalog, rather than how developers and librarians think and react. Do users take any joy or satisfaction in having successfully used the online catalog? Or is the online catalog almost completely transparent, merely a means to an end? What is the value of the activities associated with using an online catalog and finding recorded information in general? Do many users theorize about their use of online catalogs, or are they always intent on what Webster Hood (1983) calls technics and products—the outcome? Public services librarians try to encourage users to theorize about the information retrieval process, because the process is not determinate, and theorizing about the process could make subsequent usage more fruitful. But online catalogs themselves, as currently designed and implemented, may be sending contradictory signals to users about the value of finding recorded information.

61

Philosophies of Technology

There are several philosophies of technology with pertinent points about the online catalog as a technological device. The intention of this chapter is not to provide a comprehensive overview of the various philosophies of technology, but rather to explore the possibilities of intersection between these broader theories and a focused understanding of online catalogs.

Heidegger's Question Concerning Technology

In 1954 Martin Heidegger published an influential essay about the essence of technology. Heidegger's main contribution to the understanding of technology is his ability to go beyond the idea of technology as a tool. He seriously challenges the conceptual model of technology that understands it as mere instrumentality. Unfortunately, this attitude—that online catalogs are just tools—is still expressed quite frequently in librarianship. He wants to prepare man for a free relationship to technology (Heidegger, 1977; 3). Although instrumentality is considered by many people, including library and information professionals, to be the fundamental characteristic of technology, technology actually is a way of revealing (1977; 12). The mode of revealing that rules in modern technology is a challenging one (1977; 14). In the modern technological outlook, things are revealed not as objects, but as standing-reserve, ready to be exploited and used (1977; 27). Heidegger (1977; 23) terms the way in which the real reveals itself as standing-reserve as an enframing. For example, a bibliographic record downloaded in machine-readable form presents itself to the user in a different way from a card catalog card. The downloaded bibliographic record is much more indeterminate. It may be manipulated and exploited in ways a card catalog card cannot. A machine-readable bibliographic record seems to invite manipulation and exploitation.

Modern technology as a way of revealing is extremely dangerous for several reasons. Man is continually approaching the brink of the possibility of pursuing and pushing forward nothing but what is revealed in ordering, and of deriving all his standards on this basis (1977; 26). Conceptually, modern technology is a closed system. The profound poverty of values and valuation in the technological age is the result. Man does not have control over discovery itself (1977; 18). Nevertheless, Heidegger sees the possibility of a saving power in the essence of technology (1977; 29).

Heidegger also developed the concept of the clearing as the place in which Being occurs. As such, it is a spatial metaphor for a nonspatial sense of location. Users of online catalogs also suffer from a loss or diminution of spatial location within the bibliographic database. Heidegger's discussion of the clearing may be applicable to our understanding of the online catalog as a lived experience.

Our knowledge of the experience of using an online catalog allows us to test Heidegger's generalizations. The shift from card catalogs to online catalogs supports this analysis. The online catalog no longer is conceived by users as an object. In a very real sense each user creates the online catalog as she or he uses it. Remote access to online catalogs challenges space and distance. Automobiles and the telephone, not the card catalog, were its precursors. Multiple threats to loss of human control are revealed in modern technological devices like online catalogs. Many individuals feel that they have lost control over the library as a resource. Individual libraries feel that they will lose prestige, control, and patrons if they fail to automate. Professional librarians feel they are losing control over the information storage and retrieval process. This vague sense of loss of control often manifests itself in a fear that the information storage and retrieval process will become completely privatized.

In many ways the online catalog never is a complete thing. It always is growing and evolving, which also is true for card catalogs, although with card catalogs the growth may be more apparent. The online catalog never is present to the user, unless the user mistakes the display terminal for the online catalog. Finally, the order in which the records (and even parts of records) are stored in the online catalog is almost completely irrelevant and useless. A printout of the entire online catalog database of bibliographic records would be of little use to anyone.

Perhaps online catalogs differ from other tools and other automated library systems in that online catalogs do not fulfill specific needs and ends. They are systems that were designed without specific needs and uses in mind.

Critical response to Heidegger's analysis. Subsequent critics of Heidegger's understanding of modern technology lament his separation of tools and "toolness" from the true significance of technology. Heidegger argued that attention to the machines or tools of modern technology overlooks the ontological significance of technology. Later philosophers, such as Borgmann, want to examine the ontological significance of the tools themselves (Leder, 1988; 17). Subsequent discourses on the philosophy of technology have renewed interest in the tools themselves and human interaction with them.

Albert Borgmann's analysis: devices. Albert Borgmann contends that it is the technological object itself (the "device") which makes available for inspection the manner in which technology has reshaped the world (Leder, 1988; 18). Borgmann's major thesis is that modern devices, unlike old-fashioned tools, are designed with the intention of being as inconspicuous as possible. Borgmann's explanation of the device paradigm in modern technology can help us better understand what really happened when library catalogs were automated.

Borgmann (1984; 33) argues that a modern technological device is distinguished by a sharp internal division into a machinery and a commodity procured by that machinery. In the case of an online catalog, the machinery is the complete database, the central processing unit, the telecommunications equipment, and the necessary software. The commodity procured would be the user-created subset of the database. The online catalog differs radically from other catalog forms by irrevocably separating the machinery and the commodity. Users rarely consider the database as a whole. There is no incentive for them to do so. Although many users may not realize it, the essence of using an online catalog is set creation and set manipulation. An online catalog helps the user identify and retrieve a subset of the entire database of bibliographic records that may be pertinent to the current information need. Card catalogs do this only in the way they are organized. They do not create subsets actively and on demand.

Devices and tools are antithetical to each other in many important aspects. The final cause or purpose of a technological device is to render a certain commodity (e.g., material objects, desired experiences, and social goods) available in an instantaneous, ubiquitous, safe, and easy fashion. The perfect device completely unburdens the user from all concern about the availability of the desired commodity. The machinery supporting the device strives to be concealed from our attention (Leder, 1988; 18).

If Borgmann's distinction between tool and device is useful, the card catalog appears to us as a tool, while the online catalog is a device. The device, unlike the old-fashioned tool, ceases to be the locus of human effort to make the desired commodity available. The necessity of clean rooms for computer CPUs has encouraged this separation of machinery from product. The main array of public access terminals to the online catalog are often still found in reference rooms of libraries because old habits die slowly, not out of necessity. Devices are designed and improved to obviate corporal engagement by the user (Leder, 1988; 19). Most online catalogs still require the user to type (or at least point and grunt), but no longer is the user required to pull out catalog drawers and move from A to Z.

Many modern technological devices, including online catalogs, deliver more than one type of commodity, product, or output. One of the inscrutable aspects of modern technology is the recurring inability of humans to predict the impact and ramifications of a new technological device prior to its introduction and deployment. When a technological device such as an online catalog is used for communication, it communicates representations of ideas and also embodies ideas about how to communicate (see Levinson, 1988; xv). The experience of using an online catalog not only conveys bibliographic information about the items contained in the collection, it also conveys information about the structure of knowledge and the process of the dissemination of recorded information. This second type of message receives little attention during the planning and development stages of a technological device.

Each new technological device offers a promise for the attainment of a future state of affairs. The biggest promise of any technological device is the hope of future disburdenment—use of the device will make life a little easier. In the case of the online catalog, it promises to make the task of identifying and locating intellectual works easier and faster. Fast and easy has been the rallying cry of many online catalog installations.

The online catalog does possess unique characteristics as a contemporary technological device. Most technological devices exhibit a tendency toward homogeneity (see Hardison, 1989; 142). Most technological developments do not foster diversity and local variations. Yet the development of the online catalog has shattered the homogeneity of their fundamental structures, and the tendency seems to be toward even greater diversity.

Hood's five ontic structures of technology. The philosophy of technology after Heidegger has established the importance of the tools themselves in our understanding of technology. When the use of online catalogs is investigated, however, we need to consider more than just how users behave toward the online catalog as a tool. How users theorize about the whole process of information production, storage, and retrieval needs to be examined. Hood's explication (1983) of the five ontic structures of technology provides a good schema for such an examination. He identifies five ontic structures of technology: technics, products, nature, theory, and intersubjectivity.

Technics are the technological tools themselves. In this case, the technic would be the online catalog itself as a system of hardware and software. The chief ontic function of technics is to spatialize man's surroundings and to permit man to stand somewhere with regard to himself and entities (Hood, 1983; 356). We need to critically examine how well online catalogs allow users to spatialize at all, particularly in the universe of information entities. Remote access to online catalogs, in particular, has had profound effects on users' spatial orientation to recorded information. This ontic function needs to be compared to Heidegger's sense of the clearing in which Being appears.

Products are the value-added outcomes from the technics. Because online catalogs tend to deal with information, which has different properties than material objects, it is difficult to identify and valuate the product of an online catalog. Online catalog products are tied more to individual interactions and individual users than are the products of other technics. Most of the value of information depends on a specific context. We usually do not try to produce the products of online catalogs first and then try to "sell" or distribute them at a later time. Tentatively, the information contained in the records (bibliographic, piece, and authority records) as presented to an individual user can be identified as the product of an online catalog technic.

Nature is the totality of objects not related to the technic. Perhaps in this instance nature in the world of online catalogs is the universe of information and carriers of information not yet brought under some measure of control by the online catalog technic. The relationship between library catalogs and library collections has special implications in this context. Portions of the collection not accessible through the online catalog form part of the natural background of the technic.

Theory is the contemplative conception of material objects that the particular technology encourages. For many Heideggerians, the theory behind modern technology encourages mankind to view material objects as so much raw matter and energy, ready to be exploited by modern technology. For example, a forest is now seen as a reserve of so much wood pulp. The theory behind modern technology sees nature merely in terms of its instrumentality (Hood, 1983; 362). In modern technology, man appropriates the world in a radically new fashion. Controllability is the keyword (1983; 359).

Hood's fifth ontic structure of technology is intersubjectivity. Society is rendered determinate by the prevailing technology. In the case of online catalogs, the social relationship between reference librarians and users may be changing as the switch is made to online catalogs.

The five ontic structures of technology contribute to the formation of a horizon of possibilities, grounded in man's being (1983; 361). The ontological meaning of technology is that it reflects the concern man has for the Being of all entities (1983; 362). Our interaction with technology encompasses both making things through it and theorizing about it (1983; 360). Without an ontological sensitivity which releasement toward things makes concrete, man comes to regard himself as a mere factor in the world of pell-mell technological advance (1983; 362). The fundamental task in understanding modern technology, as Heideggerians see it, is to discover how the ontological dimension or condition of man makes possible the ontic determination of technology (1983; 354).

Winner's analysis. Langdon Winner finds it curious and intriguing that no agenda exists for technological change. No shared goals against which each technological innovation can be judged prior to acceptance or rejection have emerged. This certainly seems to be the case during the development of online catalogs. The technology was adopted before the need was expressed. For the most part we continue to disregard a problem that has been brewing since the earliest days of the industrial revolution—whether our society can establish forms and limits for technological change, forms and limits that derive from a positively articulated idea of what society ought to be (Winner, 1986; 52). In the case at hand, remote access to online catalogs may change forever the meaning, structure, and value of academic libraries.

Unfortunately, in general many analyzers of online catalogs rely on popular, unarticulated notions of technology. Elizabeth Dow (1988; 83), for example, believes we can predict the effects of the adoption of a technological device; she argues that we must understand *in advance* (her emphasis) how media work so that we can understand, if not control, the implications of computer applications as they are being developed.

Discussion

One cause for wariness when applying philosophies of technology to online catalog development and use is the fact that most philosophies of technology were developed in reaction primarily to modern methods of producing and consuming tangible things, rather than information and knowledge, the instantly renewable commodity handled by online catalogs.

Users

An examination of the relationship between general philosophies of technology and existing online catalog systems should focus on users and their lived experiences with online catalogs. Unfortunately, online catalog system development seems to be driven more by the interplay of the latest technological innovations and the economics of libraries than by the expressed and discovered needs of potential users of online catalogs.

Poor Lifelong Information Retrieval Skills

Because the perfect online catalog would be almost completely transparent, similar to the talkative automated daily organizer featured in a recent promotional video from Apple Computer, Inc., the online catalog as a device encourages the user's information retrieval skills to atrophy. The premise behind the design and development of online catalogs works against librarians' and educator's efforts to encourage the development of users' information retrieval skills.

Technology and Information and Users

What we can foresee as the shape of our work in the future rests only in part on what technology can offer us. The larger part rests on how we feel about what technology can do for us (Lacey, 1982; 112). Remote access, downloading of bibliographic records in machine-readable form, and the use of personal bibliographic database management software is creating a fundamental shift in the way users view information and their libraries (Rice, 1988A).

Privacy

New technological developments often raise new fears about loss of privacy, and the development of online catalogs confirms this. Few of the numerous surveys and questionnaires, however, have included questions about users' attitudes toward, and sense of, personal privacy in online catalog environments. Two separate issues constitute the issue of privacy in the use of online catalogs. Does the terminal screen and the clustering of terminals provide less privacy than the old card catalog drawer? Is transaction monitoring an invasion of privacy? As access to the online catalog moves beyond the walls of the library through remote access, the ability to identify particular search sessions with particular individuals increases (Judith Adams, 1988; 34). During a study of the transaction logs of in-house public users of an online catalog system (Peters, 1989), the frequency of potentially embarrassing searches (e.g., searches dealing with human sexuality and other bodily functions) on the unmonitored terminal in the book stacks appeared to be higher than at the main array of terminals in the reference room.

Is the typical online catalog terminal less private than the old card catalog? Is there a pent-up demand among users for more privacy in their searches? Remote access users tend to look for more potentially embarrassing information than users at the main array of terminals within the library. Over 80 percent of the respondents to the Swarthmore/Bryn Mawr survey indicated they would not feel uncomfortable if someone could see what they were searching for on the computer terminal (Walton, Williamson, and White, 1986; 395).

Loss of the Sense of Spatial Orientation

Robert Taylor (1986) argues convincingly that a human frame of reference must inform and structure the design of information systems. Yet spatial orientation, one of the fundamental frames of human reference, is largely absent in an online catalog environment. Spatial orientation can have several meanings within this context. Spatial orientation within the screen display is a context that has received much attention from designers (see, for example, Tullis 1981). Spatial orientation toward the database is another context. A third context is spatial orientation toward the subject. One aspect of this is knowledge of the narrower, broader, and related terms in a controlled vocabulary on the subject. A fourth context for spatial orientation is with the literature on a subject. Finally, the user must develop some sort of orientation, probably both spatial and temporal, with the project at hand. From the user's standpoint, this may be the most important context of spatial orientation.

The loss of a sense of spatial orientation experienced by the user of an electronic database, especially one that is remotely located, can be detrimental or beneficial to the search process. Some would argue that conceptual orientation has always been more important than spatial orientation, with spatial orientation—usually initiated by flipping through the card catalog or browsing through the book stacks—often functioning as a crutch or mask for the user's lack of conceptual orientation. Browsing in a database will never be the same as walking through a space of stacks of books, with so many different temptations for informative digressions drawing the eye (Lacey, 1982; 117).

The Evaluative Needs of Remote Access Users

Remote access users tend to have more questions about the technological aspects of remote access than about searching the catalog and interpreting the results. Gaining remote access to an online catalog seems to be much more of a challenge and triumph than other types of access to other forms of the library catalog (see Sally Kalin, 1987). Some remote access users even have questions about the best hardware and software to purchase to meet their needs. Many librarians, however, are reluctant to provide technological advice and support. Often this aspect of the remote user's need is left to the computing services staff. The distinctions between getting connected to the online catalog, searching it, and applying the results may be more artificial and bureaucratic than real, particularly in the user's eyes. The failure of system developers to understand the user's projects and their unity is evident here. For professional reasons, often librarians are reluctant to make evaluative judgments about anything.

Sense of Control

Perhaps in-house access to the online catalog is conceived now as a more or less static thing owned by the library and available in the library. Remote access may give users the sense that they have much more control over the database. The stronger bonds that users have to remote access terminals, compared to in-house library terminals, may contribute to an increasing sense of personal control over the search session and the contents of the database. If a user is able to search remote library catalogs from a personal computer located near the personal project, their attitude toward the library, its catalog, and its collection may change.

Confidentiality

The ethics of current remote access systems is another point of contact with the broader concerns of philosophy. Remote access may increase privacy but decrease confidentiality. In the case of online catalog use, privacy is the ability to engage in searching activity without anyone's knowledge, while professional confidentiality is the ability to know what users are searching for without spreading that knowledge. In the system studied, dial access sessions could be compromised before individuals are identified. For example, if FBI agents question a reference librarian about terrorists using the library to conduct research, and the librarian responds only by reporting that on a certain date at a certain terminal some user entered the title keyword search "How Build Atomic Bomb," the librarian has not named individuals, yet may have violated the principle of confidentiality. If patron confidentiality can be compromised prior to the actual naming of individual users, how can the boundaries of violation be determined?

What mechanisms and ethical standards exist to assure users of the strict confidentiality they have come to expect during use of the library in the precomputer age (Weiskel, 1986; 556)?

Declining Sense of the Local Library

Evan Farber notes that in the future many users will expect information from all parts of the world instantaneously (Riggs and Sabine, 1988; 17). If that happens, what will happen to the user's sense of the local library? Will the only bond of allegiance between the user and the "local" library be the cost difference between a local and long-distance call? Access to online catalogs via the Internet mitigates the cost of access (see Bailey, 1990). Will the funding support for local libraries erode as high-end-users increase the number of potential sources of recorded information? The nature of computer mediation reduces both the librarian's responsibility to the user and user contact with the library (Azubuike, 1988; 275).

As remote access becomes more common, the importance of user affiliations, as traditionally defined, will be questioned and overrun in the familiar manner of technological innovation. Dow (1988; 87) wants to consider the implications of the growing number of unaffiliated patrons who are using the academic library. Reappraisal of the library's definition of its primary clientele undoubtedly will be one of the last phases of this transformation of the academic library. Currently, the primary clientele of most libraries are defined geographically and or politically.

Publishing Trends

The effects of automation on the creation of intellectual works are having profound impact on the society of middlemen and consumers alike. The keying efficiencies that could be realized by fuller cooperation between producers and middlemen are immense. Electronic publishing is a much more radical innovation than document delivery. In electronic publishing the computer network becomes the primary medium for the creation, storage, and dissemination of a document (Brownrigg, 1983; 109).

Copyright and the Dissection of Texts

Online catalogs are encouraging new attitudes toward bibliographic records, ownership, information documents, and intellectual texts. They also have increased the potential controllability by the individual user of the individual search session. Some commentators have predicted that static vehicles of information, such as books, journals, journal articles, and encyclopedias, will decline radically in importance or cease to exist. Individual users will be able to deconstruct and reconstruct large bodies of information contained in automated information systems as they see fit. The reality of static, integral intellectual works may be lost. The social mores of recorded scholarship find it acceptable to manipulate the elements of citation information, as witnessed by all the competing styles for citing intellectual works, but direct manipulation of the full text is still taboo.

Part of many scenarios of the future of recorded information is the probability that, as full-text retrieval becomes more economically feasible and prevalent, users will pick apart texts and choose only those portions that they want to use. Of course, this has been done by scholars for quite a while, but now the process will be computer assisted. The concept of a text as an identifiable entity may cease to exist if users can selectively pick and choose sentences, citations, paragraphs, and graphs out of full-text files. The text, therefore, will be manipulable by the user.

Diffusion and Explosion of Publishing Power

The automation of the production of intellectual works already has had profound effects on the quantity, overlap, and individual value of those works. The burden to library collections is a perennial concern. In the past the library has depended on an arbitrary filter for ephemera, confining itself largely to the acquisition of published material, usually from the reputable academic publishers (Weiskel, 1986; 557). What will happen to the acquisition process in academic libraries if most of the important scholarly material is published or disseminated by small groups or even individuals, rather than the traditional publishers, such as Oxford University Press?

Squeezing the Library Middleman

In 1983 Brownrigg speculated that some of the traditional functions of the library were moving outside the library to other sources. In some cases the producer groups were assuming the burden of traditional library functions. Much cataloging, especially analytical cataloging, is done by the publishers themselves under other names, such as advertising and indexing. Brownrigg (1983; 108) suggests that, as the locus of cataloging moves beyond libraries, upstream in the flow of information, the locus of usership will change as well. Users may cease being library patrons and become publishing-company patrons. He sees remote access to online catalogs as the first step in weaning the seeker/user of information from the library middleman. In the flow of information scheme developed in Chapter 3, just as libraries are pushing outward into areas traditionally handled by publishers and users, publishers (and users, too) are pushing into areas normally handled by libraries.

Loss of Distinct Editions of Complete Texts

An information retrieval system should be valued and judged by its ability to help the user perform a close, informed examination of whole texts (Lacey, 1982; 111). But user attitudes toward the lengths of texts is changing. Most users of online catalogs probably do not want book-length intellectual works. The book, like the Victorian novel and the epic poem, is a dying or dead form, from a time when people (or at least a small portion of the populace) had more leisure time to read and to listen. Lacey fears that electronic storage and retrieval devices are not conducive to the production of whole, complete texts. New information access techniques will break traditional bibliographic units down into fragments better suited to users' needs (Molholt, 1985; 287). The current consensus is that most users want smaller units of text.

It appears that even the strong correlation between the physical item and the unique intellectual content and configuration of that item wanes. Library catalogs traditionally have paid more attention to the physical items than to the intellectual content. As the items containing intellectual records become radically more malleable and transmittable, the library catalog as originally conceived will have difficulty coping, and it probably will lose value. Just as the automation of the production of scholarly information eventually will lead to the disintegration of many intellectual works, the automation of the library catalog may lead to the disintegration of the library catalog. In the words of Hardison (1989), the online catalog will disappear through the skylight.

In previous eras of bibliographic technology, the intellectual work had to achieve a stasis within the bibliographic item (e.g., the book) because it was necessary to do so in order to disseminate the intellectual work across distance and time. With computer technology, at least in theory, the necessity of a static medium for the intellectual work no longer pertains. The old notion of an intellectual work may pass away, with the corresponding notion of distinct editions of texts. They will be replaced with a malleable, mutable intellectual soup, which may involve more direct interaction between the creator and the end-user. The end-user will have a much larger role in the addition of value to the new intellectual work.

Media Changes and the MARC Format

The declining importance of the formats and information currently contained in online catalog databases presents additional problems. Retrospective conversion projects were sold and supported on the basis of the argument that having catalog records in machine-readable MARC format would be a permanent resource incapable of losing value. Now there are increasing calls for the complete revision of the record structure of bibliographic citations. The death of the concepts of a main entry and of an edition of a monograph have taken their toll. The value of the information contained in the MARC fields to the actual users of the system should be a continuous research question and policy debate in the profession.

Libraries and Librarianship

A fuller examination and appreciation of the implications of the philosophies of technology increases our understanding of the ties of libraries and librarianship to technology and technological devices.

Our Philosophies of Technology

The two fears currently dominating the profession are the fear that the introduction of technological devices (e.g., photocopiers, online catalogs, database searching, CD-ROM products, and telefacsimile transmission) into the provision of information services will result in user demands and expectations the current information structure cannot meet, and the fear, perhaps related to the first, that the system of information production, dissemination, and storage will become increasingly privatized and profitable.

It is a little disconcerting to see an eminent theoretician like Buckland (1989B; 389) advocating a clear distinction between means and ends as the way to overcome what many perceive as a current overemphasis on technological devices. He suggests that we should establish the purposes of library service first, then choose and adopt techniques and technologies to achieve the established goals. If this ever was the true relationship between means and ends, it no longer applies. One of the distinctive features of modern technology is that we do not know exactly what our ends will be until the means are up and running and we have had a chance to see how we will interact with them. It is difficult or impossible to anticipate the effects a technological innovation will have on the way we conceive the world. Buckland (1989B; 390) admits that current changes are enabled less by new ideas than by changes in the underlying technologies. In effect, the means, not the ends, are dictating changes in the theory and practice of librarianship and information science.

Channeling

Timothy Weiskel (1986) sees much library automation as just an increase in the instances and efficiencies of what he calls channel switching. It seems that libraries are becoming more and more involved in two types of channel switching. The first is switching from one type of channel to another. This occurs during retrospective conversion projects, when bibliographic records in paper form are switched to machine-readable form. The other type of channel switching does not cross from one type to another. When a user downloads an online catalog record, he or she merely switches the information from the institution's machine-readable system to his or her own personal machine-readable system. The information remains on the institutional system, but now it is on the personal system also, where it may be manipulated and valuated. This type of information switching has serious implications for notions of publication, copyright, and ownership.

Of course, channel switching has been going on in libraries since they began, if we define channel switching broadly to include the switching that occurs as one reads, when the information on the printed page is processed in the mind of the reader through reading. If we bracket this special case of channel switching—perhaps the highest order of channel switching, and the ultimate end of all of the lower orders of channel switching—libraries were not much involved with channel switching prior to the advent of library automation, photocopying, and microfilming. What relative importance should channel switching assume in the library's overall mission (Weiskel, 1986; 549)?

The university library, by assimilating the technology enabling massive channel switching of information, could become an accomplice in undermining the historic principle of copyright for which it has so long fought so valiantly (Weiskel, 1986; 559).

Ownership and Access

The conceptual problem with access extends far beyond the walls of the library. Society as a whole is having a difficult time accepting and adjusting to the new norm where access to intangible information, with its unique properties, is the defining interaction between human beings. The old rules about ownership and material objects, with their different unique properties, do not apply much anymore.

The new challenge for libraries is to develop ways of using the online catalog to provide access to many resources in electronic form (De Gennaro, 1987; 37). The question no longer is how many volumes a library owns, but how effectively the library can deliver needed resources to users via the new technology (De Gennaro, 1987; 10). What present and future libraries need is a bibliography of what is conveniently accessible, rather than the much narrower concept of a catalog of what happens to be locally owned since location and ownership of copies of texts becomes a technical detail for librarians irrelevant to the reader (Buckland, 1988; 307, 308). The closer we come to accepting the principle of access over acquisition, the easier it will be to incorporate additional types of information as they become economically viable (Molholt, 1985; 285).

The value of access and the value of information. Perhaps the library and information science profession has assumed, probably erroneously, that the value of access to a unit of information has some correlation with the value of the unit of information itself. The development of online catalog systems reflects the profession's championing of the value of access, while we simultaneously assume a hands-off attitude toward the value and application of the information itself. This tandem set of professional values worked well when the production of information was experiencing an era of controlled growth, but the information explosion has greatly increased the need to valuate the information retrieved. By and large, librarians are not helping users satisfy that need. The profession has a difficult decision ahead about whether to provide overt assistance to users in their process of valuating units of information. The least we can do in preparation for that decision is to keep in mind the distinction between the valuation of access and the valuation of units of information.

There is a relationship, however, between the possibility of access and the value of a unit of information. Information that is inaccessible is at once both highly valuable (in the sense of desirability) and totally worthless (in the sense of being totally useless, because it is inaccessible). When the unit of information is accessed and retrieved, these widely divergent a priori valuations are replaced by a valuation based on the experience of examination of the individual unit of information. Freshmen composition students go through this valuation process all the time: either this bit of information will fit easily (with perhaps too much emphasis placed on ease) into the project at hand (usually a three-to-five-page paper), or it will not.

Online catalogs really present contradictory valuations from the profession and designers to the users about the importance of access to information. Positively, we send implicit messages that we value the information retrieval task so highly that we are willing to invest a significant percentage of our total operating budget in developing and operating better access systems. Negatively, the online catalog as a device, as defined and examined by Borgmann, sends the message to the user that the retrieval of information is a trivial, tedious task from which modern technological devices should liberate us. We seem to be telling the users that, although the evaluation of information may be important (so important, in fact, that we leave it to the user to perform that task), the evaluation of the information retrieval process itself is not. Online information systems are designed to make the process of accessing information as quick and painless as possible.

Tradition of Bias Against Remote Access

In academic librarianship there is a tradition of bias against remote access users of the library's services and information. Many fledgling reference librarians are taught that, if the telephone rings at the same time an in-house patron approaches the reference desk, they should help the in-house patron first, because that patron at least made the effort to physically come to the library. Patrons who come into the library usually receive quicker, better and more thorough service than remote access users.

Is the unstated premise of reference librarianship working against the efficiency of the user population? When will this fundamental premise about library use change, and what will cause it to change? Here is a specific case where the library has the efficient operation of the institution in mind, rather than the user's efficiency. The technology of remote access has made this decision glaringly apparent. Mary Vasilakis predicts that in the near future the whole attitude of the library will be different. Libraries always have been geared for walk-in users. The future is with electronically available services (Riggs and Sabine, 1988; 3).

Elitism

As noted above, a common reaction to the deployment of a new technological device is to express fears about a further erosion of personal privacy. Another common reaction is to express fears about the elitist tendencies of modern technology. Charges that library automation is elitist are scattered throughout the professional literature (see Becker, 1979). The primary users of the more sophisticated information resources will be an informed and skilled minority (Drabenstott, 1988; 104).

The push for more advanced features could lead to the charge that online catalogs are elitist systems that ignore the rank and file users of library catalogs. Nielsen (1988) proposed the thesis that reference service is essentially elitist because the service is premised on the assumption that only a small percentage of patrons entering the building ever will ask reference questions. Reference desk service, as currently conceived and implemented, cannot accommodate all users of the library.

Of online catalogs. The real drive in online catalog development has been to improve the searching patterns of the current user groups, rather than to identify and court nonusers of the system. The CLR study used a separate questionnaire for nonusers, but the findings suggested that nonuser reluctance was temporary.

The CLR study revealed that 60 percent of online catalog users are male (Matthews, Lawrence, and Ferguson, 1983; table 4). Karen Markey (1984; 11) reports, however, that the issue of gender seldom came up during the focus group interviews conducted as part of the CLR study. If there is a reason for a gender-specific aversion to online catalogs, it remains unrevealed.

The CLR study found that young people, part of the computer generation, responded favorably to the introduction of online catalogs. Older users tended to be less enthusiastic. The locus of the overwhelmingly favorable response to the online catalog is in the younger age brackets, and the bulk of users are children, teenagers, and young adults. Is it fair, however, to disenfranchise older patrons? Most commentators assume that the main reason older patrons are wary of online catalogs is because they did not grow up with computers. They argue that this resistance is temporary, and will pass away in a decade or two.

To utilize any form of library catalog the user must be able to spell, or at least be able to correctly remember the key elements of a found bibliographic citation. The online catalog is the first form of library catalog where users have been required to correctly type information.

Of remote access. Were remote access systems set up with the implicit understanding that if many or all library users utilized the system, the load could not be handled by the system? Traditional definitions of a library's primary clientele usually contain a geographical component. A primary clientele often is designated as those who work at an institution (for special, school, and academic libraries) or those who live within the city limits of a public library system. The intent of remote access is to devalue distance, which creates serious problems for traditional notions of primary clientele.

Information Science

The potential influence of philosophies of technology on some fundamental concepts and concerns in information science also is great. The philosophy of technology is concerned with the use of machines in human activities, and information science is interested in the way information is generated, collected, organized, stored, retrieved, and utilized.

Information Efficiency: Whose Efficiency?

Much labor goes into creating and maintaining an online catalog, and current systems were designed to make the production and maintenance processes more efficient than the manual systems they replaced. Much work, however, also is involved in using an online catalog, especially within the broader context of a user's information need or research project. Online catalogs do not address this area of efficiency to any great extent.

When online catalogs are referred to as efficient systems, the vantage point usually is professional. Ideas about efficiency vary among library administrators, library systems personnel, technical services librarians, public services librarians, and end-users. Perhaps we should encourage libraries to make the efficiency of the user top priority. Miriam Drake (1990; 170) at Georgia Tech estimates that the major cost associated with traditional information-seeking in libraries (e.g., traveling to the library, searching the card catalog, retrieving the items, and transporting them home) was the seeker's time and effort. For each processing task, we need to determine where is the most appropriate and most efficient place for processing to take place (Fayen, 1986; 5). Ideas of efficiency have started at the system and spread out, rather than started with the user and moved in.

One ultimate efficiency in bibliography is the situation where the basic bibliographic information about an item is keyed only once—by the original cataloger. All other users of the information would simply download and manipulate the original information. Derived cataloging is a step in the right direction toward achieving this ultimate efficiency. It is only one step however, and it does not increase the ultimate user's efficiency at all.

Are the librarian's and the user's senses of efficiency fundamentally, irrevocably at odds? Are the user and the library confined to an adversarial relationship?

Efficient production. Each stage in the flow of information is capable of realizing its own efficiencies. Authors and publishers worry about efficient production. Sometimes librarians long to exercise some control over this stage of the information process. Sometimes we wish we could make the production system a little less efficient and facile. Efficient production has resulted in an explosion of documents.

Efficient storage. Efficiencies of storage also have been changing rapidly. It is becoming much more efficient to store electronic information near the application point. Microcomputers can be used to optimize the economic trade-offs between the cost of local storage of information and telecommunications costs (Fayen, 1986; 12).

Many online catalogs store much the same bibliographic information, usually in the same format, with local holdings information attached. From a systems perspective this could be seen as a grand inefficiency. The same MARC records are stored on thousands of sites around the globe. From the user's standpoint, however, this redundancy is as it should be. The information may be stored inefficiently, but it is ready-at-hand and accessible. From a systems storage perspective, the wide distribution and replication of knowledge—perhaps a basic goal of education—is very inefficient.

Efficient retrieval. Online systems designers and programmers worry about efficient retrieval. As databases increase in size, efficient, precise retrieval becomes imperative. Two facts work against efficient retrieval. Most users of an online catalog are untrained public users, and users pay little or no penalty for conducting systemically inefficient retrieval requests.

The user also is interested in efficient retrieval—as perceived from the user's point of view, not as perceived by the systems personnel. Taylor (1986; 32) suggests that adding more search options may result in certain retrieval inefficiencies. The trend in information technologies design is to increase the number of options open to a user, on the assumption that a larger number of choices is beneficial. It may be beneficial and pleasing to the user to have a large number of choices, but the cost to the client in making the choices also will be higher.

Efficient distribution. Distribution of information occurs at all stages of the information flow. The distribution from the library to the application site is of primary interest here. Currently the user assumes most of the cost involved in overcoming the distance between the information sought and the workplace environment. As libraries begin to pay more attention to the broad issues of access in the complete information environment, they probably will assume more of the cost burden of overcoming this distance. Remote access to library files is a step in this direction, and it needs to be recognized as a major new service component for academic libraries.

Efficient assimilation and use. Efficient assimilation and use is the aspect of information efficiency of primary interest to the user. As librarians, we have a professional obligation to pay more attention to this aspect of efficiency. Information systems need to address user costs and minimize them, and simultaneously develop a more sophisticated, empathetic attitude toward user values and user benefits (Taylor, 1986; 104).

The efficiency of those who input into the online catalog system (e.g., cataloging librarians) historically has received much more attention and funding than the efficiency of those who receive output from the system. MicroLIAS at Penn State and PCBIS at the Triangle Research Libraries Network of North Carolina are steps toward rectifying that situation. Most online catalog systems have been much more interested in machine-readable input, where MARC cataloging has become the accepted standard, than in machine-readable output.[1] Machine-readable output is still in its first generation of development. Two highly efficient electronic information systems—online library catalogs and personal database management software—often are connected by an inefficient, manual transfer of data (Sutton, 1990; 43).

The negative side of software like MicroLIAS and PCBIS is that it can be used only on a specific system. It further ties a user to a specific online catalog system. Users cannot download records from other, remote online catalogs and efficiently incorporate them into a personal bibliographic database.

Every time the user searches the online catalog, he or she creates at least one subset of the database. Current system design assumes that the user's interest in that particular subset is transient. Mechanisms are not yet in place that allow the user to efficiently refer to that subset at a later time, other than using the online catalog to reexecute the search. Most online catalogs make it difficult for users to save and review the results of their searches. Michael Bauer (1988; 38–39) uses the example of simultaneously consulting an online catalog and working on a written report using word processing software. If both tasks could be performed simultaneously on the same screen of a workstation, significant time and keying efficiencies could be realized.

Beyond speed and efficiency. The suggestion has been made here that when system efficiencies are discussed, we need to question from what perspective we are examining efficiencies. It has been suggested that thinking about system efficiencies from the perspective of the user, rather than from the perspectives of librarians, designers, or systems personnel, will result in systems that are more productive and acceptable to users.

Hildreth (1989A; 46) has gone one step farther, and suggests that the tendency to focus on system efficiencies from any perspective misses some fundamental problems. Information retrieval, especially document retrieval, should be viewed as an interactive, cooperative process of mutually supportive inference by the intelligent system and the human user. Too much emphasis has been placed on efficiency and speed in the information retrieval process. Chapter 13 will raise the question whether the short-term goals of speed and ease of use are detrimental to the long-term goal of the intellectual development of the users.

Burden to Change

As technologies are being built and put to use, significant alterations in patterns of human activity and human institutions are already taking place. There is nothing secondary about this phenomenon. It is the most important accomplishment of any new technology (Winner, 1986; 11). Is the burden to change on the user or the online catalog system? To what extent should the online catalog encourage the user to critically examine his or her search?

The Value of Information

Robert Taylor (1986) has done some groundbreaking work on the activity of valuing information. In an earlier era of publishing, individual information vehicles (e.g., books) were valuable because they were rare. Today good, substantial, individual information vehicles are valuable because so many information units are superfluous. Many contain not new information but reformatted old information. Reformatting information is a value-adding process, but a relatively low-level one. The plums in the plum pudding have gained value because users are forced to digest so much more pudding in their quests to find the few good plums. User pressure to make evaluative decisions about the relevance and quality of the items retrieved will increase. Many users may look to the middleman, especially the online catalog system, to provide assistance in this task.

Every item in a library's collection has had value added to it by the developers of the collection in the past, simply because it is in the collection while other items are not. Remote access to online catalogs, and especially remote access to full texts, diminishes the worth of this unavoidable value-adding process; so also the bibliographic records contained in our online catalogs are losing value, shown by the following examples. Some fields within the standard bibliographic record are losing value as users demand other information about the items they seek; the bibliographic items described (i.e., mainly books) are losing value and market share as information vehicles; ownership is losing its monopoly as an indication to the user of ease of access—the fact that the library owns certain items no longer is crucial to users; and many information systems are being flooded by bibliographic items, and the online catalog makes little attempt to valuate each item, so users are being forced to wade through larger retrieval sets to extract the few pertinent items.

Much more analysis of human attitudes toward the technological aspects of online catalogs needs to be done. No longer is it acceptable to unreflectively apply popular notions of computer technology to discussions of the meaning and purpose of online catalog systems.

Notes

1. This new emphasis on machine-readable output could be designated by the acronym MARO.

Chapter 5

Problems with Online Catalogs and Their Use

Introduction

One major problem with online catalogs and their use is the professional belief that we know what the problems are without really going to the systems, the data, and the users themselves. We fail to make it a habit of observing how our online catalogs are being used. Or if we do observe, we do so in the spirit of managers and systems analysts, looking to determine such things as peak loads on the system. Problems are not identified in relation to users' projects. The information profession's mental model of the online catalog may be narrow, with major carryover from the mental model of the card catalog. We may assume incorrectly that there is a correct way to use the online catalog. Throughout the process of designing, implementing, and evaluating an online catalog system, extreme sensitivity to possible effects of professional biases and assumptions on system functions and use must be exercised.

What Motivates Users

The cognitive processes and motivation of users of online catalogs is of interest to researchers and designers alike. Molholt (1985) presents a good scenario of what future users will want from information systems. Motivation is an area of the user's psychology that probably cannot be changed, yet often it is assumed that instructional efforts will suddenly enthrall the users to the complex beauties of the flow of information. We need to assess the extent to which users are interested in the principles and practice of information storage and retrieval. We also need to determine how important it is to encourage them to become more interested in the process.

Users seem to have a high threshold of tolerance toward online catalogs. The CLR study and replications of it have proven that users tend to like online catalogs, even if they do not find what they seek. To information professionals, most users seem somewhat lazy and complacent regarding their search for information. What motivates them to look for information at all, if they exhibit these characteristics? Zipf's law states that people not only minimize search efforts but neither need nor want all the information on a given subject (Gerrie, 1983; 132). When it appears that a user terminates a search session early, or does not explore all the byways of the search, the user may be acting on an agenda that does not place high value on high recall.

Sue Pease and Mary Gouke (1982; 289) suggest that success (or at least the user's perception of success) is the primary motivating factor for using online catalog systems. Liking the system is at best a secondary concern. Patrons' use of the online catalog may be based more on their level of success in locating what they need, rather than on personal preference.

Users of libraries always have sought small, personalized subsets of the information contained in the larger, depersonalized library. Automation of library systems has simply led advanced users to want to realize new efficiencies. The scholar wants to create an entire series of localized, personalized databases that represent carefully selected subsets of external databases (Weiskel, 1988; 9). Although the dryness and distance of many scholarly texts seems to indicate otherwise, the scholarly drive throughout history has been to personalize information. The scholar must make the information his or her own before he or she can put the information to use.

Results. First and foremost, most users want results. Many users' desire for results is so great that they do not particularly care how the results were obtained, much to the chagrin of librarians. Users engage in long-term, inefficient search behavior because they perceive the task of learning how to use the library properly as being too inefficient in the short run. Users are motivated by the current project and must adhere to its schedule. They struggle from project to project, reinforcing their inefficient behavior within the library, until they confront a big project, such as a dissertation, that forces them to learn more about information storage and retrieval.

Borgmann's device paradigm, outlined in Chapter 4, offers one possible explanation why most online catalog users just want results. If a fundamental characteristic of modern technology is the separation of process from product, users are conditioned to expect just the results, with little insight into how the results were obtained. They expect the information product, like other modern technological products, to be served up with some flare but little history of its production. Users grow impatient when the system interface itself or some intermediary (often a reference librarian) tries to reveal how the results were obtained. If a main thrust of computer technology is to separate process from product, librarians may be fighting a losing battle in trying to generate user interest in the process of information storage and retrieval, because users have been conditioned within the broader cultural milieu to devalue process.

This observation, if correct, has profound implications for the design and use of online catalogs. The fundamental question to be answered is whether or not the lived interaction with the online catalog should provide insight into the structure of the hidden machinery (hardware, software, telecommunications, etc.). Many commentators have suggested that the user's experience should not provide a window into the soul of the machine, so they have pushed for interfaces that are as transparent as possible. Unfortunately, a transparent device may discourage human learning, especially in the long term across multiple uses of the device. This question will be examined in more depth in Chapter 7.

Information ready-at-hand and efficient. Users are more interested in precision than recall. They are interested in institutional ownership only because historically there is a strong correlation between ownership and efficient information retrieval. Users want the information as ready-at-hand as possible, in an easily assimilated form. Whether they know it or not, they always are thinking of their own productivity as retrievers of information and scholars, performing many impromptu cost-benefit analyses as they proceed. They want to find the information they need, in just the right amount and the most easily digestible form, as quickly as possible.

This is as true for the prolific scholar as it is for the freshman writing a five-page paper. Ownership has little or no impact on the desire for information, and time is a much more important variable than space. Thus the situation can and does arise where information from an online database vendor stored half a continent away is more ready at hand than a hard copy journal located a few floors away in the same building.

This overwhelming drive for temporal economies creates some paradoxes of user searching behavior. One paradox of online catalog users is that, while they are very conscious of time, their search sessions often are very inefficient (Aken, 1988; 44). The desire to find information as quickly as possible often leads the user to undervalue the processes of information storage and retrieval. Learning the processes could lead to long-term efficiencies, but most users are unwilling to make a substantial initial investment in learning the system scope and protocols. The CLR study reports indicated that many users do not want to take the time to learn how to use the online catalog efficiently.

Unfortunately, current catalog systems were designed on the premise that there is a dependent relationship between physical access and intellectual access. For a long time librarians assumed, quite correctly, that ownership and physical access were the only game in town. The electronic media have changed all that. A library catalog, defined as a guide to what is locally stored, becomes progressively less complete as a guide to what is conveniently accessible (Buckland, 1989B; 392). Users were interested in convenient access all along, and their apparent interest in physical proximity was a quirk of the state of technological development at a certain time in history, which created a strong correlation between physical proximity and convenient access. Libraries find themselves operating in a paradigm where ownership of physical items carrying intellectual works is valued. This paradigm, however, is losing some of its attraction and efficiency.

Convenient access. Historically, a library catalog has functioned as a guide to local holdings. Yet what matters to a library user is convenient access to texts. With documents on paper, what is locally owned usually is conveniently accessible.[1] With improving telecommunications, however, the physical location of an electronic text is becoming increasingly irrelevant (Buckland, 1988; 306). We need to consider what happens to the user's sense of direction and relation to the catalog and the text when both the catalog and the text are in a sense "nowhere," but for the time being it is sufficient to note that this is a growing trend.

A popular professional topic is the shift within academic libraries away from ownership of materials to an emphasis on access to information, regardless of who owns it. This may be only an illusory shift, because access always has been the primary focus of attention. Historically, libraries have emphasized acquisition and ownership simply because the economics and technologies at the time made ownership an efficient way to ensure easy access. As we move into a new era where the former efficiencies of ownership are diminishing, systems are being developed that rely less on ownership and get to the access directly.

Intellectual access, not physical access. Molholt (1988) makes the distinction between physical access and intellectual access. Most users are looking for texts (intellectual entities) rather than for books (physical vessels for the intellectual entities), and most of the time, when they are not looking for a particular item, they are looking for something good (Wilson, 1983; 7, 15). Thus the fact that the catalog does not provide much evaluative information is perceived by many users as a hindrance. The burden of evaluating the documents retrieved still rests entirely on the end-user. The kind of power users would most like to have in the library is the power to get the best textual means to one's particular goal or end (Wilson, 1983; 15).

What motivates subject searching. Access to recorded information by topic is an enduring concern and problem. A brief look at some of the main user issues regarding subject access reveals serious inadequacies. From the serious user's point of view, the subject catalog is fatally flawed, because whereas users start with a subject or problem and look for books and other materials that address that subject or problem, subject catalogers start with books and look for subjects to describe them (Wilson, 1983; 15). Some researchers investigating the use of online catalogs have strong suspicions that many users of subject access points are much more interested in precision than recall. Many users are interested in just a few relevant items, so the comprehensiveness of a search using controlled vocabulary subject headings is of little interest and use to them (Bates, 1989; 403).

What Motivates Librarians

Librarians tend to value recall more than a precise, manageable set. We tend to be expansive in this regard. One hundred books on a given topic are much better than ten good, carefully selected ones. No attempt is made to add value to the source documents by evaluating them. Sometimes a virtue is made of necessity, and policies are formulated stating that it is the user's responsibility to evaluate the items retrieved. The nature of the internal functions of a library make librarians more interested in media than in the information itself. Within the internal library systems and workflows, the bibliographic item receives much more attention and processing than the intellectual work. The item, rather than the intellectual work, holds our attention. This is an occupational hazard. As middlemen we assume a hands-off attitude toward the intellectual works themselves. They are the province of the producers and consumers. We cling to the concepts of ownership and holdings in an era when access is becoming more important than ultimate ownership. Librarians view themselves as document providers, rather than as information providers (Drabenstott, 1985; 112).

Librarians tend to ignore the productivity of the user and focus on the productivity of the internal functions, such as the production of the online catalog and other library services. The productivity of the user community is beyond the fiscal ken of most librarians. This fundamental worldview affects how information professionals view online catalogs as indicators of system efficiencies rather than as support for the user's effectiveness (Taylor, 1986; 97).

Most users are utilizing the catalog as an enabling device to advance the present project. Document identification, location, and retrieval are all intermediate processes. Our information systems have evolved to answer questions, while our users are trying to solve problems, which involves much more than finding answers to questions (Taylor, 1986; 9). Librarians tend to think of the use of information storage and retrieval devices in very small units. For example, most transaction log analyses treat each line of information entered as a discrete search. The user of a complex information system like an academic library, however, tends to conceptualize the search as a much broader thing, involving perhaps several days, weeks, or months, and several information storage and retrieval systems. There is some evidence that consumers also are thinking of information in smaller units. The market for big, baggy novels has been in decline for the last one hundred years. The computerization of the middleman's functions probably will accelerate consumer interest in the dissection and diminution of texts.

How to Classify Use Problems with Online Catalogs

All researchers into online catalog use would agree that at least some users occasionally have problems using the online catalog. The challenge is how to classify and study those problems. In an earlier study of in-house use of the online catalog, this researcher identified fourteen categories of causes for problems with the use of online catalogs (Peters, 1989).[2] Not all of these fourteen probable causes are of interest to all participants in the flow of information. If an item is not in the database being searched, systems analysts probably are not interested in the ability of the system to locate the item.

When examining problems with online catalog use, it may be desirable to keep separate the processes of problem identification and the assignment of primary blame. Some librarians may object, for example, that it is not the fault of the online catalog system if the item sought is not in the database, especially if the item sought is clearly outside the imagined boundaries of the collection. To object along these lines, however, is to conjoin problem identification with the assignment of blame. If the item sought is not in the database, that is a problem for the user, regardless of who or what is at fault. A better method of analysis would be to first identify all of the evident problems during the search sessions. Responsibility and blame, if necessary, can be assigned later.

It may be impossible to study usage problems without assuming a correct use of the system. For example, if we study transaction logs and conclude that there is a problem in the use of the system because users seem to terminate their searches early without fully exploiting the results of their queries, our professional bias toward recall over precision is revealed along with the "problem." It is frequently assumed that a successful search session must be relatively thorough.

Identifying Actual Search Sessions

The study of online catalog use always has been hampered by the problem of how to identify and study a complete search session by an individual user without compromising the user's right to privacy and confidentiality. Transaction logs of dial access search sessions are a major new research opportunity, because the system records when a user on a specific port logs on and off. Yet the user is not required to enter a password, so there is no way to establish the identity of the remote user.

Even if we are able to identify when dial access search sessions begin and end, however, we may be no closer to understanding search sessions as perceived by users. To equate a dial access session with a search session may be misleading. Dial access sessions often utilize more than one type of search, but not infrequently more than one topic is pursued during a single dial access session. It is difficult or impossible to understand and measure the relationships perceived by the user about the various topics searched. For example, if a remote user searches for information on lung cancer and throat cancer during the same dial access session, it is not clear whether two topics have been searched or just one—cancer in humans who smoke. During subject searches the user often utilizes both controlled-vocabulary and free-text searching in an attempt to find information on the subject.

User Behavior Problems

Since the intended audience for this book is library and information professionals, not public users, the examination of problems will follow from user behavior problems through user attitudinal and conceptual problems to system problems. Users probably would follow the opposite path of problem identification—from the system back to the user. For most users, the default object of blame is the system itself.

Users exhibit several types of behavior problems as they use online catalogs. For this discussion, a behavior problem is defined as an action or activity that has a significant, detrimental effect on the progress or results of the search session. It is an interesting philosophical question whether or not a user misconception or misbehavior that does not adversely affect the progress or results of the search session should be counted as a problem. Within the context of a single search session, this situation can be ignored. But if the developing information skills and knowledge of the user is the focus, the mistaken but unaffecting activity should be identified as a problem.

Users' Will to Type

Online catalogs generally require little keying, yet users expect to be active as they search the online catalog. Many users seem more anxious to interact with the computer with their fingers than with their minds. Overall, the amount of characters keyed during an individual search statement tends to be more than is required by the system for efficient and effective retrieval. It should be noted that this "will to type" is evident when the individual search statements are the basic unit of analysis. The average number of search statements during an individual dial access session remains relatively small.

Low Use of Advanced Features

Underutilization of advanced features has attracted the attention of system designers and administrators. Many of the unique features of online catalogs are not being used by the majority of users. Two types of advanced feature use were examined in this study. The first was new access points, such as Boolean searching and call number browsing. The second was search options, such as truncation, scoping, sorting, and display options (see Chapter 10). Studying the amount of use of advanced features can help determine whether increasing the number of access points beyond the traditional author, title, and subject access points is a cost-effective enhancement. Online catalogs often are purchased because of the advanced features attached (commonly referred to as "bells and whistles"), yet research of actual usage of the system often reveals that the advanced features rarely are used. Whether low use of advanced features is caused by general user unawareness of the advantages and power of the features, or by conscious user avoidance of the advanced features is a subsequent research question.

Boolean searching. Many studies of online catalog use and user attitudes have found that Boolean search options found in many online catalog systems are rarely used. It is difficult to determine in how many searching situations the use of Boolean operators would have been possible and useful, but it is safe to say that the Boolean search option is underutilized. Boolean search techniques have come under fire as inappropriate for systems with diverse groups of public users. In 1989 Hildreth published *Intelligent Interfaces and Retrieval Methods*, about online catalogs that seriously questioned the extensive use of Boolean logic in online catalog systems intended for diverse, infrequent users. There are insurmountable problems with the use of Boolean logic by such a diverse, untrained user group.

Call number browse. The ability to browse by call number reintegrates two other activities or resources back into the online catalog. The first is the shelf list, which most users do not know about and, in some libraries, is not accessible by public users. The other activity is actually browsing the shelves, which most users know about.

Some researchers feel that classification schedules and call number browsing have great possibilities among the available online catalog search options. Robert Holley (1987) for example, presents a hopeful vision of the effects the new availability of call number browsing in online catalogs will have on patron behavior and librarians' attitudes toward classification schemes.

The analysis of transaction logs presented in the following chapters, however, reveals that the call number browse option is not heavily used. Even users who like to browse through the physical items on the shelves seem to use the call number browse feature very little. Call number browsing could be very useful during the identification portion of the search process, because the newer portion of the collection (assuming that retrospective conversion is incomplete) is presented in relatively pristine condition, with nothing checked out, misshelved, stolen, or in use in-house. Since numerous studies reveal that shelf browsing continues to be a popular behavior by library users, it is difficult to explain why call number browsing through the online catalog is shunned. By call number browsing online, however, the user is cut off from all the nonverbal clues presented by bibliographic items, such as color, newness, height, and thickness.[3] The online call number browser does not have immediate access to the full text, which seems to be a major attraction of browsing the shelves.

Until retrospective conversion makes great strides, the user who knows the value of the classification schedules would be better served by going to the shelf list than by browsing call numbers online. Conversely, a user interested only in more recent books on a given subject would be better served by browsing call numbers online.

High Failure Rates

Chapter 3 discussed the concept of a successful search. The converse is to examine the notion of failure in the use of online catalogs. Failure in this context focuses on the outcome of the search session, rather than the behavior and attitudes evident during the search session. Failed outcomes can include no information, too little information, too much information, and too much information of the wrong kind (too much noise or too many false hits). Transaction analysis typically reveals only one type of failure—zero hits. If the user finds one or more items none of which are pertinent, transaction analysis fails to reveal this. It also fails to reveal most instances when the user finds more records than desired.

Reaction to large retrieval sets. When users retrieve a large set of bibliographic or authority records,[4] rarely do they revise their searches to retrieve a smaller set with greater precision. Nor do they frequently scan through all of the items in the retrieved set. The characteristic behavior involves scanning through the items in the large set and quitting somewhere before the end. It would be incorrect to assume, however, that all such searches are terminated early. From the vantage point of the system they were terminated early, because all of the information retrieved by the system was not viewed by the user. If the users want just a few items on a topic or by an author, from the users' vantage point the search is complete when the desired amount of information is found, regardless of how much more information the system wants to make available. Systems, intermediaries, and end-users all have ways of reacting to large retrieval sets. It is not clear which is the best response.

Failure in context. High failure rates occasionally are tacitly accused of being caused by the public sector nature of much information storage and retrieval. The private sector, it is implied, would not accept these consistently high zero-hit rates. For example, Kilgour (1989) argues that such high failure rates would be unacceptable in private sector information brokerage. The drive to improve the success rate of library users is seen in the context of maintaining the library's market share in the business of information provision from all of the upstart private sector information retrieval services.

Truncation Confusion

Most users do not realize the power of truncation. From the perspective of systems analysis, truncation is an expensive luxury. A search involving truncation tends to increase the system response time. Sometimes truncation is automatically supplied by the system. In the system studied, the author search was automatically right-truncated. The truncation symbol varies from system to system. Truncation could be useful if the user has doubts about the veracity of the information brought to the search or his or her spelling abilities. Truncation also is useful to increase recall or to use title keyword searches as uncontrolled vocabulary subject searches. Truncation tends to increase the size of the retrieved set, but we cannot conclude that users shy away from truncation because they do not want high recall, precise sets. Most users probably are simply unaware of the possibilities and applications of truncation.

Low Persistence/Early Session Termination

Professional opinion is divided about the persistence of users of online catalogs. Markey (1984; 14) suggests that searchers' persistence has increased as as a result of the switch from the card catalog to the online catalog. On the other hand, Hildreth (1989A; 35) contends that one problem with the use of second-generation online catalogs is the prevalence of partially implemented search strategies and missed opportunities to refine the search. Researchers need to determine what it means to terminate a search early, then study the transaction logs to determine how often search sessions are terminated early. We must not allow our professional bias toward recall influence our data collection methods and interpretation of the results.

User Conceptual and Attitudinal Problems

Besides the observed behavior problems noted above, users also exhibit (through transaction logs and other forms of observations) and express (through questionnaires and focus group sessions) conceptual and attitudinal problems in their understanding of the online catalog system.

Users' Conceptualizations of the System

Users are not passive. They will create mental models of the information systems they use (Arret, 1985; 120). Users have problems conceptualizing the scope of online catalogs, because most online catalogs are union catalogs in some sense, while most traditional card catalogs are not. Users should come to the search with a vague sense of what they should expect to find in the online catalog. Serious user misconceptions are apparent about the system coverage and the utility and means of subject searching (Steinberg and Metz, 1984; 68). Users tend to overestimate the scope and coverage of the online catalog. "Unfortunately, users often believe that the new electronic catalog is actually the ideal catalog of the nineteenth century" (Tyckoson, 1989; 11). Many online catalogs are scrambling to include records for items not held in local collections, rather than just striving to include all locally held items or intellectual works.

What are the effects of the growing number of jumps, links, windows, and gateways in online catalogs on the users' conceptual orientation? The old conceptual orientation of bibliography, heavily reliant on alphabetization, may no longer be useful in the new generation of online catalogs. If alphabetization is one of the dimensions of the bibliographic universe, much like depth is one of the dimensions of the universe of objects, many automated systems diminish the significance of alphabetization as a dimension.

Controlled Subject Vocabularies

Patterns of controlled vocabulary subject searching versus uncontrolled vocabulary subject searching during online catalog search sessions can now be studied. Should we teach and encourage patrons to use uncontrolled vocabulary keyword searching as a way to establish a foothold in the controlled vocabulary? Perhaps title keyword searching should be presented as an alternative method of subject access. In some instances the Library of Congress subject classification is not precise enough to allow selection of a retrieval set of reasonable size, even if the user enters a precise and complete LC subject heading (Lynch, 1989A; 52). As intellectual works become less formal, more current, and specific to a particular discipline (or even a small group of scholars in a discipline), a universal list of subject headings that actually reflects the way topics are currently identified becomes more difficult to achieve.

Authority Files

The user interface with name and subject authority files does not help users create an adequate mental model of the structure and purpose of authority files. Users often have difficulties understanding the purpose of authority files and their relationship to the fields within the bibliographic records. In the system studied, menu-mode users are required to pass through the name and subject authority files to gain access to the bibliographic records.

Syndetic Structure

The internal syndetic structure of the library catalog may have regressed during the era of transition to online catalogs. The syndetic structure of the online catalog may be less user friendly than the syndetic structure of card and book catalogs. "See" and "see also" references often are more difficult to conceptualize in the online environment, because the sense of alphabetic arrangement is lost. The ability to update or customize the syndetic structure of the catalog is not being exploited in the online environment. Users could begin building a partial but useful citation/influence index to the records in the online catalog, but this would require a major policy shift to allow active user participation in the structure and maintenance of the online catalog database.

Precision and Recall

Issues of precision and recall in online catalog search results persist. Most users will work with a high recall search if the results are obtained quickly, such as on the first attempt. They judge that it is easier and safer for them to supply the need for precision on the fly than to try to make the system supply a more precise retrieval set. Most users do not manipulate recall as a variable during their search sessions.

As online catalogs developed, the real drive, primarily through retrospective conversion projects was to increase recall. As online catalogs expand and mature, the movement will switch over to an attempt to increase precision. Prabha (1989) sees the problem of large retrieval (high recall)[5] as a growing problem as the size of the online catalog bibliographic database expands. In an information-rich world, precision will become much more important than recall. The library catalog, based on the assumption of a strong positive correlation between local ownership and accessibility, was one way to make the broader concept of the bibliography more focused and exclusive. As the strong positive correlation between local ownership and accessibility deteriorates, however, alternative methods of selectivity must be explored.

Lynch and Berger (1989; 380) observe that many users prefer high precision searches in the MELVYL MEDLINE database rather than high recall, comprehensive searches. In his study of the slow growth of end-user searching of commercially vended databases, Pfaffenberger (1990; 115) agrees. Most end-user searchers view online database technology as a means for finding pertinent articles, not for producing comprehensive bibliographies.

Although they often appear to be inversely related, the relationship between precision and recall is not a constant. The user's desire for precision and recall, furthermore, easily could vary over time. The user's intentions, desires, and expectations regarding recall and precision can vary from search statement to search statement.

System Problems

Even when examining the problems with current online catalog systems, we should do so from the perspective of users. The systems should be designed to complement the user and his or her projects. Taylor (1986; 57) maintains this perspective when he makes a distinction between the interfacing capabilities of an information system and its adaptability. The human-computer interface denotes the ability of the system to explain itself to users, while its adaptability is a measure of how well the system is able to conform to the shifting context and problems arising from the environment of users. Online catalog designers and critics have devoted much time to the interface, but little time on ensuring that the systems are adaptable in a changing environment of information needs and projects.

Availability Creates Demand

There is some evidence suggesting that information is not made available because there is a demand for it, but rather that there is a demand for information because it has been made available. If we put quite a bit of money and time into making the information contained in the library catalog available to the user population, the library catalog will be used heavily. That the library catalog is heavily used, however, cannot be used as a justification for its existence, if this hypothesis is correct. "When removed from all of the economic and technical distortions caused by the expense and difficulty of using the commercial online utilities, there is a good deal of evidence that databases traditionally considered as specialized resources of specific subject areas will be used in a highly multidisciplinary fashion and that mounting databases without these distortions will promote multidisciplinary use of the databases" (Lynch and Berger, 1989; 382).

Design Biases

The interface between the user and the computer has received much attention. The design of the user interface must be grounded in the user's mental model of the information retrieval process (Hildreth, 1982; 41). The concept of a user interface, however, suggests something static—as a question to be considered during the initial design stages but rarely thereafter. Researchers should think in terms of search sessions, rather than a user interface, because the idea of search sessions reinforces the fact that experiences with an online catalog occur in short bursts, complete with a beginning, a middle, and an end, like all good tragedies.

Online catalogs, like many recent technological devices, offer users a large number of search options and choices. The desire for choice is a fairly recent phenomenon, and may be peculiar to certain cultures. Design features are based on the cultural premise that diversity—giving the user as many choices as possible—is inherently good. Sometimes the user is over-whelmed by choices. A point of diminishing returns soon may be reached, where the addition of more search options actually diminishes the usefulness of the system to most actual users.

One drawback of multiple-level interface features (such as menu-mode and command-mode in the online catalog studied in this reseach) is that, although they appear to give the user more options, users get stuck in the mode they first choose. They are reluctant to move to a different mode later on, even if it now represents a more appropriate choice for them, based on their skill level in using the system. Multiple-level interfaces discourage online learning and growth.

Large Retrieval Sets

Large retrieval sets are a system problem as well as a user problem. As online catalogs grow and mature, the sizes of retrieved sets of records, even for "good" searches, are becoming unmanageable. Most users do not know how to manage and manipulate retrieval sets. The average size of a retrieved set in the MELVYL catalog, containing about five million records, is about 150, while the average retrieval set for MELVYL MEDLINE is approximately 450 (Lynch and Berger, 1989; 379).

Transaction log analysis tends to reveal more about searches that fail because of zero hits than because of large retrieval sets, perhaps combined with low precision. Evidence indicates that most users of online catalogs have a hard time refining their initial search results to improve their satisfaction. This is a skill often required by online catalogs that has little carryover from skills learned while using card catalogs.

The behavioral tendency to work with near misses and large retrieval sets, rather than revise the initial search to achieve better results, may be the waning effect of computer phobia. Many users tend to grasp onto any set, however large or imprecise, rather than attempt another access to the database that may lose their original search results. Perhaps the online catalog should store the results of the previous search so that patrons are assured that they always can backtrack and review their previous findings. This observed behavior may also be the result of the cost/benefit analysis that users and researchers always are undertaking as they use the library, or even contemplate using it. Many users seem to assume that it is more economical for them, in the context of their current projects, to work with the set they have.

Subject Access

If subject search failure rates are as high as most studies indicate, where only a small percentage of users exhibit the skills necessary to efficiently and effectively use the system, some corrective action is needed.

Users are not sufficiently flexible and inventive during the subject search state. Bates has argued that effective search formulations almost always contain more variety in terminology than typical users provide (Ercegovac, 1989; 33). The subject catalog is a substantial, venerable, costly apparatus, but approximately 80 percent of all subject searches bypass the subject catalog. Reference librarians often consciously steer patrons around the official subject structure (Gerhan, 1989; 83). Even many intermediaries lack confidence in current systems of controlled vocabulary subject access.

The subject disciplines most often searched by a group of users may affect the use of the subject access features of the online catalog. During a recent study of the variability of subject searching activity over time, Neal Kaske (1988B; 368) found that business and education libraries have their highest subject searching late in the academic term, while the engineering and science libraries have their highest use during the first half of the semester.

Costs

Online catalog systems are not cheap, especially when all the hidden costs are taken into account. Who is responsible for paying the increased price of sophisticated information-retrieval techniques? Should libraries deny this advanced service to all if it cannot be provided equally (Drabenstott, 1988; 104)? In an era of rising value for access and falling value for ownership, what is the proper balance between the two? If future online catalog systems will focus on providing access to information, regardless of where it is stored, rather than merely identifying and locating items held in the local collections, they will require much more institutional support. If all of the costs involved in creating and maintaining a library catalog are added up, a disproportionate amount of the library's resources are spent providing access to a small percentage of the library's holdings (Tyckoson, 1989; 12).

There has been a tremendous drop in the cost per character of computer storage (Drabenstott, 1988; 103). This drop has made local storage of electronic information required for a project much more attractive. Redundant storage of information is not as costly as it used to be. Remote access to online catalogs and other information databases will increase the redundancy of stored bibliographic information, but that is not necessarily a bad situation.

Retrospective conversion costs. Retrospective conversion projects have been a major cost factor in the transition to the era of online catalogs. The assumption has been that older items in the collections will not get used unless they are included in the resource most users consult first, and the only source many users consult. As the monolithic era of the card catalog passes, however, users may start to consult more sources for information. Users seem to be resigned to the pluralistic sources of information as a signature of the new age of electronic and optical information storage.

Search Sessions as Strings of Unrelated Moments

Online catalogs currently are designed on the assumption that user information needs are momentary and fleeting. Nothing in the online catalog encourages the user to return to the results of the search at a later date for review or refinement. Online catalogs should help users manage or control the information retrieved, but most do not, or do so at a primitive level—the level of a slow dot matrix printer. Search sessions cannot be saved for future review, yet transaction log analysis of search sessions indicates that users apparently return to the online catalog again and again, reexecuting the same or similar search arguments. The design of most online catalogs encourages users to begin over again, rather than pick up where they left off.

Downtime and Slowtime

Downtime is not unique to online catalogs. If downtime is thought of as those times when the catalog is unavailable for consultation, early online catalogs represented a retrogression from the earlier catalog formats, because sometimes the library was open and the online catalog was unavailable. Remote access, however, has led to advances in access to the catalog. In many libraries offering remote access to their online catalog, the catalog can be consulted even when the library is closed.

Compared to other catalog formats, variable and slow response time is unique to online catalogs. The combination of slowtime and dumb terminals without type-ahead capabilities is very frustrating for many online catalog users. Research into user behavior during periods of slow response time and downtime may indicate how willing users are to consult other document identification and locating devices. How does downtime affect users? Will they try the card catalog? Will they go away and do something else until the system comes back up? What happens to the image of the entire library when the online catalog goes down? What strains are placed on the reference staff during periods of downtime? What happens to dial access users of the online catalog when the system goes down? Often they receive no system message that the catalog has gone down, and there is no intermediary nearby to consult. Their phone lines may be tied up while they wait for the system to release them.

Other Problems and Concerns

Other problems and concerns about online catalog systems refer not so much to their actual use, but to the relationship between the online catalog and the other work processes within the library and the larger institution. These concerns are more theoretical than operational.

Online Catalogs and Other Library Services

Online catalogs have had an impact on other library services. In some instances the relationship has been problematic.

Interlibrary loan. As users employ more powerful tools to quickly identify needed local and remote library materials in printed form, they will want equally convenient and speedy access to the information itself. Unless adequate attention is paid to full text delivery, enhanced access to bibliographic and electronic information systems may create a library with glass walls, instead of a library without walls (Bailey, 1989; 182).

The University of Illinois, the number one interlibrary borrower among ARL libraries, borrowed almost four times as many items in 1988 as the second place borrower, Boston University. The director of the library points to LCS, the online union catalog connecting twenty-nine Illinois libraries, as the primary cause of the heavy demand for interlibrary loan.[6] The effects on interlibrary loan service caused by remote access to online catalogs via Illinet has been the opposite of what was expected. The University of Illinois at Urbana-Champaign, the largest library in the Illinet network, actually became a net borrower (Potter, 1986; 23).

Reference desk service. The large variations in the use of subject searching in online catalogs over time and among different branch libraries have implications for the staffing and scheduling of reference desk service, bibliographic instruction programs, and systems updating and maintenance (Kaske, 1988B; 371). The reference needs of remote users are qualitatively different than typical in-house reference demands. Kalin's evidence indicates that most users want technical assistance in establishing remote access to the catalog. Many want advice and evaluations of hardware and software (Sally Kalin, 1987). Perhaps soon they will be asking for advice and evaluations of the texts themselves.

Ratio of Collection Building Costs to Access Costs

Online catalogs also have created problems in the area of collection development. The traditional way of viewing a library's costs is to strike a balance between the costs of building the collection and the costs of providing access to the collection. Again we seem to be dealing with a pie of a definite size. Every dollar put into providing access to the collection is a dollar taken away from actually building the collection. This could be termed the "collectocentric view" of libraries.

This way of viewing the situation assumes that the value of the information contained in the online catalog is vastly inferior to the information contained in the documents themselves. For example, the bibliographic record may contain the information that pages 154–160 of a book is a bibliography, but only the book itself contains the actual bibliographic information. The collectocentric view of libraries sees the online catalog as a device to provide access to the collection and nothing else. If you put too much money into a device that merely provides access to the collection, you have achieved good access to a collection that has not grown as fast as it would have if less money had been pumped into access costs. As more users become more interested in the information contained in the online catalog itself, the catalog will become a part of the collection—the payoff information. The view of library funding that sees a struggle between the costs of collection development and the costs of access development will become untenable.

Classification of Information

Currently, information is classified by type, format, source, etc. All the patron wants to do is personalize the information. Ease of location, retrieval, digestion, and application are the primary concerns of the user. To the user, there is little distinction between journal information and monographic information, between information on paper or on microfiche. Almost all users are seeking unique intellectual works, not unique bibliographic items. The demand by the user to make the information system more personalized and seamless has always been great. That is a principal activity of every scholar currently laboring away. They are breaking down the walls of information and making it their own so they can turn around and apply it. To personalize information, however, does not necessarily imply that the information is rendered idiosyncratic. Most scholars are very careful to personalize information—to make it their own—without making it idiosyncratic. Checks on this fundamental drive in any information system come from producers and publishers, who want to maintain the concepts of ownership, publication, intellectual property, and copyright. Librarians and other middlemen are facing a crisis of allegiance on this issue. Should librarians be advocates for the users or the producers and creators of information? If we decide to be advocates for the users in the flow of information, we must push for systems designed with the users' projects in mind.

Personalized Information Systems

The notion of a personalized information system has received much support in the era of automation. What is meant by the numerous calls for personalized information systems? If we view the flow of information as a series of processes, including creation, publication, distribution, storage, retrieval, valuation/assimilation/interpretation, and application, the first two and the last two steps always have been highly personalized. Calls for more personalized information systems seem to focus on personalizing the cataloging, storage, and retrieval of information—the middle functions that are the traditional domain of libraries. Rice (1989A; 21) asserts that "an entirely new and individualized method of information access and use" is becoming available, with remote searching of online databases, CD-ROM products, online catalogs, and bibliographic database management software representing the tip of the iceberg. Another way to personalize an information system is to customize the user interface (Hildreth, 1982; 53).

Historically, libraries began as private collections of recorded information. Recent technological developments, including remote access to all types of information, may make adequate and sufficient personal libraries again feasible. Academic libraries always have felt a little threatened by personal information systems and collections. Our fear of private libraries almost rivals our fear of complete privatization of the middleman functions. Some potential high-end-users on campus, particularly in the sciences, already choose to forego the formal institutional information stores and services in favor of the construction of focused personal information databases. Remote access may accelerate the defection of high-end-users. In a generic sense, private libraries gave birth to public access libraries. In the next few decades we may see public access libraries return the favor by giving birth to high-tech private libraries. It remains to be seen how magnanimous public access libraries will be as this trend gains momentum.

The idea of the scholar's workstation, which grew out of Vannevar Bush's idea of the memex, utilizes individual freedom and control as guiding principles. Bush's idea of a memex machine stressed its speed and flexibility. The memex would become an enlarged intimate supplement to the individual user's memory (Rice, 1988A; 14). Here is a vision of information storage and retrieval systems that is so idiosyncratic that the device becomes an extension of human memory. The social interaction that nonindividualized systems demand of users may be eroded or lost.

Glenn Bacon (1986; 163) believes that the next wave of development in information storage and retrieval systems will focus on the individual needs and autonomy of the end-user, not on the internal, hierarchical functions of the institution. "The information end user's drive for autonomy is a very pervasive and potent force, one that will ultimately reshape our knowledge-based institutions." One version of the history of information storage and retrieval in the last two hundred years sees the individual end-user as a slave to institutional and public storage systems, because the economics of information flow prohibited all but the most wealthy individuals from purchasing all the information they wanted or needed. Bacon suggests that in the future the valuation of information systems will focus on convenience and subjective values, perhaps more than on institutional productivity (Bacon, 1986; 162). Libraries, nevertheless, are still intent on automating internal processing functions, such as serials control and circulation. Does this necessarily imply, however, that the institution is ignoring end-user needs? Bacon assumes that there is a fundamental conflict between the needs of the institution and the needs of the end-user. An information storage and retrieval system cannot serve both interests. Dow (1988; 85) seems to agree with Bacon. The academic library should support technological development that encourages and enables information autonomy. Dow (1988; 83–84) argues that the goal of technological development in information systems is "complete information autonomy," where the relevant information chunks from disparate sources are presented in the most individually pertinent way to the end-user.

A goal of the Library 2000 Project at Georgia Tech is to create personalized information systems (Drake, 1989; 111). New information structures need to be developed, including the ability to approach information from an individualized perspective and be drawn toward the desired information in natural steps and ordinary language (Molholt, 1988; 94). Once an individual has gathered needed information, he wants to (and should have the right to) build files based on personalized, idiosyncratic logic. Indexes will be built that are most meaningful to the individual (Molholt, 1985; 286).

Recent debate on the concept of a virtual library, based on the notion of virtual reality, should not be confused with personalized information systems. Remote access is a step toward the realization of a virtual library, because remote access begins to make time and distance insignificant. Before the library can be replicated in a virtual environment, however, more study needs to be made of our current understanding of the universe of recorded information.

The question of personalized information systems touches on some fundamental issues about human freedom, individuality, and the ability to communicate with others. We face a future where whole systems will be unable to communicate with each other, where the barriers caused by different human languages are minor compared to the higher barriers recently erected by technology and the appreciation of the market value of information. The prospect of personalized information systems needs careful scrutiny.

Postcoordination. The concept of a personalized information system comprises several visions. When Kilgour (1979; 40) defended the ability of online catalogs to display personalized results, he was referring only to the ability to postcoordinate the search results. Set creation and manipulation is a highly personalized activity, even though most users seem to believe they are interacting with a static, institutional entity. Dale Carrison (1989) assumes that systems that require conformity to a shared vocabulary or basic search strategy are bad. Anything that confines or frustrates the individual user should be avoided at all cost. Judith Adams (1988; 32) sees keyword searching capability as a "stunning blow for individual freedom." In these visions, personalization is subsumed under broader commonality of stored information.

Selective dissemination of information. Drake's idea (1989; 115) of a personalized information system is a selective dissemination of information service that is delivered via electronic mail. A paradox exists here. In the past, the burden of transporting the information on the final leg of its journey to the site of application was the responsibility of the user. The user checks out the book and transports it back to the office or dwelling. In Drake's vision, the institution will build an infrastructure for that final leg of transportation. How then can institutional encroachment into a traditional user function lead to greater personalized information? This paradox has implications for all types of remote access. Regardless, in Drake's vision of personalized information systems it is the transportation that is being personalized, not the syndetic structure of the database or the content of the records within the database.

Hypertext, hypermedia, and hyperlibraries. Hypertext is a movement to personalize the syndetic structure of stored information. Hypertext and hypermedia applications have developed first in the realm of producers and consumers of information. Hypertext creates new possibilities and responsibilities for the author. He must structure the material appropriately and provide readers with a sense of the structure of the texts (Arms, 1990B; 317). Hypertext and hypermedia also create new possibilities for end-user management of information. Now the middlemen are looking seriously at hypertext. What needs to be considered is the desirability of a library organized on the principles of hypertext and hypermedia.

Syndetic structure in the flow of information does not begin and end with the library catalog. Internal and external syndetic structure is evident throughout the flow of information. Complex associations between information, texts, and their carriers (vegetable, human, electronic, and optical) provide the pressure that makes the flow of information possible. Hypertext and hypermedia give value to syndetic structures. They strive to make the syndetic structure transparent and idiosyncratic.

The library catalog may be one of the most massive hypertext databases in existence within ten years (Drabenstott, 1988; 110). Hypertext and hypermedia take the concept of personalized databases far beyond simple postcoordination of search results. Hypertext and hypermedia were designed and based on the notion that the individual user best knows her or his own information storage and retrieval habits.

If the process of information seeking becomes as individualized as the subject matter in some academic disciplines, how will individuals be able to communicate with each other? How will a user be able to find and utilize information in another individual's personal hypertext system, unless there are shared assumptions about the fundamental methods of information storage and retrieval? The principles of research should not become as expansive and individualized as the subject matter of research. Hypertext is seen in this context as an impediment to common communication between individuals. The lack of standards for the organization of hard disks and databases also fits into this category of potential problems.

Hypertext and hypermedia encourage distributed, individualized, idiosyncratic classification of information. Support for personalized information systems is strong, and its strength seems to come from assumptions and values common to the broader culture. This drive to personalize information has a long history. Over a decade ago, Joseph Becker (1979; 414) listed the personalization of information services as one of the three main missions of the library in the age of automation. Any professional assumptions of conformity by end-users to standard procedures for information storage and retrieval often is presented in the light of the last vestiges of repressive nineteenth-century librarianly behavior. Adherence to standards seems to be seen as an activity for professionals only. Mere end-users cannot be expected to conform to standard operating procedures. For centuries libraries have forced multiple layers of conformity on their users and patrons. It is time to move away from that assumption, and tools based on hypermedia concepts offer us the opportunity to do so (Molholt, 1989; 96b). There seems to be a sizable group of critics who see any system constraints inhibiting free expression in the world of recorded scholarly information as bad.

The purpose of an automated information storage and retrieval device is not to make the world of scholarly records conform to each user's idiosyncracies, but to help each user learn and decipher the established scholarly record. As devices, online catalogs facilitate the flow of recorded information. Stated another way, the online catalog is a communications device. The online catalog should teach as well as identify and locate. The coming era seems to be one in which both the texts and the bibliographic systems supporting the identification and location of texts are losing their authority. A new dark age, based on hoarded information and incompatible systems, is not unimaginable.

Conclusion

Although the problems with online catalogs and their use are numerous, this does not imply that the systems are bad. Research attempting to identify problems should be neutral. The identification of problems is anterior to the assignment of blame.

Notes

1. There are studies refuting this assumption, proving that even when a catalog says that the library owns the volume, the chances of the user's actually being able to retrieve the item are less than 50 percent. See Kilgour, 1989.

2. See Chapter 9 for a further discussion of probable causes of the problems.

3. All of these characteristics, except color, are standard fields in bibliographic records, but the object itself presents these characteristics much more graphically, without the need for any decoding and training.

4. These were scaled at more than thirty bibliographic records or fifty authority records in the system studied.

5. Although the concept of high recall does not necessarily entail large retrieval sets, the two are often conjoined in real search situations. For example, if the collection contains only three books on a distinct topic, a high recall retrieval set is still a small set.

6. "AL Asides: Stats." *American Libraries* 20 (5) (May 1989): 389.

Chapter 6
Potential Solutions: Change the Systems

Introduction

Although Hildreth argues that the user should be perceived and considered as a major component of online catalog systems, this is true only as the user uses the system, and it is true only from the vantage point of the system designer and analyst. While the user is using the system, he or she perceives the online catalog as somehow complete prior to his or her particular session with it. There is some validity, therefore, at least from the user's point of view, in thinking of the user as separate from the online catalog system in its state as a potential bibliographic retrieval device. As will become apparent in the next two chapters, this study maintained a conceptual division between the system and users of the system.

Outline of the Basic Options

When potential solutions to current problems with online catalogs are considered, two basic options immediately present themselves: change the system to accommodate the users, or educate the users in the proper way to search the system. Ironically, this fundamental decision about how to apply the results of research into problems with online catalogs is rarely discussed in the literature. Usually the validity of one option or the other is just assumed by the reseachers and commentators.

Often systems people, such as Lynch, assume that changes to the system are the solution. The major report on the CLR study seems to assume that user education is out of the question because the user cannot be redesigned to meet the needs of the system (Matthews, Lawrence, and Ferguson, 1983; 84). This fundamental bias toward system modification, rather than user education, is evident in statements like this: "Much of the potential information in transaction logs is of interest only to the system designers, for enhancing or modifying the system" (Larson, 1983; 3). "It is unrealistic to expect our catalog users to know in advance the structure and language of our library databases" (Hildreth, 1989A; 36). Hildreth clearly is in the camp of the system designers, not the educators. The dominance of the option of modifying the system, rather than educating the user, as the preferable and feasible way to improve online catalog use is observable throughout the brief history of online catalogs.

The tacit assumption for not following the path of user education seems to be either that this is not an effective way to achieve generally successful use of the system, or that the education of users is a task far beyond the traditional mission of the library. The interesting thing about discussions of the design of online catalogs is not so much what they reveal about design principles, but what they reveal about the designers' assumptions about human capabilities.

Most practicing librarians fall into the other camp, believing that user education is the best path to follow. The small amount of research done in this area fails to support the intuitive belief that design factors should be important sources of variance in user behavior (Borgman, 1986; 394). Winner (1986) argues that people alter their behavior and beliefs to conform with the possibilities offered by the new technology.

This basically is a management decision, but is rarely made as such. Should cost be the determining factor when making the decision about which avenue to follow toward improvement?

Hildreth (1987; 660) conceptualizes potential changes to online catalogs slightly differently. He sees three basic ways to enhance the ease of use and retrieval effectiveness of online catalogs: improve the interaction between the user and the system; enrich and improve the content and structure of the database; or add supplementary databases. His first option could involve changing the system, educating the user, or a combination of both. His second option is a task for maintainers of the database and maintainers of the system. The third option is basically a management/ marketing decision to expand services (or at least to consolidate services into one central access mechanism).

Another fundamental decision to be made when searching for solutions to the problems of online catalogs is whether the principal thrust of the problem-solving effort will be directed toward putting records for different types of items into the database or toward providing other or additional information about the type of items already in the database. Proponents of the first solution would argue that the book format is losing its share of the information universe, so the library catalog should slowly move beyond the book format by providing access to journal articles, video materials, as well as gateways to other databases of interest to the primary clientele. Proponents of the second solution could argue that online access to tables of contents or even full text is a better solution. Defenders of evaluative catalogs also are advocates of the second solution. In practice, of course, strains of both solutions are inextricably mixed, but we need to note that the separate thrust of each solution is fundamentally different.

Change the Online Catalog: New Features

This chapter will examine the possible ways to change online catalog systems to improve search sessions and their results. Discussion of how to change the systems seems to center on two sets of options. The first focuses on ways to improve the current access points without major overhaul of the systems. Discussions of improved subject access dominate this first option. The second arena of discussion calls for a more radical rethinking of online catalogs.

Backup Catalogs

A first option would be to use all of the use studies of library materials to place strict temporal limits on the bibliographic records contained in the online catalog database. As the size of online catalogs increases, perhaps older, less-used materials should be made available via CD-ROM catalogs, with the online catalog providing access only to the most recent materials, perhaps only those that have been published in the last ten years.

Have automated catalogs increased, rather than decreased, the number of locating tools a user must consult? Do users really want one-stop shopping? A study of public catalog use by Ben-Ami Lipetz and Peter Paulson (1987; 611) reveals that, at least as an aggregate group, users will utilize both a microfiche catalog and an online catalog. It remains to be studied, however, whether the individual user will regularly consult more than one catalog to a library's collection.

Additional Access Points

The ability to limit search results by date, language, medium, and location is important. As online catalogs mature and expand, the ability to retrieve only recently added items in the collection will become increasingly valued. Kilgour believes that nonliterary books should be arranged on the shelves by subject, then in reverse chronological order, rather then by Cutter number.

Citation Access

Swanson (1979; 8) has argued that citation indexes were a significant improvement to traditional information storage and retrieval systems, because citation analysis is something of great interest to users trying to solve problems. This is particularly true of the high-end-users of library systems, such as faculty, graduate students, and independent researchers. The network of citations between works is of great importance to problem-oriented access to information. Online catalogs do not provide this type of access.

Spelling Checkers and Thesauri

An earlier study of in-house use of the online catalog studied here found that approximately 20 percent of searches that produced zero hits were caused by typographical errors and misspellings (Peters, 1989). An educator would see this as a failure of the educational system, and look to the educational system to correct the problem. A system designer would overlook that option and look for ways to modify the system to compensate for user failings. Spelling checkers available in many word processing software programs could be adapted for use in an online catalog system.

Bates (1989; 405) thinks that thesauri hold great potential in the online catalog environment, but their purpose needs to be reformulated. Most current thesauri are designed primarily for the indexer/cataloger, not the user.

It is imperative that the online catalog inform the user if the data entered have been altered in any way, perhaps including even automatic right truncation.

Enhancing Subject Access

The subject search session involves the confluence (or lack of same) of three human subject vocabularies: of the producer (usually the author), of the middleman (usually the cataloger), and of the user (Tague, 1989; 53). Most of the current work on subject access focuses on the relationship between the consumers' vocabularies and that of the middlemen.

The CLR study of online catalogs provided a mandate to improve subject access to the bibliographic records. For several years many researchers, notably Markey, have been working on ways to improve subject access. It has been suggested that increased attention to enriched subject classification and cross-referencing is perhaps the most efficient way to improve user access (Brownrigg, 1983; 106).

Some research suggests that subject searching is performed primarily by undergraduates in the evening. The mean number of subject searches per hour per terminal increases all the time the library is open in a day, so that there is more intense use of subject searching in the evening (Kaske, 1988A; 276). The movement to improve subject access to online catalog information, despite all the technical jargon, really is a movement to help the low-end-users of the system. Perhaps some of the schemes for improving subject access forget this fundamental fact.

It is possible to add information to the controlled vocabulary, such as chapter titles and words from the index; to increase use of uncontrolled vocabulary subject searching; to improve the syndetic structure of the online catalog, perhaps making it transparent. The Lipetz study of 1970 may have been misinterpreted by many as an indication of lack of desire for subject access, rather than the difficulty users were experiencing at the time obtaining good results via subject access. The users' perceptions about subject searching indicate wishful thinking (Steinberg and Metz, 1984; 68, 69). An OCLC-sponsored analysis of transaction logs from three libraries not using OCLC as a catalog found that subject searches result in zero hits more often than any other type of search, except Boolean searching at Syracuse (Broadus, 1983; 465).

Marilyn Lester's doctoral research attempts to measure the match success when several different automated retrieval processes, which could be designed into an online catalog, were applied to the users' failed subject terms as identified in the random sample from the transaction logs at Northwestern (Roose, 1988; 76). The research indicates that the way online catalogs process the database for retrieval of records is far more significant than previously recognized. Adding retrieval processes such as right truncation, string searching, and keyword and Boolean searching improves retrieval much more than augmenting the database with authority files (Roose, 1988; 77).

Bates' three elements of subject access. Bates (1989; 401) identifies three aspects of subject access in the online catalog environment. The very nature of the online catalog as a technological device has increased the parameters of subject access. In the card catalog format, subject headings and classification numbers comprised subject indexing. The online catalog has added a third element to subject indexing—the online search capabilities themselves. Subject search capabilities vary markedly across systems.

Change or abandon LCSH. Is is possible or prudent to have one subject list that attempts to provide subject access to all subjects known to man? Is it possible or prudent to offer one online system that is accessible by all types of users? The generality of LCSH (Library of Congress subject headings) combines with the power of an online catalog search to result almost inevitably in the recall of far too many records for the patron to use effectively (Herschman, 1987; 347).

Gerhan (1989; 86) classifies the functions of the Library of Congress subject headings into four categories: standardization of terminology, broadening the context of the title, providing a facet of the subject not indicated in the title, and clarification. Although the principles of specificity and coextensivity in the assignment of subject headings is assumed to be absolute, the research sample indicates that the database of LC subject-cataloged works probably contains a large set of records where the assigned Library of Congress subject headings are of greater generality than the actual topic scopes of the works (Gerhan, 1989; 87). The meanings of many terms and phrases have become discipline-specific. As a concept, a unified list of subject headings does not handle this situation well.

Weighting of terms. Two of the common complaints about Boolean search procedures is that all terms have equal weight or importance and the relationships between concepts are difficult to translate into Boolean search strategies. Some system designers are working to provide methods for the weighting of search terms.

Improve the syndetic structure. One service that has suffered during the transition from card to online catalogs is the user interface to the syndetic structure of the catalog, particularly "see" and "see also" references. Some writers have suggested that it is the user's burden to know variant forms of names and subject headings since it has become too expensive for libraries to provide such services (Jamieson, Dolan, and Declerck, 1986; 277). This is one small instance where a traditional function of the middlemen in the flow of information has been transferred to the end-users, not to the producers and suppliers. Some research reveals, however, that a catalog without a cross-reference structure for variant forms of names and subject headings will give its users inferior service. Keyword searching cannot compensate for the lack of syndetic structure (Jamieson, Dolan, and Declerck, 1986; 283). Jamieson, Dolan, and Declerck, however, base their conclusions about the failure of keyword searching on a one-stage search process only. The great value of keyword searching is to get a quick, fairly precise, small set of bibliographic records, then use this toehold to analyze the retrieved records and initiate controlled vocabulary searches as necessary. The keyword search can be used as an entry point into the subject of interest to the user. Third generation online catalogs will not assume that the display of a full bibliographic record represents the end of the search process. The system will ask the user if she or he wants to view linked records with common data elements (e.g., author, subject headings, series title, call number) (Hildreth, 1987; 657).

Bates (1989; 406) thinks we need to greatly expand the scope of the syndetic structure of the catalog, with "see from" references written in the vernacular. The primary purpose of the syndetic structure of the library catalog is to help the end-users use the catalog, not to help the middlemen in the flow of information maintain the catalog.

A common feature of the design of online catalogs is to undervalue or discount the importance of making a decision whether or not to pursue "see" and "see also" references. If the ability to pursue references electronically is built into systems, the systems often pursue them automatically. In the case of "see also" references, the professional bias toward recall over precision is revealed. Systems are designed on the assumption that most users want to "see also" most of the time.

Relevance feedback. Relevance feedback also has been proposed as a way to improve system responsiveness. The system would ask the user if the fully displayed item is relevant to the user's information need. If so, the system would use information contained in the full bibliographic record (probably assigned subject headings, author and corporate author names, or call numbers) to perform revised searches for the user. Relevance information should be sought from a user only when the system can detect that a user is being fairly persistent (Walker, 1988; 29). As noted above, however, the concept of relevant items is almost as thorny as the idea of a successful search.

Stemming. Systematic weak or strong stemming would increase recall. It is hoped that weak stemming would increase recall without adversely affecting precision. Strong stemming would provide dramatic improvements in recall, but probably at the cost of a serious deterioration in precision. Both of these stemming options are designed to improve recall. One conclusion of the present study, however, is that, for various reasons, a significant increase in recall is not a top priority item at this time.

Keyword subject searching. Keyword searches of the title and/or subject fields also hold promise. Only 15.52 percent of nonpreferred topical subject headings of a synonymous nature were able to retrieve bibliographic records in the sample database via keyword searches of all MARC fields (Jamieson, Dolan, and Declerck, 1986; 279). When these successful keyword searches throughout all MARC fields for nonpreferred, synonymous LCSH topical subject headings (i.e., a subset of the "see" references in LCSH) are examined, however, the distribution rate in the MARC 650 field (topical subject heading) and the 245 field (title statement) is almost identical (approximately 41 percent) (Jamieson, Dolan, and Declerk, 1986; 282). Thus title keyword searching seems to be a valid subject search, as successful as a controlled vocabulary keyword search for unused access points.

Lester's doctoral research indicates that keyword and Boolean subject searching seems to be the system enhancement that would improve online catalog subject searching success rates the most (Roose, 1988; 77). Keyword searches of subject fields would overcome unnatural word order, a major stumbling block in the use of card catalogs. In the system studied in this research, keyphrase searches of headings and subheadings of assigned subjects were possible, but not keyword subject searches.

Use of classification schedules. In the United States the agenda for changes in, and expansion of, verbal subject access is firmly established, while the potential for the use of the classification scheme in the online catalog environment has only begun to be considered (Holley, 1987; 67). Classification schemes are unique as access points in an online catalog because they are the only nonverbal methods of subject access to the bibliographic records. Several commentators and researchers have argued in recent years that classification schemes and class numbers are grossly underutilized as access points to bibliographic records. Janet Hill (1984) suggests that it is not wise to use classification numbers primarily as location devices, rather than for subject access. At odds here are the two concurrent main purposes of the library catalog as currently conceived—to identify and locate bibliographic items. Creators of intellectual works and classifiers share something in common. The main purpose of any form of subject access—the title, the dust jacket, the call number, or a subject heading—is to provide some indication of the content of the work to the potential user without requiring the user to first read the entire work.

Elaine Svenonius (1983) presents a good discussion of the conjoined use of verbal subject searching and classification numbers. Because class numbers indicate the perspective of the intellectual work toward the subject, classification schemes have a natural advantage over controlled vocabularies. A book on iron, for example, will be classed according to its orientation toward the subject (Chan, 1989; 533). Bibliographic records could contain more than one call number from the same classification scheme, as well as call numbers from other class schedules (e.g., LCSH and DDC), so users could choose which class schedule they feel most confident in searching. Lois Mai Chan (1989; 531) even presents a case for the use of call numbers for efficient retrieval of known items comprising broad subject areas, short common titles, numerous editions, or from prolific authors.

One of the forms of browsing most libraries have neglected is the shelf list (Taylor, 1986; 80). If we assume that items that circulate have more value for the user population than items that do not, browsing the shelf list is better than browsing the stacks, because nothing is checked out, stolen, or misshelved. This is particularly true when the user is not interested in immediately retrieving the full text. Of course, items that are not in their proper places on the shelves are not as accessible, so if accessibility is a primary motivation of the user, shelf browsing is better than shelf list browsing. Shelf browsing also allows the user to go from bibliographic record to the full bibliographic item itself, particularly subject-rich areas such as the table of contents, the index, and the reference lists and bibliographies. This is information of interest to many users that most online catalogs do not provide.

Classification schemes do have inherent drawbacks. A class number is a nonverbal method for locating an intellectual work within the universe of knowledge. Compared to verbal subject headings, class numbers are one more step removed from the user's notion of a topic. Classification schemes, even more than controlled lists of subject headings or descriptors, are doomed to be perpetually out of date, unwieldy, and somewhat pompous and reductive. Miksa (1987) is one commentator who suggests that a neat cosmology of knowledge, complete with a little music of the spheres, no longer is useful to many scholarly research projects.

The evidence from transaction log analysis indicates that call number searching is not used much by public users. "Used together, key words, controlled vocabulary, and class or call numbers can achieve the best subject retrieval search results by complementing one another to improve both precision and recall" (Chan, 1989; 536). The results of research conducted in 1989 by Kurth and Peters indicates that dial access search sessions combining more than two subject access possibilities are not uncommon. It would be foolish to enhance call number access in online catalogs without educating users about the advantages and disadvantages of call number access to intellectual works.

Analytics: tables of contents and indexes. The need for analytic catalogs is increasing, because the average size of intellectual works is decreasing, and they often are grouped with other intellectual works in a single bibliographic item. There seems to be wide agreement that future online catalogs should contain more information from the intellectual works themselves than is contained in current MARC bibliographic records. This trend of expanding the contents of the bibliographic records probably will continue until the full text of most or all intellectual works in the collection are available through the online catalog. At that point the online catalog will become an online library, and the current proliferation of multiple bibliographic items containing the same (or similar) intellectual work may decline or cease altogether.

Several studies have suggested that tables of contents and indexes should be analyzed to improve and expand subject access to monographs. Effort also should be made to improve the contents pages and indexes in books so that they become more content-bearing (Atherton, 1978; 87). There is a vague hint here that the burden of improving subject access should be on authors and publishers—the producers. Proposals such as these intend to take a portion of the uncontrolled vocabulary surrounding a book and make it respectable and semi-official.

Hildreth (1987; 661) points out that two separate benefits would be achieved by adding data from tables of contents to bibliographic records. First, they would improve subject retrieval, since the current language of the discipline and topic probably would be found in the table of contents. Second, the option of displaying tables of contents from retrieved bibliographic records would help the user begin evaluating and determining the relevance of the retrieved records.

Title keyword searching. Uncontrolled vocabulary subject access provided through title keywords is a form of subject access previously unavailable through the card catalog (Bates, 1989; 401). Perhaps some librarians, especially technical services librarians, are reluctant to condone title keyword searching as subject searching because they perceive it as a waste of years of work to create and maintain a controlled vocabulary. Relying more on title keywords for subject access also puts pressure on creators and producers to provide titles that are descriptive of the contents. Although this has been successful in certain segments of the producing population, notably the hard sciences, some librarians seem reluctant to force the entire set of producers to assume a greater portion of the burden of providing subject access through title keywords. Titles serve other functions besides subject access. Nevertheless, during one study of the efficacy of title keywords for subject access, it was found that fully 76 percent of the sample records would offer some degree of subject access via title keyword searching (Gerhan, 1989, 85).

Some recent studies support the retention of controlled vocabularies as the principal method of subject access. Gerhan (1989; 87) found that searchers will retrieve more citations in fewer tries by making use of Library of Congress subject headings before trying title keywords when searching by both options. Gerhan's method may be flawed in that he assumes that users make no use of the retrieved relevant records to identify valid subject headings. The title keyword search can be a good first step because it often results in highly precise retrieval sets that are not too large. The found items can then be analyzed to go back and try official subject headings searches.

The debate over controlled versus uncontrolled subject vocabularies should not focus, as Carolyn Frost does in her 1989 study, on the degree of similarity between the two vocabularies. If a quick title keyword search helps the user identify relevant items and relevant controlled vocabulary subject headings, the uncontrolled vocabulary subject search has fulfilled its purpose, regardless of the similarities or dissimilarities between the title keywords and the assigned subject headings. In fact, a title keyword search could help the user identify promising subject headings much faster and easier than would a trip to LCSH, even if LCSH is available online. If the user wants only a few pertinent items, title keywords could be used to locate the items with no intention of resorting to controlled subject vocabulary to increase recall.

For the users of an online catalog, the line between legitimate and nonlegitimate indexing terms is blurry (Bates, 1989; 406). Title keywords as a means of uncontrolled vocabulary subject access seem to be gaining use. Approximately 20 percent of the users of an automated circulation system early in the 1980s admitted using the title access as a form of subject access (Carole Moore, 1981; 296). During a study of selected months of 1988 and 1989, at least 6.5 percent of all dial access sessions utilized title keywords for uncontrolled vocabulary subject access (Peters and Kurth, 1990).

Arguments against additional subject access. Even if technology is an answer to improving subject access to the online catalog, it does not address the more basic question of how best to help online catalog users find all the information they seek (Lawry, 1986; 127). Primarily for economic reasons, the adoption of an even more controlled system driven by strict professional standards does not appear to be the correct direction to pursue (Beckman, 1982; 2047).

Precision and Recall

Earlier studies by Moore and Norden revealed users' perceptions that insufficient recall, rather than lack of precision, is still a problem (Steinberg and Metz, 1984; 66). This study suggests that many users are much more interested in a small, manageable, precise set of hits than a high recall, large retrieval set.

If a system is designed to tolerate or correct user errors so that precison and recall are not impaired, do the errors, by definition, cease to exist? For example, it is traditional cataloging practices that have created the impression that searching for an author by entering the first name first (in natural order) is an error. If most or all online catalog systems could accept author searches entered in natural order, entering the first name first would cease to be an error.

There seems to be a growing awareness that certain systems and technological devices can encourage the user to strive for precision or recall. The style of online database technology stresses comprehensiveness (recall) over evaluative judgments of quality (precision) (Pfaffenberger, 1990; 21).

Output Control Design Features

Of the two categories of output control identified by Hildreth (1982; 137)—the visual presentation of bibliographic information and user manipulation of search results—the first has received much more attention. This is odd, because the act of searching an online catalog is dominated by the creation and manipulation of sets. The online catalog does not provide much guidance and help in assisting the user with the management of retrieved information.

Improved sort options. Sort options for sets retrieved from online catalog databases include random sorts, by date, by author, by title, and by numeric value, such as accession number (Hildreth, 1982; 142). From the user's perspective, four useful sort options would be by title, by author, by year of publication, and by call number. Many of the newer online catalog systems have a default sort set in reverse chronological order, so that the newest books in the retrieved set are listed first. A title sort would help users identify known items within a retrieved set of bibliographic records. The author sort would be good for a user who wanted to incorporate the retrieved set of records into a working bibliography.

The best sort is dependent on what the user intends to do with the retrieved set of bibliographic records. Perhaps a call number sort should be adopted as a default sort on many systems, rather than by author, title, or year, so that the retrieved set would be displayed as a microcosm of the larger universe of knowledge. It is surprising that call number sorting was not one of the original design features, considering the common professional assumption that most users utilize the online catalog just prior to heading to the stacks.[1]

Improved output options. The three basic output options are to a screen, to paper, or in machine-readable form to a disk or diskette. Many online catalogs have become hung up on the first output option. If remote access to online catalogs increases, the demand for the third output option will increase correspondingly. Some online catalog designers are starting to develop software that will help users manage machine-readable bibliographic records on personal computers. MicroLIAS at Penn State is an example of personal computer database management software designed to be used in conjunction with a mainframe online catalog (Rice, 1989B). Only when the results of an online catalog search can be saved and manipulated in machine-readable form will the possibility of significant user efficiencies be attainable.

Change the Online Catalog: New Emphases

The first set of changes to the system entailed improvements to the catalog's performance without radically changing its purpose or scope. The next set of system changes are more radical.

Encourage Two-Way Communication

Most of the online catalog systems currently operational do not support direct communication among users, unless the users happen to be standing next to one another at the main array of inhouse public access terminals. Current online catalog systems, unlike electronic conferences, do not foster direct scholarly communication. Perhaps at the very least online catalogs should allow users to communicate comments to systems personnel and reference librarians. Crawford (1987; 6–8) thinks that online catalogs should allow users to send more messages to the system, such as signed and anonymous questions, requests, and messages, holds and recalls, purchase orders, and interlibrary loan requests. The OOPS command on the MicroLIAS system at Penn State allows users to enter free-text messages (Carrison, 1987; 50). These forms of two-way communication focus on the library systems and the physical bibliographic items, rather than on the intellectual subjects and the texts.

Online catalog systems need more information from users about the relevance and satisfactoriness of the retrieved information. Hildreth (1987) outlines ways this additional information from the user could be utilized by the online catalog system to execute subsequent searches.

Regarding the question of whether to allow users of online catalogs to generate messages and transmit them electronically to library and systems staff or other users, at issue is not feasibility or probable demand, but rather the library's sense and articulation of the boundaries of its primary mission (Buckland, 1987). If system managers and designers wanted to encourage interactive scholarly communication between producers and consumers, they would dissociate the library catalog from the static texts in collections.

Evaluative Catalogs

To begin making online catalogs overtly evaluative would be a direct intrusion into functional areas that have been the responsibility of the user of information systems. Some commentators argue, however, that the profession's fixation with subject access fails to satisfy a major motivating factor for many users: they want to find a few good books on a specific topic. Often the availability of a few good books on another topic is sufficient motivation to make the user switch topics. Lowell Arthur Martin (1974) suggests that librarians are so subject oriented toward information documents that they completely overlook the psychological, motivational aspects of the search process and the quest for knowledge (Taylor, 1986; 90).

The next step in systems development is to go beyond the organizing and retrieval of graphic records to those activities necessary for filtering, analyzing, and evaluating information for use (Taylor, 1986; 125). In some ways, however, this direction of systems development could be seen as a nefarious version of idiot-proofing, because we want to have the system perform some of the intellectual decisions regarding worth and relevancy that have been performed by the user.

Even if we accept the inevitability of evaluative catalogs (some argue that library catalogs always have been evaluative, only covertly), the questions reman: how and to what extent? Hildreth (1989) envisions a cooperative synthesis of intelligent systems and intelligent users. An effective information retrieval system supports and facilitates the user's assessment of the relevancy of a document (Hildreth 1989A; 47).

There are at least two senses of the phrase "evaluative catalogs." The first and perhaps most obvious is a catalog that contains evaluative information about the items it catalogs. All catalogs already do this minimally or covertly, if most users want current information on their topic, and the catalog lists the date of publication. Many users assume that the existence of an item in a library collection in and of itself is a statement of basic value by the library.

The second sense is a catalog that somehow evaluates the user of the system, performing a sort of reference interview as the search session progresses. For example, Walker (1988; 29) reports that future plans for the Okapi system include redesigning it to detect and adapt itself to the knowledge, experience, and aptitude of the individual user, being more or less helpful and providing wider or narrower ranges of options according to the ability and needs of the individual user and the apparent success of the current searches. Care must be taken to ensure that the system detects learning that occurs during the course of the search session, so that the user, based on his or her early fumblings, is not needlessly locked into an easy to use but weak search mode.

The value of information (macro and micro). Although in the aggregate the value of information may be rising, in individual instances the value of a package of information may be falling. As it becomes increasingly easier to massage, repackage, reformat, and reproduce information, the value of any information presentation becomes less valuable and more suspect. We may be facing a crisis of confidence in the value of any given text. Attention will gradually shift from the technology for handling information to the quality and usefulness of the information itself (De Gennaro, 1987; 38).

What are the qualities of information that make it valuable? If fewer people know or have access to the information, does that increase its value? If the information package contains a fair amount of truth, wisdom, or knowledge, does that make it more valuable? Does the amount of human effort that went into the creation of an information package make it more valuable?

Regardless of the source of value in information, some commentators argue that what most users want is good information (however goodness is defined) rather than a glimpse of the totality of information readily available on a subject. What they want is high precision, not high recall. Many of these same commentators have suggested that online catalog systems should at least help users begin the evaluative process. According to the flow of information scheme developed in Chapter 3, the online catalog, controlled by the library, should begin to move into the area of evaluation. Brownrigg (1983; 114) believes that online catalogs also should start addressing the users' demands for evaluative comments by providing reviews and evaluative, annotated bibliographies online.

One obvious method for counteracting the effects of the information explosion is to increase the amount of evaluation performed on each incoming piece of information, and include in your database only the better material. It is a false model of learning to assume that knowledge is the sum total of accumulated information. Kenneth Boulding has commented that the advancement of any field of knowledge requires the orderly loss of information that is determined to be redundant or simply wrong (Lacey, 1982; 116). What seems to be required is more selective evaluation of the contents of electronic databases, including online catalogs.

The evaluation and filtration of information seems to be an area that will grow substantially in the coming years. If academic libraries are feeling pressure from publishers and bibliographic utilities for market share during the early stages of the information flow (outlined above in Chapter 2), and if academic libraries are concerned about survival, it is natural to look toward helping the user with the final processes in the flow of information.

Most librarians assume that the catalog cannot be expected to reflect value judgments, except insofar as it reflects value judgments involved in acquisitions decisions (Wilson, 1983; 9). Making catalogs more descriptive and evaluative would force a fundamental shift in how librarians view their role in the information storage and retrieval process. Most reference librarians argue that our professional duty is to show the patron the way to find most or all of the information available in the library on the topic, then let the patron decide which information is good and pertinent.

If online catalogs did provide overt valuations of the texts identifiable and locatable in the online catalog, the maintainers of the catalog probably would value incorrectly, not because their powers of valuation are rusty or fundamentally flawed, but because the value in question is relative to an individual user's specific situation and purposes (Wilson, 1983; 15). Perhaps no one but the end-user can determine if a piece of information is valuable and pertinent to the problem at hand. Most users do not care as much about the absolute quality or verity of a text as they do in its ability to help with the project at hand. After a cursory reference interview, reference librarians and other intermediaries may know a little about the user's current project, but online catalog systems themselves know nothing about users' projects and intentions in using the catalog. Since the task of evaluating texts is context sensitive, it would be difficult to design a catalog that could provide substantial assistance with the task of evaluation. Of course, the accepted quality of a text varies over time, but the pertinence of a text for the project at hand can change in a moment.

Wilson (1983; 178) also suggests that, in general, the demand by users for assistance from librarians or automated library systems in the task of evaluating texts is lacking or at least latent. Online catalogs were introduced without previously strong user demand, but to turn online catalogs into systems that facilitate a fundamental responsibility of the user would be foolish and presumptuous.

An attempt to create an evaluative catalog tied to a value-free collection would be an unusual endeavor. To attempt to provide evaluative information about texts represented by bibliographic records in the online catalog without trying to control the quality of texts entering the collection is like, to turn an old adage inside out, trying to close the barn door after all the farm animals have crowded inside.

Make the Online Catalog Less Online

There is a movement to decrease the information community's dependence on large, centralized storage and processing computers. The bibliographic utilities have encouraged distributed processing on microcomputers for some time. Online catalog development has lagged somewhat on this front.

Use of microcomputers. The more advanced microcomputers now have the capacity to efficiently operate many libraries' online catalogs, yet development in this area has been sluggish. Emily Fayen (1986) makes a plea for more use of microcomputing capacity in the online catalog system. Micros are being used to take some of the computing burden from the central processor (1986; 2). Intelligence can be added at the most appropriate point: situation-specific and site-specific help screens and other instructional information (1986; 3). Much of the input validation, such as checking for syntactical errors, could be done by the microcomputer.

The main point here is that the state of technological development and the economics of electronic memory probably will make distributed processing and storage more efficient over the years. This leads to the observation that many online catalog systems are quite old. The software and the system configuration may be based on economies of efficiency that no longer exist.

Developers and maintainers of online catalogs also should think beyond a strict dependence on being online. The era of the technological and cost advantages of centralized database storage and processing may be over. Since most users of online catalogs are interested in only a small set of records within the large database, perhaps the system should encourage the user to first perform a high recall search (including many "or" Boolean search arguments), download the records to a personal workstation, then perform subsequent, more precise searches on the downloaded subset of the institutional database. This would speed up processing time for the user and conserve computing resources for the centralized online catalog.

Many librarians and automated library system designers have failed to fully appreciate the effects of the microcomputer revolution on the process of scholarly communication. Within the library itself, many microcomputers are being used as workstations dedicated for a single purpose, rather than as multipurpose workstations. Librarians may argue that contractual agreements or lack of standardization in the technology force them to use microcomputers as dedicated workstations, but the call from librarians for multipurpose microcomputer workstations has been noticeably faint.

Use of optical storage. Optical storage media are particularly suited for information that does not change rapidly or is rarely accessed. Retrospectively converted records for older materials could be stored on optical discs to minimize the load on the CPU and to maintain adequate response times for the online catalog proper. The big disadvantage of CD-ROM systems is that the workstations must be linked via a local area network, so true remote access is impossible. This works against the goal in most academic environments to provide students, faculty, and researchers with access to information from wherever they may be (Fayen, 1989; 133).

Locally mounted databases and CD-ROM products are second-generation batch searching devices. The database is static (usually updated every quarter) and controlled by the producers, not middlemen (see Cuadra, 1986; 12).

The question of where bibliographic data should be stored, and whether they should be distributed to several local sites, involves more than the economies and technological possibilities of electronic data storage. There are psychological, social, legal, and even ethical aspects of these decisions. For example, most users seem to want some control over the data of interest to them in the light of their current projects. Socially responsible middlemen should help users realize that control.

Make the Online Catalog More Than a Library Catalog

During the early stages of online catalog development, developers by and large did not question the value of the information contained in the online catalog. The early focus was on developing a user interface that would help most people find something most of the time. Now, however, the value of the information contained in the online catalog has been questioned. The debate has become much more fundamental than which MARC fields to index. The real research and development push now is to add other types of information to the online catalog systems. Carol Mandel (1985; 10) suggests that the online catalog is changing from a single store into a bibliographic shopping center.

The decision about how to expand the online catalog beyond its current confines seems to be based primarily on economics. The technology for all of the options outlined below is already available. Some are just more costly than others. Making the online catalog less online, by using alternatives outlined above, should legitimately be driven by technological advances and cost efficiencies. The potential solution of making the online catalog more than (or at least other than) the traditional concept of a catalog, however, should look to other spheres for guidance.

The online catalog also should move beyond the intellectual confines of the concept of catalog as traditionally conceived. The essential functions of the library are not wedded irrevocably to books. There is no functional reason why the book should be the center of a library's attention (Weiskel, 1986; 547). Users expect to have the same type of easy, free access to journal articles, newspaper articles, and many other types of information (Fayen, 1989; 132). Micros could be used to provide intelligent or transparent gateways to numerous online databases and services (Fayen, 1986; 5). Patricia Culkin (1989; 173) thinks that online catalogs no longer are within the conceptual realm of the idea of a catalog. She thinks online catalog systems should include book reviews linked to the local holdings, citation counts linked to journal articles, and circulation counts for individual titles (1989; 175). Again, these improvements are designed to facilitate the user's job of making evaluative judgments about the information she or he is finding.

These improvements also keep the contents of the online catalog focused on the local holdings of the library. In the MEDLINE subset loaded onto the Dartmouth College online catalog, only articles from journals actually available at Dartmouth were loaded (Klemperer, 1989; 140). Although this decision was made to minimize storage space, in principle this improvement seems to be a step in the wrong direction, reinforcing the concept of the catalog as a finding tool for local holdings only. The decision assumes that not all users want to know about journal articles, however vital to their subject search, if the articles are not located physically close to them. It also fails to anticipate rapid advances in the transmission of data, of which telefacsimile transmission is just the beginning.

Expand scope to include journal articles. Nothing seems more natural than providing access to a library's periodical literature through its online catalog (Hildreth, 1987; 662). Eliminating the artificial distinction between books and journal articles must be one of the great priorities for library automation in the next decade (Lynch, 1989A; 54). The long-standing division of access, borne of economic necessity in the nineteenth century, between the book catalog and the periodical index, will fall as technology advances (Drabenstott, 1988; 110). Culkin (1989) from CARL provides a good overview of the costs, technical issues, and intellectual issues of providing access to the journal literature through the online catalog.

Barbara Quint (1987; 88) sees this as a movement being led by (or burdening) public services librarians. The public services staff may shortly find itself challenged as to journal holdings coverage—not titles held but titles of articles available in the journals held. Almost all libraries spend the bulk of their acquisitions budgets on serials. Omitting periodical articles when developing the library's primary access tool disregards the investment the library has already made (1987; 87).

Lynch and Berger (1989; 373) cover many of the major obstacles to integration of periodical article databases with automated library catalogs. One fundamental decision libraries need to make when they decide to provide local, automated access to periodical indexes is whether the indexes will be presented as bibliographies (with no claims made regarding holdings information) or as extensions of the library catalog (with holdings information attached). Caroline Arms (1990A; 33) thinks that locally mounted databases are more satisfactory and less expensive than CD-ROM networks.

Provide gateways to other databases. As gateways between different automated library catalogs are established, the incompatibility of these systems quickly will come to roost with the profession. The lack of a standard interface design and common command language will frustrate users much more when they want to search several different systems during the same search session.

Load machine-readable versions of standard reference books. Electronic versions of encyclopedias, dictionaries, and thesauri have been made available through a few online catalogs, particularly in Colorado and Arizona (Culkin, 1989; 175). This seems to be the first step toward providing online the full text of many works.

Add locally created databases. Database creation also has evolved into a era of decentralized creation. The economics of database creation, including the number of person-hours involved, seem to favor distributed creation. If locally created files are to be added to the online catalog database, they should be in the form of standard bibliographic records, created by technical services staff (Herschman, 1987; 344).

Automate the administrative functions. Some online catalog systems have pursued development of automation of all administrative functions within the library. Some commentators are enthusiastic about the possibilities of electronic mail within an online catalog system to increase communication between all groups of users and maintainers of the system. The conjunction of electronic mail and online retrieval systems, such as online catalogs, can extend the benefits of each technology (Buckland, 1987; 266).

There are problems and concerns about automating administrative functions within an online catalog system. Pamela Stoksik (1985; 53) expresses reservations about the incorporation of administrative functions into a bibliographic system. Adding administrative subsystems to an online catalog system would increase the ties between the institution and the online system. This branch of development is designed to increase the library's efficient operation, but not the user's efficient retrieval and application of information.

Integrated information systems. What some commentators and developers envision is a seamless, one-stop shop for any type of information of potential interest to the library's primary clientele, however primary clientele will be defined in the future. What Dartmouth wants to create is an integrated campus-wide information system, including everything from rental housing notices to commentaries on the *Divine Comedy* (Klemperer, 1989; 144). This will blur the distinction between formal scholarly information and informal communication. The gap between the visible and invisible college will narrow.

Discussion: extended content versus extended access. The days of trying to replicate the card catalog in an online environment are over, but commentators still envision the online catalog becoming more like other known devices, particularly the search software offered in conjunction with commercially vended databases. Buckland (1987; 269) for example, suggests SDI service for online catalog users, where new bibliographic records on an individually tailored topic would be sent to the patron via electronic mail at specified intervals.

Extending the content of the catalog and extending access to the catalog are two distinct propositions. Extending the content and structure of the catalog, through things like enhanced MARC records and locally mounted databases, has received much more attention than the problems and possibilities of extended access. Both of these aims may be enabling steps to the ultimate goal of providing better access to intellectual works commonly used in academic situations.

Against Idiot-Proofing

The assumption that user-friendliness is the ultimate goal of online catalogs may be a crucial error. If system designers try to make online catalogs idiot-proof, over the long run does this encourage idiocy? Do we really want to design online catalog systems that require only that the user be able to point and grunt? Users want to learn and master the system and feel in control of their searching (Judith Adams, 1988; 33). Menu-driven online catalogs may become so easy to use that they will fail to encourage users to learn (Arret, 1985; 118).

Against a Universal Command Language

Culkin (1989; 176) argues that a universal command language for all online catalogs would be an insult to users. An online catalog system needs to develop a voice and tone that both reflect institutional personae and accomplish quick rapport with users. There is some indication from the transaction logs generated by the online catalog system studied that some users are confused by the different command languages used by various online catalogs in any given metropolitan area.

Against Automatic Closest Match Drops

More and more information storage and retrieval systems are designed to drop the user into an appropriate alphabetized file based on the closest match to what the user entered. This means that the user always gains at least partial entry into the database, even if it proves to be a completely useless drop. This technique makes it extremely difficult to study failed searches, because the computer system makes no value judgments about the quality or intent of the input data. Whatever the user enters, even if it is gibberish, is where the computer drops the user. Simply dropping the user into the alphabetic location in the controlled vocabulary subject list, based upon the characters entered by the user, only hides a multitude of misconceptions and failed access attempts.

Against Transparent System Functions

The quest for transparent systems is a major motif of technological advance in this century. Perhaps we believe that a transparent system will help us punch through the pasteboard mask of existence (see *Moby Dick*). The rage of transparency is curious and pervasive, extending far beyond automated information storage and retrieval systems.

The early calls for speedy and reliable access to electronic bibliographic records have been augmented by a push for increasingly transparent access. The subtle messages sent by a transparent system to the user should be examined. User-friendliness often means making the system do more (and thus the user less) in a more transparent fashion. A transparent system conveys the assumption to the user that the task of bibliographic searching is not inherently worthwhile and instructive. It is better, the design of the online catalog seems to say, to make the machine do as much of the work as possible. These retrieval tasks are tedious. It is an insult to users to require them to pay attention and make decisions.

If the system is forgiving and makes many translations of user input that are transparent to the user, the system effectively has cut the user off from realizing that an error has been made, thus precluding the possibility of learning from one's mistakes. Although an interface greatly facilitates searching for novice users, it also masks the workings of the system to the user, making error diagnosis by users difficult (Baker and Sandore, 1987; 195). The online catalog should assist experienced and inexperienced users by revealing its inner working organization (Carrison, 1987; 46). What is transparent in one system, such as switching personal names input naturally into inverted order, and therefore assumed proper by the user, may not be transparent in other systems.

A transparent system should make itself available for user comprehension, if the user is inclined to know. The online catalog should not present a dissembling, user-friendly interface. The main current of the philosophy of technology reminds us that one of the fundamental characteristics of the technological age is the alienation of product from process. An online catalog should not make the problems and intricacies of bibliography and scholarship transparent to its users.

Not all transparency is degrading to the user. Most users are not interested in the processing and telecommunications aspects of the online catalog they are using, so it is inappropriate to reveal those workings to the users. Dial access still requires users to be somewhat conversant with telecommunications procedures and protocol. John Abbott and Jinnie Davis (1988) think the parameters of dial access, such as parity, word length, and stop bits, should be made invisible to remote users.

The question of transparent automated library systems is on the verge of becoming a moral debate. An irony of the remote access movement is that, while system personnel were trying to make the system more transparent to the users, the users became more transparent to the system.

Transparent Connectivity Between Systems

The question of transparent connectivity between different automated information storage and retrieval systems is a related, but separate issue. Again, the big design push has been to make the connectivity as easy and transparent as possible. The real danger in totally transparent connectivity is the total disorientation of the user, not only about the origin of the information displayed on the user's microcomputer or workstation, but also about ultimate authorship and ownership. The ideal of a virtual information system will need to account for the possibility of total user disorientation.

Many commentators have defended this aspect of transparency as well. "For a workstation to be useful in providing a non-technical user with access to the available applications and resources, transparency of access is paramount" (Bauer, 1988; 42).

Against Icons

There is little or no conceptual difference between icons used in information retrieval systems and a picture of a bag of french fries on a cash register key at a fast food restaurant. Both uses of icons are fast and efficient, yet somehow demeaning and retrograde. Again, the mistaken idea that an information storage and retrieval system should be as quick as possible may lead to widespread use of icons with long-term detrimental effects on the ability of users of the system to understand the output. It is ironic that icons are popular in systems that record scholarly textual information. Although icons may be efficient, we must seriously consider whether they are appropriate in a purported educational setting. Even used in the context of a command system for computer software, icons sacrifice much of the subtlety of direction available through the use of alphabetic commands (Levinson, 1988; 152 note 17).

Conclusion

The purpose of an online catalog includes much more than merely helping any and all users find as many bibliographic records as quickly and as painlessly as possible. Hildreth (1982; 136) suggests that each online catalog has a distinct personality. An online catalog's personality should be scholarly and communal, not harried and idiosyncratic.

Notes

1. See Crawford (1990) for an expression of this common assumption.

Chapter 7
Potential Solutions: Educate the Users

Introduction

Human beings are very adept at assimilating information. An important component of what is assimilated is called language. Language in turn functions as a tool for further assimilation. In the coming years, the protocols emanating from the symbiosis of human beings and intelligent machines may become an equally important component (Hardison, 1989; 326). In a sense, all users of computer systems must be bilingual. This does not mean that all users must be programmers, any more than that all automobile drivers must be mechanics. But to be able to use a computer system effectively, the user must know the messages acceptable to the system, as well as the meaning of the responses from the system. Whether it is provided from the system itself or from an outside source, some instruction in the use of the online catalog is required by all users. The instruction need not be separate from the actual use. Many users can and do learn on the fly. But some learning must occur.

All aspects of online catalog instruction and learning remain open to doubt and study. Unfortunately, the methods for studying online catalog use and the expected outcomes have not been particularly rigorous. "A survey showed that the students found that the system was easy to use and saved time" (Arms, 1990B; 315). Statements like these abound in the research reports surrounding information storage and retrieval systems. Ease of use and time savings seem to be the two prime movers of online catalog development. Intellectual stimulation and instructive situations are barely mentioned. This neglect raises questions about the commitment of library and information science professionals to teaching users about the processes of information storage and retrieval. If human participation in the flow of information were perceived and valued as a worthwhile endeavor, the impulse to make online catalog systems as transparent and as inscrutable as possible would not be so pronounced. Many aspects of current online catalog systems do not encourage users to assess their own personal knowledge bases and choice of access methods. Many information

127

storage and retrieval activities are not intellectually interactive, and the trend seems to be toward less engagement between the mind of the user and the database.

Online catalogs are textual systems tied to collections of texts. The collections of texts are not random, but rather deliberate attempts to collect items that record and preserve scholarly information. "What is available online is not information in a strict sense, but rather text, which requires the kind of text-decoding and judgment capabilities normally associated with subject expertise" (Pfaffenberger, 1990; 160). To make sense of this guide to a collection of scholarly texts, users need some training.

It is safe to claim that all users of an information storage and retrieval system must develop a sense of the structure of the system. They may develop a grossly misconceived or stunted sense of the system, but develop one they must. One task of online catalog development is to decide to what extent and how the system should aid the user in developing a sense of its structure. This design problem is much more murky than system architecture and screen layouts, so it is difficult to address directly.

Users should approach an online catalog search session as a no-lose situation, but many apparently do not. The worst that can happen is that nothing (or too much) will be retrieved. Using an online catalog usually involves no cost to the user, at least not in visible, monetary costs. Carlos Cuadra (1986; 21) suggests that, if this situation existed in the arena of online database searching, searches should become better and more successful. Yet many online catalog search sessions are neither exhaustive nor noticeably inventive. User lethargy may be a more fruitful subject of study and cause for professional concern than user impatience.

Perhaps librarians as middlemen have striven too hard to make the online catalog reassuring and pacific to former card catalog users. One assumption about the public user population of online catalogs is that most of them were former card catalog users, who simply migrated to the new catalog format. Many online catalog users, as evidenced by searching behavior recorded in transaction logs, have not redrawn their cognitive maps of information-seeking activities. The middlemen in the flow of information must assume partial responsibility for this failure. An entire generation of students and academics may have missed the power and possibilities of online catalogs because of the lingering sense that an online catalog is just an automated card catalog.

An online catalog offers users many more access points and functonal options than did previous library catalog formats. Any technological device that increases user power and flexibility should challenge users to question the goals and methods of their projects that utilize the device. The development of word processing has triggered a rethinking of the creation (i.e., writing) and production (i.e., publishing) stages of the flow of information, but, by and large, online catalogs have yet to foster a radical rethinking in the public user population of the retrieval stage in the flow of information.

Change the Users

Another way of approaching the need for improvements to the retrieval stage of the flow of information is to bracket the question of system changes and enhancements and concentrate on educating the users of the system. How much knowledge and skill should an online catalog system expect from the majority of users? At least the users should be able to spell and type most of the time. Beyond this, there is strong disagreement about what should be expected. Kilgour (1984; 320) for example, is solidly in the camp of system designers who believe that online catalogs should minimize the amount of memorization and conceptualization required by users. A prevailing attitude in online catalog systems design seems to be that any system feature or response that challenges or frustrates users is necessarily tedious and undesirable. An alternative conception of online catalog design, where the system provides strong encouragement for the intellectual growth of users, even at the cost of slight temporary user frustration and system inefficiencies, deserves consideration.

Commentators who argue that users should be educated, rather than having the online catalogs changed, can do so for a variety of reasons. Even though some critics may argue that the commentators who call for user education tend to be dreamy and impractical, a hard-edged, pragmatic argument could be made that user education is much more cost effective and cost efficient in both the short term and the long term than system redesign and modification.

Another argument also can be grounded in the premise that the tasks faced by online catalog users are new types of task, at least within the field of public information retrieval. Users of previously developed catalog formats had no control over set creation and output options, so an attempt to somehow educate users seems logical. Although Hildreth (1982; 33) is not in the forefront of the movement for user education, he states the basic premise for this argument. The techniques used in computer-aided information retrieval are new and will not have been previously experienced by most catalog users. The type, methods, and location of education efforts are all subsequent issues to raise and address after the basic need for education is recognized and accepted. Much of the profession seems unwilling to accept that basic need, which translates into a basic professional responsibility, particularly within the context of an educational and research institution.

A core assumption of this book is that instruction and learning that occurs during actual search sessions are much better and more effective than external instructional efforts, regardless of the form they take—printed brochures, lecture demonstrations, etc. The development of external computer-assisted instructional programs seems to neglect the computer-assisted instructional possibilities of actual search sessions, where users are highly motivated to look for information they really want to find.

Some system designers of online catalogs acknowledge the need for user instruction. However, often their calls for user education are based on the desire to improve the efficiency of the operation of the system, not the intellectual development of the user. System designers often want to shape the behavior of the user toward activities that are best or most efficient for the system (Hildreth, 1982; 36). Users' projects and system processing efficiencies are not always at odds, but users' projects, not its own internal efficiencies, are the raison d'être of the system.

Culkin (1989; 173) believes that automated library information systems could become active components in the educational process and change users' conceptions of how our intellectual heritage is organized. She sees online catalogs as educational tools, not as systems that should take the user from a human need to a systematic answer or solution as quickly, painlessly, and transparently as possible. Technical innovations in libraries have very little impact on library users unless the innovation forces a change in the habits or behavior of the user (Lee Jones, 1984; 152). Because of this, online catalogs have received much more attention than shared cataloging, automated acquisition systems, and automated circulation systems. For the first time in a long while, perhaps since the introduction of photocopying equipment, libraries are offering an automated service that probably will change the behavior of library users. Online catalogs have a much greater instructional potential than photocopiers. Online catalogs require a fundamental change in the way library users get access to information about the local collection (Lee Jones, 1984; 153). Reed suggests that the design of user interfaces should follow the path of constructive assistance rather than error prevention (Ercegovac, 1989; 28). Online catalogs should help people learn about the structure of databases and the intricacies of the retrieval process, not lead them down a yellow brick road of error-free, mind-numbing searching.

It is easily forgotten that most online catalogs in academic settings are used primarily by undergraduate students. The teaching mission of the academic institution is particularly strong at the undergraduate level. Bibliographic instruction librarians yearning to develop collaborative teaching programs with classroom instructors should not overlook the online catalog as an ideal venue.

Little research exists that examines how users learn to effectively utilize online catalogs. Some studies have relied on questionnaires to ask users the source of the information and instruction they received on how to utilize the online catalog, but this does not really answer how users learn to search.

Observed patterns of behavior in certain learning situations need to be compared to observed (not reported) online catalog use patterns. If, for example, the type of recorded behavior a trial-and-error learning pattern would produce were known, transaction logs of online catalog use could be studied to search for those patterns. To test the hypothesis that user interest in the information contained in traditional bibliographic citations is waning, perhaps research should be undertaken to investigate the hypothesis that the searching behavior for bibliographic information differs substantially from the searching behavior for holdings information. Perhaps the learning patterns of a user who wants to simply identify texts differ from those of a user interested in retrieval of the full texts.

Instructional Efforts

A prerequisite of any online catalog instructional effort is a firm understanding by the instructors of how online catalog users learn about the online catalog. Perhaps this basic understanding is lacking at present. Librarians rely very heavily on the skills of computer literacy to achieve their goals of information storage and retrieval, without really understanding how these skills are developed (O'Connor, 1984; 152). The desire to reduce searching errors on a search statement–by–search statement basis may be counterproductive, because trial and error may be an important method for learning both the scope and searching techniques of the online catalog.

Others argue that the problems with online catalog use instruction rest not so much in the lack of a firm pedagogical foundation as in the problems with the online catalog itself as a device with a specific function. "The difficulties in teaching online catalog use lie principally in the design and implementation of the catalog itself and not in the technique of teaching its use" (Bechtel, 1988; 32). This approach has a tendency to slip back into the need for system modifications.

Program goals, structures, and formats. Most online catalog training programs teach in situations external to actual unsolicited user searching. These programs need to cover at least four broad areas: database content, requirements and techniques for communicating with the system, the contents and meanings of various displays, and the evolution of the system (Van Pulis, 1985; 8). Baker and Sandore (1987; 192) argue that narrow training programs that focus only on procedures are insufficient. All users will form a mental model of the system they are using, and one goal of online catalog instructional programs is to help users form an accurate mental model. Technological innovation evidenced by online catalogs forces the instructional librarian to balance instruction about the procedural aspects of searching with instruction about the conceptual aspects of searching.

Some librarians have expressed concern over their observation of large numbers of users who place inordinate faith in the reliability and comprehensiveness of automated information storage and retrieval systems. Finding the best way to encourage appropriate preparation for and use of online subject searches is not only a matter of finding technological solutions to troublesome questions, it also is a matter of recognizing librarians' responsibility to teach by ensuring that cautionary advice becomes an integral part of reliance upon the new medium (Lawry, 1986; 130). This instructional philosophy is allied to the idea of online catalogs as essentially a winnowing device. Just as the system should weed out unwanted items as quickly as possible, the instructional program should exclude false assumptions. Online catalog instruction should be perpetually remedial. The results of the Steinberg and Metz (1984; 70) study at Virginia Tech demonstrate the magnitude of the user-education task by showing that, even where very active library-use instruction programs exist, serious misconceptions about the online catalog persist.

Lawry (1986; 129) is an advocate of presearch instruction, believing that the main instructional effort regarding online catalogs should be to anticipate and correct erroneous expectations. For example, a preamble of what not to expect from a subject search of the online catalog should be presented to users prior to searching the online catalog. He suggests that the value of the a priori search strategy became greater with the introduction of online catalogs, because no online catalog can supply, or even suggest, a search strategy for the user (1986; 127).

Instructional efforts presented to potential users prior to actual searching are not worthless, but, in general, instructional programs external to the catalog itself and the perimeters of the search session will lose value as more users access the catalog from remote locations. Training sessions and printed brochures probably are unknown to the majority of remote users. The motivation to learn how to use an online catalog is very fragile and does not survive long outside the context of the user's current project.

Some libraries offer formal instructional sessions on the use of the online catalog, at least for certain users. The problems with training sessions are that they are very labor intensive and they typically reach only a small percentage of all users of the system. Perhaps users who need the training the least tend to show up for the training sessions. Those users who do attend training sessions are less motivated to learn than they are during the heat of an actual search session. Because of the constraints of training sessions, much of the information is presented outside the context of a specific information need or project. Training sessions of necessity emphasize the system rather than the users' projects and needs, including the value of the system to those projects and needs.

Printed instruction can complement an online catalog system. Often the material contained in brochures also is available on-screen, but many users do not read all the information on the screens. Thus the printed material compensates for interface problems with the system itself. Sometimes printed material gets used for scratch paper, but little else.

Instructional features should be included in the system itself, especially as more users of the online catalog become remote users. Many librarians have felt that an online catalog that requires external teaching devices and aids to produce adequate usage somehow fails (Baker and Sandore, 1987).

Such a rigorous criterion rarely is applied to other forms of library catalogs.

Correcting perceptions and beliefs about scope. Many users have major misconceptions about the scope of the database. They assume that at least all bibliographic items within the local collection can be identified and located via the online catalog. Librarians and systems designers should not validate users' erroneous perceptions of the online catalog as the single complete access point to the world of information, but rather clarify the scope of the online catalog and give users correct information about the nature and challenges of subject access. Some users of online catalogs may believe that the system reveals everything that has been or can be known about the topics under investigation (Lawry, 1986; 126). Many users seem to be misinformed about the relative strong and weak points of card and online catalog formats (Lipetz and Paulson, 1987; 612). These misconceptions often operate on a higher plane than the procedural matters of searching, but this does not preclude the possibility of revealing aspects of the scope of the system during the process of searching. Scope is not necessarily learned outside the search session.

Users' misconceptions about online catalogs may be influenced by broad social values toward technological devices in general. Advertising messages pertaining to various technological devices often stress the ease of use, speed, and comprehensiveness of the new devices. Although early publicity efforts by librarians tried to portray the online catalog as a new, better replacement for the card catalog, many users may have perceived it as primarily a computerized technological device. The failure of the profession to consider online catalogs in the light of modern technological devices may have hampered instructional efforts.

Steps Toward New Instruction

Online catalog instructional efforts can improve online catalog use by encouraging uncontrolled vocabulary subject searching, by advocating playfulness and flexibility during search sessions, and by discouraging user functional fixity.

Research by Lipetz two decades ago established the tendency of catalog users to sublimate subject searches as known-item searches in a catalog inhospitable to subject access. Most librarians would see this practice as lamentable—as a failure of the catalog system to meet the needs of the user. The introduction of online catalogs, however, has made uncontrolled vocabulary subject searching, especially via title keyword searching, a viable alternative to controlled vocabulary subject searching, especially if it is true that many users prefer a few precise hits on their subject search rather than a large retrieval set. The distinction between controlled and uncontrolled vocabulary subject searches, never too clear and rigorous, has become more confusing in the online catalog environment. For example, a keyword search on the assigned subject headings falls somewhere in the middle ground. Evidence of uncontrolled vocabulary subject searching via title keyword searching in the transaction logs of remote access users of the online catalog studied has been found (Peters and Kurth, 1990).

Too often the choice between uncontrolled and controlled vocabulary subject access is presented as an either/or proposition. Uncontrolled vocabulary subject searching can be useful for certain topics with unsettled terminology, certain stages of a search session (e.g., to gain an initial toehold in the database or after other access points fail to provide access), or where a small, precise set of records is sought. Uncontrolled vocabulary subject searching can be used as a stand-alone method or in conjunction with controlled vocabulary subject searching.

Perhaps online catalogs should encourage more creative, instructive playfulness. Users can play with online catalogs in at least two ways. Topical playfulness involves trying different topics of interest or variant phrases used to gain access to materials on the same topic. Functional playfulness entails trying the different system functions and access points. Transaction logs record few instances of either type of user playfulness.

"Freedom of choice" is a phrase often used in the areas of marketing and the service industries, but when the ideas of freedom and choice are separated, their differences become apparent. Most online catalog systems offer lots of choices, reflecting a trend in social preferences that seems to have accelerated during the last decade, but little challenging freedom. Rather than give users a plethora of choices about the parameters of their search request (as if they were ordering fast food to go), and thus claim that the new library catalogs are versatile and liberating, online catalog systems should be designed so that no one search is tacitly presented as the proper and recommended way to search the database. For example, uncontrolled vocabulary subject searching should be presented by the system with as neutral a valuation as controlled vocabulary subject searching.

Functional fixity is a situation where the dominant function for a device actually impedes problem solving, because the user has become conditioned to think of the device as having only the familiar function (Corsini, 1984; 298). As an example from another era and set of tools, a user who uses a screwdriver as a shoehorn has overcome functional fixity toward the screwdriver. Many online catalog users suffer from functional fixity, perhaps because the systems encourage the notion of official functions. For example, many users assume that the title search can be used only if the title is known. Many fail to realize that the title keyword search in an online catalog can be used for uncontrolled vocabulary subject access to the database.

The question of whether an automated system should encourage the belief that there is a right way to use it is not as clear-cut as it appears, especially in a university environment. A balance between predictable, functionally fixed user behavior and creative, playful, perhaps inefficient, behavior involves many lost opportunities. Similar searching behavior within a user population allows for replication of searches, focused instructional efforts, and communication between users. Functional fixity encourages interpersonal communication about search techniques. It is small evidence of shared socialization in scholarship. But individualized play also is an important part of the process of learning to use an online catalog (Matthews, 1985; 90). Ercegovac (1989; 31) argues that the online catalog should be designed to assist users in breaking their mental patterns and overcoming an attitude of functional fixity toward the automated system. He suggests that idea tactics should be designed into online catalogs to help the user overcome functional fixity. This is an unusual situation where the ultimate goal of changing the user is pursued by arguing for modifications to the fundamental design of the system.

The Online Catalog as an Instructional Device

The online catalog certainly was not designed and developed to function primarily as an instructional device. But the intensely interactive nature of online catalog search sessions enhances the possibilities of using the online catalog for instructional purposes. An online catalog *is* computer-assisted instruction to a degree unimaginable during the era when the card catalog and card-assisted instruction dominated academic libraries.

Unfortunately, data from transaction logs and other sources suggest that online catalogs often are not intellectually stimulating and liberating for many users. Users often have short, conservative interactions with the system. Using an online catalog should help the user appreciate the flow of information. To achieve this goal, however, the online catalog will need to be taken seriously as an instructional device. The emphasis of development will need to shift from making the systems as easy to use and as transparent as possible to making them supportive of the user's development of concepts and skills related to information production, storage, retrieval, and utilization. Perhaps the librarians and the system designers undervalued or misappraised the activities involved with using a library catalog. Using an online catalog may be a cultural activity, akin to reading a novel or listening to music, where the participant picks up a wealth of subtle hints about a complex, structured world. Using an online catalog is more than a menial task that should be expedited and made transparent by an automated system.

Although online catalogs initially were intended to be self-instructive, most libraries have gradually shifted the burden of instruction to other modes, such as printed handouts, class lectures, and assistance from the reference librarian on duty. The facts remain, however, that the online catalog has great potential as a teaching device, and that the current generation of systems does not tap that potential.

If we neglect our responsibility to instruct online catalog users not only in the techniques of retrieving information, but also the principles, the long-term effects on the viability of the academic library as an information storage and retrieval system could be significant. Libraries can improve access to recorded information by creating an environment within which users themselves can develop and exercise maximum ingenuity and resourcefulness (Swanson, 1979; 12). Although the position taken by this study is that the user is external to an online catalog system, rather than an integral part of it, our professional responsibilities point more strongly to the education and development of the users of our systems than to the development of the systems themselves.

A goal of online catalog research and development, than, could be to develop the human potential for locating, retrieving, and evaluating scholarly information rather than to shift the tasks and burdens of information retrieval to the system. If a significant portion of the user population becomes remote access users, far removed from the reference desk and a printed copy of the *Library of Congress Subject Headings*, we may rue our gradual migration away from the ideal of the online catalog as a self-contained teaching system.

The value of a library catalog is not in the information it contains about local holdings and institutional ownership, as Buckland suggests—that which distinguishes the catalog from a bibliography—but rather in its ability to acculturate the individual user to the information production, storage, and retrieval habits of the scholarly community. The experience gained through the use of an online catalog could help users better understand and exploit the universe of recorded scholarly information. The information contained in a bibliographic citation cannot be decoded and utilized by the user without the application of knowledge learned through experience (Pfaffenberger, 1990; 64).

Miksa (1987) argues, however, that most library catalogs, with their quaint classification schemes for all knowledge and perpetually outdated subject headings, do not reflect the purposes, methods, and productions of contemporary scholarship and research. Designing information systems flexible enough to keep up with the fluctuations in scholarly communication is no small task.

The retrieval of information usually is not an end in itself. Most users utilize online catalogs in order to be able to continue with another task. Use of an online catalog almost always is undertaken within the context of a larger project. In academic libraries this larger project usually is called research.

Socialization Aspects of Online Catalog Searching

It is commonly lamented that many library catalogs in all forms are unforgiving of the idiosyncrasies of individual searchers. The users often struggle against the unyielding aspects of the system. There has been some discussion of modifying the user interface to accommodate individual needs. Searching an online catalog is perceived as a very private affair.

In some respects, however, searching an online catalog, like other information retrieval behaviors, is a process of socialization. Pfaffenberger (1990) asserts that the retrieval of recorded, scholarly information is a social act. The individual user is learning the proper and acceptable etiquette for retrieving information from the world's store of scholarly information. If the automated information storage and retrieval system fails to help the user learn and decode the procedures and etiquette of scholarly communication, the user may have more problems knowing how to behave at a later stage of the flow of information, when he or she wants to somehow apply the information. The more online catalog systems are forgiving of user errors and idiosyncrasies, the less socialization occurs within the individual user. In effect, errors and idiosyncrasies are positively reinforced. When the user tries to retrieve information from a system that is less forgiving, the user will be frustrated and bewildered, because he or she has not learned the proper way to behave in a scholarly information environment. Acceptable behavior in the realm of recorded scholarly information is not an immutable constant, but it also should not be presented as a free-for-all. Even though not all users of online catalogs are scholars, the values of good scholarship should be projected and encouraged through the use of online catalogs.

The language and grammar of scholarship. If the record of scholarship is likened to a language, the intellectual works themselves are the words, packed (one can only hope) with meaning. The structure of scholarship, both formal and informal, is its grammar. The structure of an online catalog is part of the grammar of the record of scholarship. Jean Tague (1989; 49–50) discusses the language and syntax of online catalog systems, but she does not relate the syntax of the system to the grammar of scholarship. Online catalogs should encourage users to become acquainted with the grammar of scholarship as they identify and study the words of this unique language. Learning how to seek scholarly information and how to use specific tools of scholarship, and learning the subject matter are all part of the acculturation process.

Perhaps online catalogs and other automated information storage and retrieval devices have resulted in unanticipated changes in the grammar of scholarship. If the designers and maintainers of online catalogs intend to make fundamental changes to the grammar of scholarship, they should do it openly, rather than simply through transparent systems, buoyed by arguments of economic imperatives and technological destinies. Current online catalog systems tend to be designed for librarians, faculty, and scholars adept at evaluating and applying information found in texts and bibliographic records for texts. Almost all surveys of online catalog users in academic settings find, however, that most users are undergraduates and others who probably have not honed their skills in evaluating texts. The grammar of the cataloging system should reveal the structure of formal scholarly communication to its users as it reveals locally held items.

Expressive use of online catalogs. Hardison (1989; 236) makes a distinction between "classic" and "expressive" applications of technology. During classic uses, the technology is used to do more easily, efficiently, or better what was already being done before the design and development of the new technology. Expressive uses of technology utilize the unique capacities of the new technological device to do previously impossible activities. Online catalog users seem to be mired in thinking about online catalogs in classic terms. The blame for the noticeable lack of expressive uses must be placed to a certain degree on the design and presentation of online catalogs.

An apparent contradiction needs to be clarified. On the one hand, the argument of this book calls for the development of systems that encourage creative use and discourage functionally fixed uses. On the other hand, I have expressed wariness toward personalized information systems while reminding the profession of the socializing function of the online catalog into the established structure and language of recorded scholarly information. The call for creative yet communal use of online catalogs seems internally inconsistent. In many current online catalog systems, however, the functionality of the system is fixed and prescribed, while the sense of a communal collection of recorded scholarship is in flux. This argument advocates a nurturing of the opposite situation, where search sessions are more creative and even idiosyncratic, while the resultant sense of the body of recorded information includes a realization of shared social goals and attitudes.

Instructional Goals and the Goals of System Development

Much research and development has gone into lifting the burden from users' shoulders of remembering and applying search details. The working design assumption seems to be that a user liberated from these petty annoyances will become more intellectually and conceptually involved with the structure and content of the database. The goal of saving labor must be examined very carefully when the activity being rationalized is something like the intricate intellectual process of searching for intellectual works. An online catalog system in a higher education environment should not discourage and confound the development of users' critical thinking skills by reinforcing the idea that it is better in both the short and long term to let the system perform as many tasks as is technologically possible.

Are There Really Two Distinct Solutions?

The issue is rarely debated, and certainly not resolved, whether current online catalog systems are primarily service points or educational devices.

The two broad categories of potential solutions to online catalog use problems presented in the last two chapters are not as separate and distinct as imagined. The goal of online catalog design and development should be to help users identify and locate potentially useful items in a manner that educates the user, not necessarily by the fastest or easiest means. Designers, intermediaries, and users undervalue the process of finding information as a way of discovering the structure of a body of language. The two options—either change the systems or change (educate) the users—have been examined separately, although any real solution probably will be a synthesis of the two methods.

National Standardization

Some commentators have suggested that national or international standards for various aspects of online catalog systems would greatly improve searching activity and results. An argument could be made that, until the systems achieve greater standardization, so that a user who has used one online catalog could use them all, searching activity and search results will be disappointing. The gaps and inconsistencies in indexing practices may lead to demands for standardization as the population and mobility of online catalog users grow (Hildreth, 1982; 118–119). Remote access to online catalogs, particularly through national networks like the Internet, has been a quantum leap in the "mobility" of users.

Other commentators agree that the standards, the conventions, and the philosophies developed for a card catalog environment are inappropriate today. But the technology is too unstable and changing to be conducive to standardization (Beckman, 1982; 2047).

Inaction as a Solution

No action (or modification) is another possible solution. This is tantamount to claiming that there never was a problem in the first place. Librarians and systems designers are in error when they assume that any user frustration or problem using the system is a bad thing. If users are not slightly frustrated when confronted by a problem, how will they learn and hone their facility with the system? All learning involves trial and error. Healthy, constructive trial-and-error learning may be interpreted as problems and unacceptable zero-hit rates by those who monitor systems and analyze transaction logs. Perhaps online catalog users already are being coddled.

Is there evidence from transaction logs, however, that an individual user or users as a whole make fewer errors over time as they learn how to use the system? If trial-and-error is a significant method of learning during the search sessions, there should be some evidence that searching improves with time, both individually and as a group.

At Stake: Human Intuitive Judgment

It may seem odd that a book about online catalogs should work around to an examination of the educational function of academic libraries. By thinking about online catalogs and other automated information storage and retrieval systems we have arrived at a rethinking of one goal of human development.

Pfaffenberger (1990; 173) among others, would like to see the development of a technological device capable of exercising the activities of judgment now left to end-users. The impulse to transfer an intellectual task to someone or something else endures. He suggests that future research and development in the area of commercially vended databases should strive to make effective and efficient use of the database "less dependent on specialized subject expertise and advanced educational skills" (1990; 171). This may be an admirable goal for the private-sector, commercially vended database market, but specialized subject expertise and advanced educational skills are desired outcomes of students graduating from institutions of higher education. The design of online catalogs in academic settings should encourage human development of these skills, not pump money into surrogate, machine intelligence. The money would be better spent educating the end-users to make better judgments for themselves (see Pfaffenberger, 1990; 175). In all the discussion of generations of online catalog systems, we should not forget that the primary interest of institutions of higher education should be generations of human beings.

The library profession seems reluctant to admit that the online catalog is an instructional device. The use of an online catalog still relies heavily on the user's intuitive judgment. This is true both for the act of conducting a search session as an event (or series of events) and the act of evaluating the results of the search and their relevance to the information need or project. Scholarship places great value on intuitive judgment. Unfortunately, some of the trends in online catalog development (and computer technological development as a whole) tend to diminish the frequency and importance of individual human judgment. "An intellectual technology is the substitution of algorithms (problem-solving rules) for intuitive judgments" (Bell, 1973; 29).

Granted, the long-term effect of even a poorly designed online catalog on the development of a student's intuitive judgment will be minimal, but a catalog designed to foster and encourage the user's faculties, rather than sublimating the tasks within the hidden machinery of the technological device, could make a significant contribution to the mental, social, and scholarly development of the user. Four centuries ago Sir Philip Sidney wrote in his apology for poetry that its function was to teach and delight. The function of the online catalog should be to teach as well as to expedite.

What needs to be done is not self-evident. Even if the general tenor of this argument is accepted, specific design modifications do not leap forth to be implemented. What is not needed is more help screens and off-point-of-use training. The process of identifying, retrieving, and assimilating information should be self-instructive.

Most users come to the record of scholarship with mistaken notions. Often they underestimate the amount of information available on a subject, or they do not know the terminology and structure of the subject. The problem confronting the information storage and retrieval profession, including librarianship, is what to do for these users. Should we educate the users, or should we design systems that overcome user misconceptions and deficiencies? An undeniable fact remains: a user cannot make good use of an online catalog unless she or he understands somewhat the structure of the catalog and the structure of the written documents on the subject in question. This understanding is fostered by education, regardless of the nature of the educator—human or computer.

Chapter 8
Ways to Study and Evaluate Online Catalogs

Purpose and Goal of Research

An online public access catalog is a system capable of being studied and evaluated. A distinction needs to be made between pure research into online catalogs by disinterested researchers and evaluations of systems for management, development, and acquisition purposes. Researchers investigate how the system performs and how users utilize the system, while evaluators look at factors like cost-benefit ratios. The relationships between research, evaluation, and development remain unclear. Many use studies express the hope of influencing future research and development, but little formal action is undertaken to bridge the gap between the two types of study. Borgmann (1984; 24) notes that an attempt at an explanation for an event gets underway only when it is clear what problem is worthy and in need of explanation. The number of studies of online catalog use indicates that something is in need of an explanation. What is the impetus that makes an explanation of online catalog use so desirable?

Research into online catalogs can have various goals. Some studies want to discover who is using the online catalog. They seek to uncover the demographic characteristics of the user population. Other studies focus on user acceptance of the online catalog system. They want to know if the user population enjoys using the system and finds it useful. These studies emphasize user attitudes and opinions about the system. Other studies may try to reveal why people use online catalogs. What are the information needs or projects that bring people to online catalogs, and what are the factors that encourage or discourage use of the system, both before and during search sessions? Some studies focus on successful and unsuccessful uses of the system. They may try to identify and assign responsibility for problems with the use of the online catalog system.

Other studies, including the present study, primarily want to reveal how the system is being used. The attitudes and opinions of users are of secondary importance to what they are actually doing with the system. The goal of this type of research into online catalogs is examination of the experiences of the user (especially remote access users) with the online catalog. Attitudes and behavior are just two convenient referents within the complex interaction between the computer system and the human being. Many studies of online catalogs fail to specify whether the system itself is being studied, or the users, or the interface between the system and the user. This study wants to focus on the event known as the search session, particularly remote access search sessions. The dynamics of the search session and its place in the larger flow of information were outlined in Chapter 3.

A distinction should be made between users and use. A demographic study of users is concerned with identifying and categorizing them, whereas a cognitive use study is concerned with users' information needs and information-seeking behavior (Kuhlthau, 1988; 259). Many catalog "use" studies really have studied the demographic characteristics of catalog users, with little attention paid to actual use of the catalog. This study attempts something closer to Carol Kuhlthau's idea of cognitive use studies. We want to disclose the parameters and dynamics of actual search sessions using the online catalog. The tendency to become interested in the users themselves needs to be questioned.

Some researchers take the question of research goals very seriously and refuse to undertake research projects until their goals and objectives are meticulously clarified and stated. Most online catalog research, however, seems to err toward the other extreme. Much of the early research on online catalog use and user attitudes seems to have been undertaken simply because of an ill-defined but strong professional interest in the impact of these new devices. Impact studies flourished. The effects of catalog automation on internal library processes received the most attention. Institutional impact was studied much more than the impact on users' projects and users' concepts of bibliographic storage and retrieval.

Perhaps the study of a technological device is plagued by the same conditions surrounding the use of devices. Just as designers and developers cannot accurately predict how a new technological device will be used until it is actually used, so too are researchers unable to determine a priori what is worth studying about the use of a technological device until the system has been implemented and used, and the researchers are able to gather and study the raw data. The purpose of most research into online catalogs should no longer have the tacit agenda of helping the reader of the research report choose an automated system. This type of research and report will continue to be useful, but other types of research are needed.

Lack of Conceptual Models

A dominant model of online catalog searching behavior has yet to emerge. Without a conceptual model, researchers will need to continue studying behavior with an isolated variable approach. Taylor (1986) argues that a user-centered model of the value-added processes of information systems will make online catalog research more useful. This study suggests that the dynamics of trial-and-error learning and user playfulness may be underrated traits of many search sessions.

The Quest for Predictive Models of Online Catalog Use

Some commentators argue that research into online catalog use and user attitudes will not mature until it has been proven to have predictive power. Online catalog use and user studies are still merely indicative, not predictive (Cochrane and Markey, 1983; 360). For example, Hildreth (1989A; 43) believes that theoretical models of automated information retrieval environments can have predictive power. On the other hand, Lynch and Berger (1989) suggest that the use patterns and impact of the MELVYL MEDLINE project could not be predicted prior to actual implementation of the system in a real situation. Furthermore, projections of use based on use of the MEDLINE database in other environments had a detrimental effect on the design of the project. The designers of the project now realize that they made hasty assumptions about how MEDLINE would be used in the MELVYL environment. Use of the same database varies over time, location, and user population. Online catalogs and other technological devices are being used in unpredictable ways. Predictive research regarding the use of online catalogs probably should not be pursued, because predictive research could influence the design of future systems. If the design of the system itself is a variable partially determining how users actually use the system, predictive research could become a self-fulfilling prophecy.

Self-Reflexive Qualities of Research

All research should be self-reflexive to some extent. It should be fascinated not only by the subject under study but also by the process of study itself, particularly the effects of the research activities on the object of study. This study is self-reflexive in that it is interested in the ways our professional assumptions and biases affect not only the design and implementation of online catalog systems, but also our interpretations of use and users of online catalogs.

History of Online Catalog Use Studies

Online catalog use studies quickly became a major current in the information flow in the field of library and information science. To a large extent, the methods and goals of online catalog use studies are a carryover from earlier studies of card, book, and microform catalogs. Again, both the use and the methods of studying use are influenced by historical patterns and precedents.

Studies of Online Catalogs

The focus of this book is on how online catalogs are being used, so we need to review and recap studies of online catalogs. Of particular interest, partly because of the focus of this book, and partly because of their relative rarity, are use studies, rather than studies of user opinions and acceptance. What we need to do is examine the purpose, direction, and gaps in research about online catalogs. The object of interest here is not so much system performance in isolation (e.g., response time, the fluctuation of demand on the system, or the efficiency of the software), but rather the performance of the user utilizing the system. Perhaps system designers and librarians should be embarrassed by the fact that, even in the online catalog environment, most searches are still by author, title, and subject. We seem to have encouraged (or at least not discouraged) patrons to view library systems and services in fixed, limited ways.

Hildreth's study. If we think of the computer-human interface as a window, Charles Hildreth's classic book (1982) on the online catalog interface assumes the vantage point of an informed user, and examines the window and the computer. His research did not investigate to a great extent the actual behavior of users. The research presented in this book could be perceived as the obverse of Hildreth's approach. This research attempts to assume the position of the computer, and examine the user and the window—to be on the inside looking out.

Some commentators have lamented the prospect of online catalog interfaces' never becoming as standardized and uniform as the card catalog interface. Hildreth's book and other research reports attempt to encourage standardization across the online catalog industry. An implicit agenda in online catalog research may be to nudge designers and developers toward standardization.

The CLR study. Another classic study of online catalogs was sponsored by the Council for Library Resources in the early 1980s. The survey instrument of the CLR-sponsored study of online catalogs was designed and tested by J. Matthews and Associates, the Research Libraries Group, and OCLC. It was intended to analyze user requirements and behavior (Cochrane and Markey, 1983; 340). The focus of the study again was on the human-computer interface. What the CLR study primarily sought to do was to determine users' attitudes and levels of satisfaction about a variety of operational online catalogs in order to aid the future design and development of these catalogs. The study failed to make a sharp distinction between attitudes and behavior, and what the designers and conductors of the study called use was of interest to them mainly because studying it should point to ways of altering the design, particularly the human-computer interface, of present and future systems. The CLR study, like most online catalog studies that rely primarily on the questionnaire, tended to imply that a system that is satisfactory to the majority of users is a successful system.

The CLR OPAC Evaluation Projects centered primarily on users' acceptance of online catalog features and their acceptance of the online catalog as a new medium for the library catalog (Cochrane and Markey, 1983; 359). The study helped shape the first generation of research into online catalogs, in terms of goals, focuses, and methods. Developers of the new type of catalog were eager to see if the product was being well received by the users. Although most libraries fall within the public service sector, librarians are just as interested as private producers in knowing whether their products and services are accepted and liked. The CLR study was a market survey testing the library consumer's response to a newly packaged product (Hancock-Beaulieu, 1989; 26). The study and replications of it have answered that question: most library users, when asked, report that they accept and like online catalogs.

The three objectives of the CLR online catalog project were to produce data and interpretations that will enable designers of online catalogs to improve system interface features; to produce data and interpretations that will enable libraries to improve the implementation and support services (the organization interface) for online catalogs; and to enable libraries to remove barriers and extend service to potential users (Larson, 1983; vii). The study wanted to provide an opportunity for as many comparisons as possible—between libraries with the same type of online catalog, between professed users and nonusers of online catalogs, between libraries with different types of online catalogs, and between different types of libraries (Markey, 1984; 25).

Several methods were employed to analyze library patrons' reactions to online catalogs, users' behavior, system features, patrons' use of and reactions to system features, and system performance (Cochrane and Markey, 1983.; 341). The survey methods used included questionnaires, focus group sessions, and transaction log analyses. The dominant method, however, was the survey questionnaire. It is lamentable that they relied so heavily on questionnaires as their principal method of data collection, because questionnaires reveal users' attitudes and perceptions, not their behavior.

One of the major limitations of card catalog use studies—their institutional bias or study-specific findings—was overcome through the use of standard data collection instruments (Matthews, Lawrence, and Ferguson, 1983; 2). The fact that all users responded to the same set of questions gives the study a unity and power unachievable to piecemeal, local research (Broadus, 1983; 459). Both users and nonusers were questioned (Matthews, Lawrence, and Ferguson, 1983; 5). The overall response rate was 59.6 percent for users and 52.2 percent for nonusers (Broadus, 1983; 460). Incomplete questionnaires were accepted. They were not accepted in the replication of the study at the University of Missouri in 1988.

It would be erroneous to think of the nonusers as a control group or as a representative sample of the entire set of people who have not used an online catalog. Nonusers were selected to complete the questionnaire when they entered the library (Matthews, Lawrence, and Ferguson, 1983; 6). The nonusers surveyed were frequenters of libraries who reported not having used the online catalog. No attempt was made to identify and interview potential remote users of the online catalogs.

The study failed to make a clear distinction between attitudes and behavior. They stated that the intent of the data collection and analyses was "to describe user reactions, attitudes, and problems" (Matthews, Lawrence, and Ferguson, 1983; 8). The study assumed that respondents understood the intent and nuances of the questions and that they answered honestly and fully, but the possibilities of misunderstanding and accidental or intentional misrepresentation remain unresolved (Matthews, Lawrence, and Ferguson, 1983; 8). The University of California portion of the study was unique in that they administered the questionnaire online. They also did not question nonusers.

Some critics of the CLR study have suggested that online catalog systems were too loosely defined. The working definition of an online catalog used in the study, which affected the individual systems studied, may have been too broad. The CLR study included circulation systems with limited bibliographic access, pilot systems with small databases, and both OCLC and RLIN, neither of which was ever intended to provide patron access (Crawford, 1987; 2).

The major findings of the study were that users perceive the online catalog as inadequate because it excludes most nonbook media and provides poor subject access (Judith Adams, 1988; 33). These findings may have influenced the emphasis on adding new supported formats to the online catalog and improving subject access in the years after the CLR study. If asked, users will say that in general they like the new catalog format. They have rising expectations.

The study has been criticized on several points. The Council on Library Resources' support of discussion about online catalogs had a moderating effect on experimentation with the design of library catalogs (Cochrane and Markey, 1983; 338). The CLR study treated users as isolated individuals, not as social beings (1983; 74). The social aspects of the use of an online catalog in an academic setting were ignored.

Online catalog research after the CLR study. Research needs to turn its attention to other areas and methods. Just as online catalogs have entered their second and third generations, as defined by Hildreth, research into online catalogs should move away from studies of user attitudes and acceptance to user behavior. Perhaps the CLR study was a case where the normative force was applied too early to an area of research and development. How important is it for research to not be system specific and replicable? This was one advantage of the CLR study; it has been replicated several times, almost always with the same or similar results.

Replication of CLR study at Virginia Tech (1983). A replication of the

CLR study was undertaken at Virginia Tech in 1983. Steinberg and Metz (1984) report on the replication. Users again expressed satisfaction with the results of their searches. Of the respondents, 78.8 percent considered their searches to be somewhat or very successful (Steinberg and Metz, 1984; 67). Again users were encouraged to compare the online catalog device with the dying card catalog device. A large majority, 81.2 percent, considered the system easier to use than the card catalog (1984; 67). Respondents reported that they looked for items most often by subject, followed by title, then author (1984; 68).

Replication of CLR study at Wyoming (1986). The CLR study was replicated again at the University of Wyoming in 1986. The online catalog had been made available to patrons for only about one year when the study was undertaken. A survey of nonusers was not made. Evidently dial access users were not specifically included in the survey (Baldwin, Ostrye, and Shelton, 1988; 20). Surveys were distributed during two-hour blocks of time over a three-day period in early November 1986 (1988; 20). The computer had become an everyday device for many online catalog users. Approximately 55 percent of the respondents reported that they used a computer other than the online catalog on a daily or weekly basis (1988; 21). Most respondents indicated that they were looking for items on a topic, using keywords or subject headings as their access points (1988; 22). The additional features most wanted by respondents were the ability to browse a list of words related to their search words, display of circulation information, and improved printing capacities (1988; 23). Notice that improvements to the bibliographic record were not listed. This desire to view the authority files of the system contrasts with the evidence of user misunderstandings concerning the authority files in the online catalog studied in this report. Baldwin, Ostrye, and Shelton suggest that user preference for the subject and keyword access points over the author and title access points is a function of both the ease of keyword searching and the final cause of online catalog use at Wyoming—research and coursework. This comment is interesting, because it seems to straddle the issue of whether system design or user purposes is the main determinant of usage behavior. Baldwin, Ostrye, and Shelton (1988; 23) suggest that card catalog use in libraries with online catalogs has sharply declined since the original CLR study. They conclude that many users seem to not understand or to misunderstand the scope of the online catalog, punctuation, Boolean operations, and truncation (1988; 25–26).

Replication of CLR study at Missouri (1988). Using a slightly modified questionnaire instrument, the LUMIN (Libraries of the University of Missouri Information Network) Users Committee, composed of library systems people and public services librarians from the four campuses of the University of Missouri, supervised a replication of the CLR survey in 1988. Again, 85 percent of users reported general satisfaction with the online catalog system. The enhancements users wanted most (when presented with a finite list of possible enhancements) were lists of related subject terms, improved printing options (beyond a simple screen print), keyword subject searching, and the ability to bridge from a relevant item to other items on that topic (*LSO Update* [June 20, 1988]: 1).

Research Methods

The major and minor online catalog use studies rely on a fairly small set of research methods. The remainder of this chapter examines some of the characteristics of the major methods. Research procedures in library and information science rarely are scrutinized, and they often are adopted from the social sciences. Compared to other disciplines, applications of the methods tend to be rather simple. Perhaps we formulate and investigate questions that we know our procedures can readily answer, rather than ask questions that would necessitate a major rethinking of the entire research methodology of library and information science research. The dominance of the questionnaire method alone warrants an examination of other ways to study online catalog use. Six methods for studying online catalog activity will be examined briefly: questionnaires, focus groups, protocol analysis, controlled experiments, real-time unobtrusive observation, and transaction log analysis.

Questionnaires and Surveys

The survey questionnaire remains the most popular research method for studying online catalog use, not to mention most other research topics in library and information science. Markey's research (1984; 17) into the history of traditional catalog use studies confirms its popularity.

One basic assumption of the questionnaire method is that not only do respondents know what they are doing when they search an information storage and retrieval advice (even if they do not know the terminology used by information professionals), but also they are able to articulate all the nuances in the form of responses to the questions. Most questionnaires also assume that there is a strong positive correlation between the respondents' expressions of satisfaction and the success of the information storage and retrieval device. Questionnaires place a high value on users' opinions.

Questionnaires measure the users' attitudes and behavior as reported by the users themselves. If the researcher's primary concern is whether or not users are accepting the online catalog, and if aggregate figures of the volume of usage of the system are not adequate, the questionnaire method is perfectly acceptable. Surveys function well within the framework of an impact study, but answers to survey questions do not gauge all facets of impact.

Surveys are good instruments for measuring what users know and think about the problem at hand (the information need), the search system (the procedures of searching), the database (scope, record structure), and the intended outcome of the search. Like all surveys, however, only user opinions are measured. All opinion polls suffer under that limitation.

The relationship between opinion surveys and online catalog use remains in doubt. Carrison (1987; 48–49) questions all of the user attitudinal studies masquerading as use studies. Survey and questionnaire data measure perceived (by the user) success or satisfaction, while experimental data (including transaction logs) measure actual success (Borgman, 1986; 394). It must be remembered that the user makes the final decision (actually, the only decision) about the satisfactoriness of an online catalog search session. User satisfaction measures the effectiveness of the relationship between the information provider and client (Hannabuss, 1987; 122).

Relying on the measure of user acceptance of a new technological device can distort the profession's own conception of what the new technological device is all about. Most questionnaire surveys ask respondents to compare their satisfaction with, and acceptance of, the new online catalog against their prior experiences with the card catalog. This procedure, innocent enough, reinforces the notion in the minds of both the professionals and the users that the online catalog merely replaces the card catalog and should be evaluated using criteria left over from the old card catalog use studies. "The librarians' somewhat arrogant and naive assumption has been that whatever is provided [in the way of automated library catalogs] is better than the old card catalog, so patrons are bound to like it" (Weiskel, 1988; 22). Early online catalogs were evaluated in the context of card catalog use.

Focus Group Sessions

Focus group interviews can be seen as a doubly obtrusive form of questionnaire survey. Not only does the questioner intrude, but the users' peers do as well. Unlike the other research methods mentioned in this chapter, the best focus group sessions are interactive, allowing the researcher to follow spontaneous lines of discussion. It is possible to depart from the script, allowing users some control over the direction of the session.

Focus group sessions can make the user more at ease and willing to share the particulars about his or her online search sessions with the group. These sessions can be useful in conjunction with one or more of the other methods. "The [focus group] interview remarks provided much insight into transaction log analysis" (Markey, 1984; 35).

With focus group sessions, the temptation to the user to mask the realities of the search behavior probably increases. These sessions about online catalog use can quickly change into instructional ones, where either the moderator or the users themselves share searching techniques and tips.

To public services librarians in general, this may be a desired outcome of the focus group session, but to the researcher interested in the actual behavior as reported by the users themselves, this sort of transformation can be very misleading.

As a research method, focus group sessions may be too free-form and subjective. Most of the previous research on subject access of online catalogs has been based on subjective research methods—observation and/or interviews (Roose, 1988; 76). Two additional disadvantages of focus group method are the failure to randomly select participants and the inability to quantify the results of the sessions (Markey, 1984; 35).

Protocol Analysis

Protocol analysis—the thinking aloud technique—was developed by Leu Vygotsky in 1962 (Kuhlthau, 1988). It has been used to study the behavior and decisionmaking patterns of catalog users who are looking for information on a topic. Protocol analysis as an online catalog research method is the analysis of subject searchers' spoken thoughts as they perform their subject searches at the catalog (Cochrane and markey, 1983; 345). This method was used by Sullivan and Seiden in a study of user attitudes, responses, and search strategies at Carnegie-Mellon University (Lunde and Copeland, 1989; 109).

Protocol analysis is the only method employed in researching the use of traditional catalog forms that approaches the ability of automated catalog systems to record every online transaction between system and user (Markey, 1984; 17). As such, it is a precursor of transaction log analysis, or a hybrid between transaction log analysis and point-of-use focused individual interviews. Like real-time unobtrusive observation and transaction log analysis, protocol analysis records user behavior and responses at the moment of use, whereas questionnaires and focus group sessions fail to capture anything from actual search sessions.

Protocol analysis is a form of obtrusive observation that can make the user very uncomfortable. Many users feel self-conscious as they attempt to think out loud. The analysis affects the behavior being analyzed. Like controlled experiments, it does not preserve the natural search state. It assumes that the user knows what search protocols are being used and is able to verablize that knowledge. Although protocol analysis may be a precursor of transaction log analysis, it does force the user to make a conscious translation or verbalization of decisions and behaviors that normally are not verbalized. The data used for transaction log analysis are obtained in a completely unobtrusive manner that requires no translation by the user.

Controlled Experiments

Controlled experiments studying the use of online catalogs are relatively rare. They tend to require more time, equipment, and financial resources than research using the other methods. Furthermore, any introduction of artificiality into a complex human behavior like information seeking makes controlled experiments suspect. Betsy Baker and Brian Nielsen (1984) at Northwestern University conducted some experiments using control groups and experimental groups to test hypotheses about the learning and use of online catalogs.

Controlled experiments allow researchers to compare the experimental group and the control group. This leads to greater validity of the conclusions regarding the effects of the variables on the experimental group. Variables can be isolated and studied in isolation. Graduated changes in a key variable can be tested and compared to estimate an optimal value for the variable. For example, if response time is gradually varied in a controlled experimental environment, researchers may be able to determine the response time that is most comfortable for most users in the experimental group, making them feel neither hurried nor impatient.

Controlled experiments are not real-life situations. The controlled testing environment may not simulate the users' motivation and perseverance when conducting their own searches in the catalog (Markey, 1984; 21). What we really want to know is how online catalogs are really being used. Controlled experiments require expertise on the part of researchers that many practicing librarians may not possess. Funding for the research may need to be sought from outside sources.

Unobtrusive Observation: Real Time and Delayed

Unobtrusive observation can take one of two basic forms. The observation can be done in real time, with the possibility of some sort of intervention policy and mechanism, or it can be done after the fact, with remedial correction as the only possible intervention.

Real-time observation. Real-time unobtrusive observation—secretly watching users while they use the online catalog—would be a good method to note aspects of user behavior that transaction logs do not record, such as facial expressions and body language. Transaction logs record only verbal behavior. It also could be used to note the basic demographic characteristics of the users, such as age and sex. This information could be combined with information gleaned from transaction logs to piece together a more complete picture of users and their behavior. There are basic ethical questions, however, about the use of transaction logs and real-time unobtrusive observation as research methods.

The use of camcorders to record the nonverbal aspects of patron use of online catalogs for further study and analysis at a later time has real potential here. Unfortunately, another real potential with real-time unobtrusive observation is a serious invasion of user privacy and/or confidentiality. With focus group sessions, controlled experiments, protocol analysis, and real-time unobtrusive observation, it is possible to identify individual users. This is less likely with most questionnaires and transaction log analyses.

Since many libraries have developed pluralistic catalog environments, real-time unobtrusive observation also could be used to study how users search two catalog systems, such as an online catalog and a card catalog, when two catalogs are readily available. Real-time unobtrusive observation could determine if most users resort to the card catalog only after they have become frustrated with the online catalog.

Finally, real-time unobtrusive observation could be used to determine where most users go after they leave the online catalog. A prevalent professional assumption seems to be that most users head into the stacks to retrieve the full texts. The increasing popularity of remote access will force the profession to study this further. After using an in-house terminal of an online catalog, do users resort to the card catalog, go to the reference desk to ask questions, head for the stacks to retrieve full texts, consult periodical and newspaper indexes for other types of materials on their topics, or head straight for the exits?

Real-time unobtrusive observation is a very labor intensive method that relies on inferences about the purposes behind the observed behavior. Librarians as researchers may not be adequately trained to correctly interpret the meaning of the observed behavior.

Transaction Monitoring

Online catalogs differ from all previous forms of the library catalog in that most online catalog systems are able to record and monitor usage of the catalog. Dog-eared pages of a book catalog, dirty sections of the card catalog from frequent thumbing, and frayed COM catalog reels were the only rough signs of use recorded by previous catalog forms. MELVYL at the University of California, MSUS/PALS at Mankato State, and SULIRS at Syracuse were early online catalogs that collected statistical information about user transactions (Cochrane and Markey, 1983; 347).

Transaction log analysis may serve as a replacement for the survey method as the dominant method for studying library catalog use. Nielsen (1986; 31) points out that interest in transaction log analysis as a research method stems in part from dissatisfaction and problems with the survey method.

There are two forms of transaction log analysis: macro and micro. Macroanalysis is interested in aggregate usage loads and patterns. Neal Kaske's (1988A) analyses of transaction logs, for example, use macroanalysis. Although macroanalysis is particularly useful to management and systems personnel who need to monitor the load on the system, it also can be of interest to designers and observers who are more interested in the instructional aspects of online catalog use. Early macroanalyses of transaction logs focused on system performance and loads. The architecture of the system, rather than the users' projects and behavior patterns, commanded attention.

Microanalysis focuses on the dynamics of individual search sessions. Emphasis is placed primarily on the search session, and secondarily on the performance of the user and/or the system. Within the context of a single search session, why does the user make the decisions he or she does? Is there evidence that the individual user learns how to use the system over the course of a single search session? John Tolle's (1983) analyses of transaction logs tended toward microanalysis of search states within isolated search sessions.

Transaction log analysis can reveal the performance of the system, the performance of unidentified individual users, and the behavior of the aggregate group of users. It can indicate the total number of online transactions and/or online search sessions over a given period of time; the frequency of commands entered by users; the mean length of a user's online search session; the size of the retrieved sets; the frequency of use of access points; the number of errors and their types; patterns of searching and relational characteristics among searches; patterns of searches that tend to involve errors; and the demands on a system and its performance for a given period of time (Cochrane and Markey, 1983; 347, 349).

Commentators differ over the purpose of transaction log analysis. Cochrane and Markey (1983; 352) emphasize system performance and modifications. Transaction logs can help system designers decide which user problems warrant careful and immediate attention, and identify for modification (or removal) those system features that are rarely used. Online system monitoring reports are valuable for assessing users' behavior, users' input, and system performance (1983; 350). Crawford (1987; 13) identifies the two conflicting purposes—to perform statistical analyses of system performance and use, and to provide direct analysis of searching behavior and problems. Hildreth's (1985B; 3) two purposes both fall on the systems/macroanalysis side—to improve system performance and to make the system useful to users. Note that Hildreth writes from the viewpoint of a systems analyst, assuming that user behavior is a constant, or at least not worthy of study.

Monitoring and studying transaction logs is another way to directly observe selected features of user behavior at the online catalog terminal. It is particularly useful as a method for studying aggregate group behavior. The purpose of a transaction log is to record and display at a later time what the users of the online catalog actually entered into the system, and what the system sent back in response. If we want to study user behavior online, we should rely more on transaction log analysis and expert observation than on statistical analyses of self-administered questionnaires completed by online catalog users and nonusers (Cochrane and Markey, 1983; 341).

Transaction logs can be matched with questionnaire data, unobtrusive observation, and protocol analysis. Data from some transaction logs can be enhanced by replicating the searches to see exactly what the user saw. Online catalog databases, indexes, and authority files frequently change, however, so the researcher cannot be certain that the replicated searches produce the same results as the original searches.

Transaction log analysis is a significant advance over the questionnaire survey as a method for studying user behavior. The survey method lacks reliability as a measure of user behavior (rather than user attitudes or levels of satisfaction) primarily because many users cannot articulate their searching behavior as answers to questions, or they perceive sufficient reasons for concealing their actual behavior when using the online catalog. Users may want to appear to be better searchers than they actually are.

Like all methods, transaction log analysis has several limitations. Only selected verbal events within the catalog search session are recorded, and the context within which the catalog search session occurred is not revealed. Most online catalogs do not require users to log on and log off, so often it is difficult to determine when individual search sessions begin and end. To further complicate matters, an individual searcher during a single session at the online catalog may have several topics or items to search for. Even if the transaction monitoring device can identify search sessions, the software's idea of a search session may have little or no correlation with the user's idea of a search session. Information about the states of knowledge with which users approach the catalog or social and cultural differences that may affect the ways in which users approach the cataloged information is not readily obtainable through a secondary analysis of use of the online catalog (Estabrook, 1983; 73). Transaction log analysis often must assume omniscient users, who never have incorrect or incomplete citation information for known items. Transaction log analysis will not give answers to user intentions, attitudes, and preferences (Hildreth, 1985B; 6).

Transaction logging software usually is highly selective in what it records, often with an emphasis on user input rather than system output. One negative aspect of transaction log analysis is that in many ways researchers simply substitute the filtering and masking of the events by the user with filters and masks supplied by the system. The filters change, so the data captured change, but the total experience of searching an online catalog remains uncaptured and unexpressed.

One lamentable aspect of transaction log analyses of remote access search sessions is that the potential users who cannot establish a remote access connection are not recorded. Only users who are able to make a connection are capable of being studied. The most basic aspect of access—the ability to log on to the system—is below the threshold of information recorded on the remote access transaction logs.

Lack of standard transaction monitoring data have hampered intersystem comparison, replication, and application. Nothing of the intersystem scope of the CLR study has ever been attempted with transaction logs.

Tolle's study reveals that the type and amount of data recorded by the transaction software vary greatly from system to system (Markey, 1984; 28). Both the present study and the Baker and Nielsen (1984; 134) study at Northwestern University identified several key data elements within the ideal transaction log, such as terminal ID, date, time, command used, content of the user input, and the size of the retrieved set.

Transaction log analysis does have many limitations, and we must not allow the limitations of much of the current transaction monitoring software to determine what we really want to know about online catalog users and use. There is a real threat of allowing the new technologies to define the limits of the possible and desirable. The equipment of the new technologies may not only determine what we will study, but also what will be accepted as meaningful data (Lacey, 1982; 114).

It may be a great error to assume that usage patterns (as revealed by transaction analysis) provide insight into a user's a priori information needs. To do so would be to deny that users alter their a priori information needs to achieve search efficiencies within the particular information systems they are searching. In other words, the architecture of the information system probably affects the user's perception or redefinition of her or his information need. The user subtly negotiates with the system to reconfigure the a priori sense of an information need into a strategy that will produce efficient or effective results.

Another danger of transaction log analysis as a research method is its versatility. Unlike most of the other research methods briefly examined in this chapter, transaction log analysis can be used to generate ongoing management reports for library and system administrators. A general problem with transaction log analysis as a new method for studying online library catalogs is that library automation has led to increased administrative demand for performance analyses of these systems. A transaction log analysis project may have several conflicting goals, and the goals will influence the methods of analysis. The use of transaction log analysis may get muddled because it is not clear from the start whether the logs are being used to analyze use, users, and search sessions or to monitor system performance, such as response time, performance during peak demand, and the relationship between development costs for specific features and actual performance/use of the features. Both goals may be pursued simultaneously as long as they are kept distinct. In essence, this distinction boils down to whether transaction log analysis will be used to modify the design of the system or to modify instructional programs and techniques.

Transaction log analysis reveals how people search the database and use the system, but it does not reveal their thought processes, particularly the decisions they make during their broader purpose of conducting research. The real dynamic aspects of information identification, retrieval, and assimilation remain hidden. Research technologies that allow us to easily access large amounts of information may cause our ability to frame the substantial questions of scholarly research to deteriorate (Lacey, 1982; 115–116). Conducting research is far more subtle and encompassing than conducting a database search. When users search an online catalog, they almost always do so in the context of a larger project or need. They do not use the online catalog just to be using it.

Most transaction logs tell us only when users fail to retrieve anything. They fail to report when users find too much. A count of searches that produced zero hits is not an accurate method for determining all types of failure in the use of the automated system. Poorly conducted search sessions need to be reviewed in other ways. During the present study, the dial access session beginning at 2:11 P.M. on January 27, 1989, provided a good example of an unrealistic search session, where the user used the title keyword search to look for "physics." The search certainly did not produce zero hits, but it probably failed to find a known item, if a known item was sought.

The relevance of what the user retrieves to his or her information project cannot be determined. When transaction logs were used as part of the CLR study as behavior records, they were intended merely to supplement the attitudinal surveys that provided the bulk of the data (Larson, 1983; vii). Patron attitudes were perceived as much more valuable than actual user behavior.

Transaction monitoring has raised some ethical concerns. Weiskel (1986; 555) thinks the library's undetectable ability to monitor user transactions is ominous. Identification of an individual's searching activity is potentially more dangerous than specific identification of the borrowing history for a patron or an item (Crawford, 1987; 13). Transaction logs can reveal what a user was searching for, whereas circulation records indicate only what the user actually, officially took out of the building.

Paradox of Studies of Technological Devices

All six of the methods outlined above are designed to study actual or intended use of the system, or a combination of the two. Transaction log analysis, for example, reveals much about how the system is being used, but little about what users would like the system to do for them. Focus group interviews and surveys attempt to study both actual and intended use, focusing on user attitudes and opinions about the system, rather than how they actually behave toward the system.

If it is true, however, as suggested in Chapter 4, that it is impossible to determine how a new technological device will be used before it is actually used, studies of online catalogs can only recommend ways to facilitate the observed uses of the system. It may be impossible to utilize catalog use studies to make predictions about future use of the system.

Conclusion

Dubois (1987; 251) argues that we should look beyond an insular analysis of system performance and evaluate systems based on a broader notion of results, defined as the benefit perceived by the user resulting from the use of the system within the context of research or organizational goals. Note that the organization referred to is the one to which the user belongs, not the library organization. Hancock-Beaulieu (1989; 30) echoes this concern about the basic assumptions of most or all catalog use studies. They tend to concentrate on the use of the catalog in isolation, rather than on understanding the user's task. Catalog use studies tend to be placed in the institutional context, not the context of the user's current project.

Chapter 9
Introduction to Remote Access to Online Catalogs

Introduction

At the very least, remote access is a distinguishing characteristic of online catalogs, and it may be their essence. Sometimes the essence of a thing and its distinguishing characteristics are different. For example, risibility (i.e., the ability or inclination to laugh) may be a distinguishing characteristic of humans, but few would argue that risibility is our essence. The development of online catalogs may have changed the way users perceive time, but it certainly should have changed the way they perceive distance. Much attention has been given to the unique interactive qualities of online catalogs, but little attention has been given to the way the online catalog can negate distance. This negation of distance will have profound effects on the way online catalogs are used and the value and nature of library collections.

When early advocates for the development and acceptance of online catalogs argued that these catalogs have more access points than previously developed forms of catalogs, the access points they referred to were within the standard bibliographic record. Online catalogs, it was believed and argued, would free users from the tyranny of that old triumvirate: author, title, and subject. Many arguments in favor of online catalogs did not stress the new possibilities in additional *geographic* access points, both within the library and without.

The two unique characteristics of electronic media, compared to other text-bearing and image-bearing objects, are that they can be used from a distance and by more than one person at a time (Buckland, 1989B; 392). These two fundamental alterations in the flow of information are slowly changing the professional conceptualization of the purpose of information storage and retrieval. Eventually these two small facts probably will change how libraries define their primary clientele. Perhaps the concept of a primary clientele will come to mean the people who actually use the library, regardless of where they or the library are located. Primary and secondary clientele currently are defined a priori, prior to use, typically along political

159

and geographic lines. For most academic libraries, the primary clientele consists of the faculty, students, and staff of the institution.

The two basic facts also probably will have long-term effects on the funding structures of libraries. Geographic limitations already are falling. The negation of distance in the storage and retrieval of information has far outpaced the negation of geography in the funding structures of libraries and other information middlemen. Online catalogs remain fiefdoms in an era of national and global information storage and retrieval.

Remote access to online catalogs, revitalized in the last decade, may lead to fundamental changes in the way libraries deliver information, services, and materials to patrons. It may also change the way patrons think about the library, and the way librarians think about patrons. Remote access to online catalogs represents a quantum leap in the distribution of access to a library's holdings. It may also mean a fundamental change in the way users search the online catalog.

Only recently has remote access become widely available. In 1985 about 50 percent of ARL libraries had functioning online catalog systems. Approximately 55 percent of the ARL libraries with online catalogs offered remote access. Almost all of these libraries intended to offer remote access soon (Jamieson and Dolan, 1985; 6).

Until now a few controlling arguments, scenarios, and metaphors were presented repeatedly as reasons for supporting remote access capabilities. These controlling ideas seem to have been created prior to actual remote access use, evolving out of arguments presented to funding bodies as good reasons to support remote access. For example, the ability of remote access to make the online catalog available at all hours is frequently lauded. One function of research in this area is to question, verify, or debunk these a priori controlling images of remote access.

History of Remote Access to Catalogs

When book catalogs and accession lists were common, remote access to a library's holdings was possible and common also. A book catalog is difficult to update, but easy to tote to remote work sites. The card catalog precluded remote access. All users had to come to the physical location of the card catalog to consult it. Telephone reference was the only service that somewhat eased the strict spatial constraints of the card catalog, but telephone consultation of the card catalog merely introduced a search intermediary and transferred the burden of overcoming distance to the reference staff. The introduction of online catalogs immediately revived the possibility for distributed access to the catalog database. Terminals could be placed throughout the building wherever they seemed convenient for patrons and staff. Remote access (i.e., access to the online catalog, often via dial access from a location outside the physical confines of the library building) could be seen as just one more step toward greater distributed access.

Remote access may form the conceptual core of the new online catalog technology, but it was rarely the first thing implemented. Usually the online catalog was made available in-house to the public long before remote access systems were implemented. The Maggie's Place online catalog at the Pikes Peak Library District may have had a unique development. Dial access to the database became available in June 1980, while in-house access was not made available until May 1981 (Hildreth, 1982; 3). By and large, remote access to the online catalog was perceived by the profession as a frill, not part of fundamental library service. Weiskel (1989; 9) argues that distributed or remote access should have been one of the primary purposes for automating the library catalogs, not just an added feature. Librarians have given little attention to creating effective links between the online catalog and the scholarly computer applications.

More Than Just Distributed Access

Remote access, however, is more than just another step in distributed access, because remote access users are using the online catalog database differently from in-house users. Remote users have the ability to download bibliographic records in machine-readable form and alter them to fit their specific needs. Some online catalog designers have developed microcomputer database management software to use in conjunction with downloaded online catalog bibliographic records. Some software, such as Micro-LIAS at Penn State, offers not only distributed access to the online catalog system, but also encourages distributed processing at the use end, rather than at the production end, of the flow of information through the online catalog. The immediate purpose of remote access users is not to get a call number so they can retrieve the full text of the item from the stacks. In fact, we need to question the assumption that full text retrieval is the ultimate goal of many remote users of the online catalog.

Remote access users may not be a portion of the library's traditional primary clientele. The installation of remote access capabilities is not just a matter of offering access from remote locations to the same user population. A remote access service seems to attract new user groups. Remote access can have important public relations implications. The decision to develop remote access, however, more often is made because of the attractions of high technology than the desire to attract a new user population to the online catalog.

This development has put a serious strain on the ownership premise of the online catalog. Just as geographic access points form a subtext to the dominant debate of access points within the bibliographic records, the relationship between ownership and access vis-à-vis the collection of texts forms a subtext to the dominant debate of ownership of the bibliographic records within the online catalog database. Ownership no longer is the primary indicator of easy access to information. Joseph Matthews, for instance, believes that the online catalog has the potential to function as the key to total information access (Drabenstott, 1985; 108). The online catalog quickly is moving beyond the conceptual constraints of the traditional library catalog. No longer is there a strong positive correlation between what the library owns and what the users have access to.

Technical services librarians have led the way with distributed processing, motivated primarily by the desire for cost containment. Public services librarians, responding to users' needs, are just beginning to cope with the prospect of distributed access to the library's holdings. We need to find out if cost containment was a motivating factor in offering remote access to the online catalog. If so, a valid research question is whether, and for whom, the actual costs of access have decreased.

With remote access, libraries are getting into the business of distributing information to the worksites of the actual user population. This final leg of the distribution process traditionally has been the responsibility of the end-user. Granted, most libraries still are not delivering full texts to worksites, but remote access to bibliographic records is a step in that direction. This extension of service into a traditional user domain is rarely debated in discussions of remote access.

Remote access is a major step toward full realization of online catalog systems—a step that moves the online catalog beyond its initial status as a replacement technology for the nineteenth-century card catalog. Remote access to an online catalog is more akin to an all-hours automated bank teller machine than a card catalog (Lipow, 1989; 865).[1] Providing remote access is an expansion of the scope of the mission of the academic library, which may have detrimental effects on services provided to faculty and students, the current primary clientele (Brunning, Josephine, Sager, 1989; 7).

Remote access is friendly access in the sense that the place of access (home or office) is familiar and comfortable to the user. The user invites the catalog into his or her environment, rather than having to enter the library environment. The universe of recorded scholarly information is beginning to separate itself from the physical library environment. This could have long-term effects on the way users perceive the online catalog and the library. Remote access may have a greater impact on users' perceptions of the user-friendliness of the system than all of the tinkering with the user interface ever accomplished.

Types of Remote Access to Online Catalogs

Currently there are three types of remote access to online catalogs. Dial access, the focus of this study, provides remote access to the online catalog to users who seem to be located primarily off campus but within the local calling geographic area. For most libraries offering dial access, access is free to users as long as the phone call is not long distance. These users may be part of the traditional primary clientele of academic libraries (e.g., a professor compiling a reserve reading list from a personal workstation at home) or unaffiliated users (e.g., a researcher in a local law firm). Their access to the full texts of the bibliographic items stored in the database is not immediate, but possible. Dial access may simply allow users to separate the processes of identification and location from the retrieval of the full text. It allows them to come into the library and head directly to the stacks with call numbers in hand.

Campus networks often provide remote access to the online library catalog for users located on campus, in dorm rooms, offices, or classrooms. Where campus networks are far advanced, it is difficult to tell where the library ends and remote access begins. In essence, the library becomes part of the total university communications network and ceases to be just another building on campus. The library is transformed from the sentimental heart of the campus into its vital blood.

The third type of remote access is available through the growing national and international system of computer networks. Numerous online catalogs, for example, currently are accessible through the Internet. This is truly remote access. Network users do not have easy access to the texts identified and located through the catalog. Intercampus network access to online catalogs may be the sector of remote access that will experience the most growth in the next few years.

These divisions of remote access are similar to those outlined by Buckland (1987; 267). He identifies four ways online catalogs can be accessed: first and most commonly, by dedicated terminals, usually located in libraries; second, via telecommunications technology, both dial access and through local area networks; third, by a computer network functioning as a virtual terminal; and fourth, as a database server.

Each group of remote access users may exhibit distinctive usage patterns of the system, quite different from each other as well as the group of in-house users. The segmentation of the online catalog user population, normally limited to a division between staff and public users, has accelerated with the advent of remote access.

Remote access to online catalogs is not the first telecommunications network developed in the field of library and information science. Libraries require communication networks for two aspects of their activities. They need links to other libraries and bibliographic utilities to aid processing, and they need links to their user population. Historically, most libraries have concentrated on the first network function (Arms, 1990A; 30).

Service Needs of Remote Access Users

Early evidence indicates that remote users have unique service needs. Remote access to online catalogs will renew the push in research and development to make online catalogs more flexible, user-friendly, and independently instructive. When most of the users were in-house, libraries could use printed documentation and human intermediaries as supplemental sources of information about searching techniques.

Sally Kalin (1987) has written on the subject of the public services needs of remote users. Because of the unique nature of the development of technology, remote users currently are an elite user population, with opportunities available to them that are unavailable to in-house users. Remote users usually can search the catalog even when the library is closed, and they can store, retrieve, and manipulate the bibliographic information in new ways. Crawford (1987; 112) thinks that people working at workstations, rather than at a dumb terminal, should be able to perform many functions not available at the dumb terminals. Others suggest that microcomputer bibliographic database management software, such as MicroLIAS, represents the future of catalog and database access because it is an integrated, easy to use package that accomplishes a complete range of information management functions and emulates the search language of the user's catalog (Rice, 1987; 315).

When we consider the financial costs of providing remote access to online catalogs and other automated library systems, services, and sources, the problems and the potential benefits should be examined from the vantage points of both the library and the user. For the library and the institution, the economic costs of providing remote access may be relatively low. For example, the executive director of the Metropolitan Library System of Oklahoma City estimates that the start-up costs for a dial access program in mid–1989 were $3,324, with an annual operating budget for six phone lines of $3,600.[2] However, the political costs of providing indiscriminate remote access, especially in privately funded libraries, may be high. Dial access to most online catalogs, unlike remote access to database search services, is provided free of charge to the user. The user no longer has to assume the cost of bringing relevant bibliographic citations to the worksite. If utilization of remote access increases dramatically, libraries may regret that they initially decided to provide the service for free.

Sally Kalin (1987) claims that telecommunications set-up and troubleshooting is the most heavily demanded service requested by remote access users. They have many more questions about their hardware, software, and telecommunications problems than about the problems of searching the online catalog itself. This will be a new service area for many libraries, requiring technical knowledge about products. Remote users may press libraries to offer evaluative suggestions on the best system to purchase for remote access to the online catalog. The possibility of an approaching era of evaluative catalogs suggests not only evaluative comments about the intellectual works within the collection, but also evaluative comments about access methods to the catalog.

To an efficient remote access user, when the online catalog is available is much more important than when the library is open. Some of the overhead costs of keeping a library open could be reduced. Staff could encourage remote users to search the catalog when the library is not open — later at night and earlier in the morning.

The new ability of remote users to download and manipulate bibliographic records raises new problems and prospects. Will downloading create new problems and questions regarding copyright, ownership of information, fair use, and payment for services (Crawford, 1987)? The creation of library catalog subsets stored and searched at the individual user's workstation will grow. Such subsets of the database will not be current and will not provide circulation status information, so they cannot replace the central online catalog, but they can take some of the burden off the central processing unit (Crawford, 1987; 115).

The widespread ability to download information in machine-readable form will fuel new user demands, and users will judge the performance and product of the online catalog against other downloadable databases, such as databases available from commercial database vendors. Pressure will come from users, particularly graduate students and junior faculty, to make the university library, especially the online catalog, respond to the user's personal information storage system in much the same way other databases respond and are importable (Weiskel, 1988; 21).

The effects on public service departments in academic libraries as more users access the online catalog from remote locations remain unmeasured (Jamieson and Dolan, 1985; 1). Griffiths observes that an increasing number of users will access information resources directly, causing a decline in internal library use, but an increase in remote use (Drabenstott, 1988; 102). Dow's (1988, abstract) doctoral dissertation seems to corroborate this hypothesis. Remote users go to the library about as frequently as they did before they began remote access, but they use the library less as a place to work, use the professional staff less, and browse less. In a sense, remote users of online catalogs return to a closed stacks arrangement (Estabrook, 1983; 71).

Weiskel (1989; 10) argues that the future role of the research library in the total research process hinges on the library's ability to provide bibliographic (and authority and holdings) information to the end-user that is easy and efficient for the researcher. If libraries do not provide useful database management software along with the online catalog, the university library itself will be bypassed as the primary research facility of scholars in the electronic age. The main failure of most online catalogs in research libraries is the inability to provide the information to the end-user in machine-readable and machine-manipulable format.

User Characteristics (Demographics)

Who are these remote access users, and what are they doing with the online catalog? Are they a portion of traditional patron groups, or are they an entirely new one? Brunning, Josephine, and Sayer (1989; 6) divided remote users into four loose catagories: the traditional library patron, the computer-literate student, businesses, and computer users who stumble upon the online library catalog as a source of information. Until it is proven that remote users exhibit the same needs, perceptions, and behavior patterns as the established user groups, they must be regarded and treated as an entirely new group of users. This does not imply that, individually, remote users are new users, but rather, considered as a whole, remote users are using library services, particularly the online catalog, in new ways. To find out their demographic characteristics, a questionnaire would have to be administered, because no information about the users can be gleaned from the transaction logs.

A questionnaire, perhaps administered online, could establish the ratio of their remote use to in-house use. In one recent survey of remote access users, about 91 percent of the respondents reported that they have a current library card for the library offering the remote access service (Magrath, 1989; 535). An entirely new area of research will be the relationship between remote use of the library and in-house use by the same individual. Now that users have two viable options, how will their behavior patterns change?

Currently this user group accounts for only a small percentage of total use of the online catalog. The group must be taken seriously, however, because the potential for growth in the group's size seems great. Already 10 percent of total use of the MELVYL system is made via dial access (Mary Moore 1988; 24). They tend to be at the high end of library users, such as librarians and other professionals. In general, research into the use of computerized information storage and retrieval devices reveals much about the highly experienced users of information retrieval systems and the users of online catalogs with little experience, but little about the users of information retrieval systems with little experience and the highly experienced users of online catalogs (Borgman, 1986; 395, figure). Dial access to the CARL system in Colorado is heavily used by businesses and individual professionals (Pitkin, 1988; 770). Remote access users of the online catalog studied here seem to be lawyers and legal services personnel, other libraries (especially for interlibrary loan verifications), librarians and other information professionals, scholars, and ordinary citizens. By and large, remote access users do not seem to be composed mainly of the university library's primary clientele, based on the types of searches conducted and the topics searched.

At the study site there is no way of knowing how most users learn about dial access to the online catalog. If they go through library channels, the public service staff asks them if they are willing to add their names to a directory of remote access users. The directory is for internal use only. If changes are made to the remote access procedures or system, users in the directory can be notified. The names in the directory as of 1988 tend to be individuals, libraries, and corporations and firms from the Kansas City metropolitan area. In the traditional way of dividing clientele into primary and secondary groups, it appears that many remote access users fall into the group considered secondary clientele. This can have important administrative, economic, and political ramifications.

One hypothesis in need of verification or refutation is that remote users are an older population group than in-house users. Several studies have begun to confirm this. Almost 81 percent (154 of 191) of respondents of Dow's (1988; 45) doctoral research who dial into the LIAS online catalog system were between the ages of 25 and 55. Again, early studies indicate that the overwhelming majority of remote users of online catalogs are men. Approximately 85 percent of the respondents to Dow's (1988, abstract) questionnaire were men. Perhaps the socioeconomic status of remote access users has a strong influence on the other variables of age and sex.

Most remote users of online catalogs are not considered the library's primary clientele, as traditionally defined. One way to view this fact is as a problem: either the library will have to redefine its primary clientele or discontinue remote access service if the situation demands it. The unique characteristics of remote access users also could be viewed as a marketing tool for the library and institution. Remote access may be a great public relations device, because the service is used by unaffiliated patron groups the library wishes to attract.

Lynch and Berger (1989; 374) and others have suggested that online catalogs are fundamentally biased against scholars in the hard sciences because journal citations normally are not included. They suggest that the amount of time and money spent on the development of automated library catalogs has favored scholars in the humanities and the social sciences at the expense of the need of scientists for better access to the journal literature. Yet early studies of the subject interests of remote access users indicate strong interest and use from professionals in the hard sciences. Over 50 percent of the respondents to Dow's (1988; 46) survey who dial into LIAS and who are affiliated with Penn State were from the hard sciences and engineering.

User Attitudes

Unlike in-house users of online catalogs, few studies have been undertaken to measure and study the attitudes of remote access users. In general, it seems that remote access to an online catalog increases the user's sense of control (over both the bibliographic records and the search session), accomplishment, and responsibility.

One major variable to be studied is the effect of remote access on the user's attitude toward the library. When users dial into an online catalog, do most of them feel that they have brought the library into their homes, or that they have found a new way to visit the library? Which space are they consciously occupying, the library or the home, as they remotely search the online catalog?

Remote access may further distort user perceptions of the basic mission of the library. Individuals who do not come to the library are less likely to understand the nature and scope of work that goes on or to develop loyalty and ties to the library (Estabrook, 1983; 71). Dow's (1988; 75–76) survey research supports this thesis. Remote users of LIAS who are unaffiliated with Penn State were more involved than the affiliated university population with other possible remote access sources of information. Unaffiliated remote users of the local university online catalog are less dependent on it for their information.

It appears that the majority of dial access users learn how to gain access to the online catalog from friends and colleagues, not library staff. Remote users at Pikes Peak Public Library reported that they are most likely to access the CARL database, the database of bibliographic records in several academic and research libraries in Colorado (Magrath, 1989; 535). Many seem to be using the remote access service offered, funded, and maintained by the local public library merely as a gateway service. Again, the political implications for the funding body are important.

When potential remote access users approach staff for information, they seem to be somewhat more demanding than the average in-house seeker of information retrieval assistance. Remote access users tend to desire evaluative comments and opinions from the professional staff about hardware and software brands and configurations. Remote access to online catalogs creates user pressure for more remote services and rights, ranging from document delivery to downloading, reconfiguring, and retransmitting the bibliographic records retrieved from the online catalog (Arms, 1990A; 26).

Perhaps remote searchers of online catalog databases do not have the same aims and attitudes as trained searchers of commercial databases. Online catalog users display no desire to search in the disciplined, highly structured, linear manner of trained search intermediaries who want to produce well-defined lists of citations for end-users (Hildreth, 1987; 657–658). Perhaps they feel more adventuresome toward the database, without the card catalog looming nearby, with its fading siren call of author, title, and subject access methods. From the Pikes Peak survey of 1988, 66 percent of the remote users, compared to 62 percent of the in-house users, responded that they usually find what they are searching for in the online catalog (Magrath, 1989; 535).

Remote users may experience a closeness or allegiance to the system because they feel they have bypassed the library and the library staff as a mediating presence. Perhaps they feel more in control of the bibliographic identification and retrieval process. The consumer may sense that the distance between the producer and the consumer has been shortened. This may be a step toward greater communication between authors and readers. Everyone in the Pikes Peak survey who responded to the particular question (92 percent of all respondents) agreed that remote access should continue to be offered (Magrath, 1989; 536).

Some commentators have argued that remote access users of library catalogs respond to and evaluate the service only in the much broader context of personal research projects and supporting information systems. "Even in circumstances where university libraries have developed easily operated systems of remote access to online catalogs, scholars will tend to use them only to the extent that these catalogs can present themselves as helpful bibliographic databases within a much more broadly conceived system of electronic information access" (Weiskel, 1988; 7–8).

Currently it appears that knowledge of computer technology (particularly modems and telecommunications software) has more influence on users who actually access online catalogs from remote locations than their need for the information contained in the online catalog itself. The new technological service determines the need for the information available through the service.

The fact that a nondedicated personal computer often is used for dial access may have more impact on the attitudes of remote users toward the system, the database, and the search session than the remoteness of the access. Most users are much more attached to personal computers than to in-house online catalog dumb terminals. The sense of a personalized microcomputer and the drive for a personalized information system could have profound effects on the way information is institutionally organized and stored.

User Behavior (Research Method)

The next few chapters will describe a research project to study the dial access use of an academic online catalog in a metropolitan setting. The focus of the research is on the search sessions themselves. The remainder of this chapter begins describing the system and the methods of analysis.

Description of the Online Catalog Studied

The research presented in this book is based on in-house and remote use of the online catalog of the University of Missouri. The use study was made at the Kansas City campus of the university between 1987 and 1989.

LUMIN (Libraries of the University of Missouri Information Network) is a union catalog used by all four campuses of the university (Columbia, Kansas City, Rolla, and Saint Louis). It is a modified version of software originally purchased from the Washington Library Network (WLN). A command-mode interface is used by the staff, and a menu-mode interface is offered to both in-house and remote access users. When LUMIN was first offered to the public in 1983, menu-mode was presented to the public as the main interface. Command-mode proper was not available via remote access during the study period, but a hybridization of command- and menu-modes, known as slash command-mode, is available during remote access search sessions. Slash command-mode allows users to search by additional access points, such as ISBN (international standard book number) and OCLC numbers. Circulation information about materials checked out through the automated circulation subsystem became available on LUMIN in mid-1988.

Remote access users of the online catalog have almost the same access to the database as in-house users. At the time of the study, the system was available six days a week from 7 A.M. until midnight, and Sundays from noon to midnight. After the user has logged on, the master menu screen appears, briefly describing the types of searches offered. The screen has been slightly modified to include information about how to log off. The keys users need to press to perform selected functions, such as to backspace and to erase to the end of the line, will vary depending on the communications software people are using and the terminal they are emulating. At in-house terminals the special function keys are clearly marked.

Approximately 70 percent of the university libraries' holdings have been added to the online catalog. At the time of the study, no additional databases were available through the online catalog. Information displayed on the screen during the various phases of each search describe the techniques of searching. There is no help key the user can press to see more detailed, situation-specific help information. If the user enters a search without qualification, the system searches the bibliographic file only for items held at the campus where the search originated. In both menu and command modes, however, users also may search for materials held at the other three campuses, either singly or as combined union holdings.

Description of the Menu-Mode Search Options

The menu-driven interface first asks the user to choose one of twelve search types. The twelve types of searches are described briefly below. The online catalog system studied here seems to be near the high end, in terms of the number of search options offered. The low end is the OKAPI system at the Polytechnic of Central London, which originally offered only two types of searches: "books about something" and "specific books" (Walker, 1988; 21).

The user then proceeds through a series of data-entry and option-selection screens until the desired information is found or she or he decides to terminate the search session. Some searches, such as Boolean searches, require more option-selection screens prior to the entry of user-provided data than other search types. Some search types, such as the author, subject browse, and official subject searches, require that the user pass through a controlled vocabulary list prior to viewing bibliographic records. There are no dead ends in the menu software. Searchers may return to the master menu screen at any point of any search (see Table 9.1).

Description of the System Searches

Four main types of system searches are used by public users of the online catalog. This division of searches is almost transparent to users of the system. They are not informed by the system that the twelve search options boil down to four basic types of searches of the various databases within the system. The TERM and BROWSE searches provide access to the various authority files maintained within the system. The SELECT search normally is used to select items from a retrieval list for a different type of display, usually a full display of a bibliographic record. Occasionally the SELECT command can function as a BROWSE command, when users are selecting blocks of bibliographic or authority records from a large retrieval set. The FIND search provides access to the file of bibliographic records. Only FIND searches accept scoping options. A fifth type of search recently was added to the system when the circulation functions were automated. The users now can search for local holdings circulation information. Regardless of the access points utilized, each search session is composed of a series of one or more of these system searches.

Description of Transaction Log

The transaction log provides a chronological listing of the searches conducted by users at the in-house terminals and remote access users. Each line on the transaction records a step in the search session. However, not all steps in the search session are recorded on the transaction log. Relatively minor steps in the search sessions, such as paging down, paging up, and returning to the master menu screen, are not recorded on the log because they do not entail access to the central processing unit.

First the log indicates whether or not the search on that line produced any hits. This is the only output data recorded by this particular transaction recording software.[3] Then the month and day are indicated. The year is recorded elsewhere on the archival tape. The hour, minute, and second of each transaction are recorded. The remote access port currently in use also is recorded. This piece of information is valuable in determining when individual dial access search sessions begin and end, particularly when several remote access sessions are undertaken concurrently. Then the menu-mode search type, translated into a command-mode search by the system, is presented. Finally, the characters entered by the user are recorded.

Table 9.1: Menu-Mode Search Options

Letter	Type	Explanation
T	Title keyword	Takes the user directly to the bibliographic records whose titles contain the keywords entered. Right truncation is allowed, but is not automatically supplied by the system for this search.
A	Author	This personal and corporate author search takes the user into a union (four-campus) name-authority file, from which the searcher chooses the name of interest to see the items indexed under it. Automatic right truncation always is added to the data supplied by the user.
K	Corporate Author	A keyword search for corporate authors (corporations, governmental agencies, conferences, societies, etc.).
S	Subject Browse	Allows the user to browse down (but not up) through the union (four-campus) list of utilized Library of Congress subject headings. When performing this search in menu-mode, the user cannot enter a subject beyond the primary subject heading.
M	Medical Subjects	Allows the patron to browse down through the union list of utilized Medical Subject Headings (MESH).
O	Official Subjects	This search allows the user to enter the entire string of Library of Congress subject headings and subheadings (LCSH). It provides more direct access to subject headings, but does not allow indefinite downward browsing. Each subheading entered is automatically "anded" as a Boolean search of the subject authority file.
W	Series Browse	Allows the user to browse down through the traced series title union authority list. The user must know at least the first word of the series title.
X	Exact Series	The user must know the entire correct name of the series, including stopwords (unique to this search).
Y	Series Keyword	Series title keywords. This is a search of bibliographic records with the sought words in the series field. Since all items in the series are retrieved, rather than just series titles, hits lists tend to be larger than for the other types of series searches, but direct access to the bibliographic records is possible.
Z	Corporate Series	Corporate author series keyword search.
B	Boolean	In command-mode all three Boolean operations are supported. However, only the "and" and

		"or" Boolean operations are available in menumode. First the user must choose which two sets to create: author/author, author/title, author/subject, title/subject, or subject/subject. Then the user must decide which operation to perform on the two created sets. This is the only search that requires the use of the tab key.
C	Call Number	Allows the user to browse through the shelf lists of items with machine-readable bibliographic records. Accommodates LC, Dewey, NLM, and local call number schemes.

A typical single search statement from a remote access session looks like this:

*1214 153126 XV05 FIND T industrial ventilation

This is the archived record of the fact that on December 14 (1988) at 3:31:26 in the afternoon, a remote access user through the fifth port into the campus computing network performed a title keyword search for items with "industrial" and "ventilation" in their titles, and was informed by the online catalog that no title with both words exists in the local campus holdings of the database.

Because the transaction logs were not examined until at least a month had passed, and because users are not required to enter an individualized password of any kind, the transaction log tells us nothing about the identity or even the demographic characteristics of the user who initiated that search.

Difference Between User Searches and System Searches

Any research project must decide on the basic units of measurement. Often there are differences between the search session as perceived by information professionals and by the users. Professionals tend to define searches in very small units. For example, each data entry search statement by the user into the system may be defined as a separate search of the database. The user, however, usually is visualizing the search session in much broader terms—probably most often in terms that extend far beyond the online catalog. Users often are thinking in terms of a large project, and use of a library's online catalog is just one small phase in the project.

If a user conducts nine known-item searches that produce zero hits before the tenth search produces a hit, a minutely defined concept of search success might identify this as a problem search session, with a zero-hit rate of 90 percent. To a more broadly defined user-based concept of the search process, the tenth search is the payoff, more than compensating for the nine prior searches that produced nothing, with the nine previously unproductive searches quickly written off as a necessary part of the trial-and-error process of finding information.

The question of the basic unit of a search has important implications for how we understand user behavior while searching online catalogs. Neal Kaske (1988B; 369), for example, has studied online catalog use at the University of Alabama. He seems to assume that subject searches potentially require more mediation by professional staff. When users are conducting know-item searches on the online catalog, they usually do not need a librarian's help. Because it is evident that, at least at the University of Alabama, more subject searching is done in the evenings and during weekends, staffing should be increased to help mediate those subject searches. However, perhaps the noticeable increase in the amount of subject searching as defined by the online system reflects not a real increase in subject searching as defined by the user, but a sharp decrease in the efficiency of subject searching commands. Kaske's research cannot really answer this question, but he assumes that, because the number of subject searches as defined by the study increased, there was a real (i.e., as perceived by the user) increase in the amount of subject searching. Perhaps a subject search that requires five subject search commands during the day, when the searcher is fresh and the mediating professional is nearby, increases to fifteen subject search commands per real subject search during evening and weekend hours.

What we really want to know is how the user utilizes the online catalog and other information sources to satisfy his or her information need or to advance toward the completion of a project. Little research has been done to determine the relationship between searches as defined by the user and as defined by the system. For example, do proficient users of online catalogs require more or fewer searches (as defined by the system) to complete one search as defined by the user?

Methods of Analysis: Unique Data-Entry Searches

One of the temptations of transaction log analysis is to treat each search statement as having equal value in the context of the search session. This makes the computer generation of usage statistics much easier. As noted in Chapter 8, however, some search statements have more value than other search statements. When analysis of the transaction logs began, it became apparent that some transactions clearly were more important than others, and that the transaction log analysts would have to establish criteria and winnow the transactions to retrieve meaningful and useful statistics. If human analyzers add a little value to the analysis by categorizing the searches in a meaningful way that cuts across the grain of the system architecture, interesting patterns emerge. For example, in the online catalog system studied, a FIND search retrieves records from the database of bibliographic records. Some FIND searches, such as the title keyword search, require data entry, while others merely require the selection of line numbers from a numbered list of authors or subject headings. Rather than lump all FIND searches together as if they had equal value, it makes more sense to give more value to those searches that require the user to input data not prompted by the system. Access to the desired information is at greater risk during these data-entry searches.

The transaction log records two basic kinds of searches—data-entry and option-selection. During a data-entry stage of a search session, such as the example given above, the user is required to enter some data he or she brings to the search, such as a title, author, subject, series title, or call number. During an option-selection portion of the search, the user merely chooses one of the options (usually a number or a single letter) listed at the bottom of the screen. For example, in the midst of a subject browse, the user merely enters "b" to continue browsing down through the list. The transaction log records all data-entry searches, including the command to log off, but only preselected (by systems personnel when they were establishing the transaction monitoring software) option-selection searches are recorded.

The decision was made to try to isolate and analyze the nonrepeating data-entry transactions, because these transactions should reflect how well the users, based on the information they bring to the system, are able to enter the database. The isolation and analysis of just the unique data-entry searches allows the analyzers to study the ability of users to formulate information needs or problems into a question understandable by the online catalog. The isolation and analysis of the unique data-entry searches is important because it overcomes an erroneous assumption of some transaction log studies that treat each line of captured data input as having equal value in the context of the user's search session. A search statement where the user finally enters her or his topic idea is more important than the search statement where the user merely selects an item from a numbered short display of bibliographic records. Transaction log analyses should valuate these search types and focus on the important searches. In this study, the unique data-entry searches receive the most attention, but the total number of searches also are often provided as part of the analysis.

All of the analysis was performed by hand and visually from printouts of the monthly transaction logs. All dial access search sessions into the inbound modem pool at one campus of the four-campus university were examined.[4] The first step in the analysis of the logs was to retranslate each unique data-entry search back into its original menu-mode search type.

This research attempts to study the usage patterns of remote access users of a single online catalog system. Usage patterns are analyzed by types of searches (e.g., author, title keyword, etc.), by the hour of the day, by the day of the week, by the week of the year, and by the month of the year. On most of the graphs presented below, three dependent variables are plotted. The total searches are based on all searches, excluding logoff procedures, recorded on the log. As mentioned above, the total searches recorded on the log include all data-entry searches and a subset of all option-selection searches. The total searches performed by remote users may be of particular interest to systems personnel as they try to assess the demands of remote users on the system.

Remote access searches performed by the author over the months of the study were not removed from the data set. Although some of the author's remote access search sessions were easily identifiable, all search sessions performed by the author could not be positively identified. They represent a very small percentage of the total searches recorded.

Second, the unique data-entry searches included on many graphs are nonrepetitive data-entry searches. They represent at least some of the information the user contributes to the remote access search session. If the user merely repeated the same data-entry search, without any different intervening data-entry search, the repeated searches were not counted. Such repetitions occurred quite often, especially after zero-hits data-entry searches. This search state was dubbed a state of incredulous repetition, because evidently the user could not believe the results he or she was receiving.

Third, the number of search session starts also are plotted on many graphs. Because the dial access port and time are recorded, and because the researcher knew that the remote user automatically was bumped from the system after ten minutes of no searching activity, the researcher was able to identify the beginning and end of each remote access search session.

Notes

1. Note that this analogy emphasizes the diminution of temporality realized by remote access rather than the devaluation of distance. With an automated teller machine, the user still must travel to it, even if it is available anytime.

2. *Library Hotline* 18 (30) (July 31, 1989): 4–5.

3. After the study was completed, the ability to display the number of hits on the log was made available to the researcher.

4. Because of problems with the logging apparatus, on certain days some activity was recorded twice. Because of this, some original dial access activity may not have been recorded on the log.

Chapter 10

Dial Access Use by Search Type, Zero-Hit Rates, and Likely Causes of Problems

Introduction

The availability of transaction log data and the growing use of remote access in many online catalog systems make it possible to study in depth the searching patterns of remote users, without relying on responses from the users themselves.

Reminiscent of the transition from card catalogs to online catalogs, early predictions about dial access and other forms of remote access were that the remote access user would use the online catalog in ways similar to in-house users, only from the comfort and privacy of offices and homes. The full potential of a technological innovation like remote access to online databases is not realized until long after the innovation first becomes available. As users learn to access the library's online catalog from their personal computers they will begin to use it in new and unforeseen ways (De Gennaro, 1987; 22).

Studying remote access use presents special challenges. In an early study, Jamieson (1985, abstract) had difficulty collecting data on the amount of remote access use. Analysis of transaction logs of remote access search sessions at the University of Missouri–Kansas City reveals some trends. Remote users do much less subject searching. Title keyword searching is by far the most popular type of searching. Often users seem to be searching from prepared lists of known items. Other libraries in the metropolitan area seem to use dial access to check interlibrary loan requests from their patrons against the library's holdings. Users will continue with the same type of search much longer than the average in-house user of the online catalog.

Remote use of online catalogs must be compared to something. In-house use of online catalogs and remote use of commercially vended databases are two possibilities. This research project assumed that remote users should be compared with in-house users of online catalogs, with

177

in-house users serving as a surrogate control group. Compared to in-house users, remote access users of online catalogs do behave differently during their interactions with the system. A greater percentage of their searches are data-entry searches, rather than option-selection searches. They tend not to browse through, and select from, lists of names, titles, subjects, and call numbers as much as in-house users. In other words, dial access users do proportionally fewer TERM, BROWSE, and SELECT searches than do in-house public users. The ratio of unique data-entry searches to total searches is much higher for remote access users than for in-house users. Remote access users tend to stay with the same type of search for a relatively long time. They infrequently jump from one type of search to another. Unlike in-house users, who have difficulty understanding the system and keying the information, remote access users know enough about the system so that, of all unique data-entry searches that produced no hits, over 80 percent seem to be caused by the fact that the item sought was not in the database.

Most of these tentative observations can be tested via transaction log analysis. The remainder of this chapter describes a research project at the University of Missouri–Kansas City that is attempting to study the searching behavior of dial access users of the online catalog.

Usage Patterns

As noted in Chapter 9, little is known about the demographic characteristics and attitudes of remote access users. The primary goal of this research, however, is to determine how online catalogs actually are being used, and how those revealed usage patterns may affect the conceptualization of the system by designers, maintainers, and users of the online catalog system. Since remote access represents a relatively new type of access to online catalogs, the focus of this research is on the usage patterns of this unique subset of the total group of users of the online catalog. Many studies have been made of the in-house, public access use of the online catalog, significantly fewer studies have been made of use of the online catalog system by professional and support staff, and almost no studies have been made about remote access use. It should be remembered, however, that these three groups of users probably are not completely separate groups. Considerable overlap probably occurs. For example, the same staff person may use a staff terminal, an in-house, public-access terminal, and remote access during a single day, depending on the time of day and the location of the staff person. When studied as a group, however, remote users display unique searching behavior.

By Type of Search

A first step toward understanding dial access use is to study the frequency and distribution of search types. Twelve types of searches were available in the menu-mode interface of the online catalog studied. Are dial access users similar to in-house users in not making extensive use of the newer search options—by series, by call number, and by Boolean combinations? How are the scoping and truncation options being used by dial access users? What type of zero-hit rates are evident for each type of search when performed in-house or through dial access?

An earlier analysis of the transaction logs of in-house users of selected public access terminals can serve as a point of comparison (see Peters, 1989).[1] As Table 10.1 reveals, title, author, and subject searches are used by in-house users on a fairly equal basis, with subject searching dominating somewhat and author searching lagging somewhat as the three main types of searches.

Transaction logs from four in-house terminals were studied. One terminal at the main array of nine stand-up terminals of the main library on campus was studied for four consecutive months—from October 1987 through January 1988. Another terminal in the main array was studied for the first two months of 1988. A terminal in the reference room with seating and a printer attached was studied during February 1988, as well as a terminal located near the main stacks of books on an upper floor, away from staff work areas and service points.

The total number of terminal-days during which the transaction log was generated and analyzed was 202. A total of 36,848 menu-mode transactions were recorded, of which 10,240 produced zero hits, resulting in an overall zero-hit rate, before the unique data-entry searches were isolated and studied, of 27.8 percent. The average number of recorded menu-mode transactions per terminal per day was 182. Of all menu-mode transactions, 13,258 (36 percent) were unique data-entry searches.

Notice that the three controlled vocabulary subject searches (s, m, o) together account for the largest percentage of all searches, approximately 40 percent. Title keyword searching is the second most heavily used type of search. Author searches comprise a respectable 23 percent of all searches. Among in-house users of the public access terminals, subjects, titles, and authors account for over 97 percent of all unique data-entry search statements. The residual effect of traditional card catalog access points and the order in which the search options are listed on the master menu screen may have some effect on the continuing popularity of these access points.[2]

The low use of advanced features is evident. If series, Boolean, and call number browse searches are thought of as advanced features or untraditional searches—new to the online catalog environment (even though some series searches were possible in most card catalogs, and many academic libraries had public access shelf lists)—less than 3 percent of all unique data-entry searches conducted by in-house users of the system at the public access terminals studied utilized these advanced features.

It is impossible to retrieve a null set during the data-entry stage of an

The Online Catalog

Table 10.1: In-House Use by Search Type
(Oct. 1987–Feb. 1988)
Unique Data-Entry Search Statements

Search Type	Searches with Hits	0-Hit Searches	Total Searches	0-Hit Searches as % of Type		Type of Search as % of Total	
T	2,558	1,996	4,554	43.8		34.3	
A	2,062	893	2,955	30.2	31.0	22.3	23.2
K	63	62	125	49.6		0.9	
S	4,227	XXXXX	4,227	0.0		31.9	
M	121	XXXXX	121	0.0		0.9	39.7
O	437	473	910	52.0		6.9	
W	34	XXXXX	34	0.0		0.3	
X	0	6	6	100.0	44.4	0.0	0.7
Y	15	33	48	68.8		0.4	
Z	1	1	2	50.0		0.0	
B	and 27 or 22	and 75 or 5	and 102 or 27	73.5 18.5	62.0		
B1 A/A	and (4) or (0)	and (10) or (0)	and (14) or (0)	71.4 –			
B2 A/T	and (14) or (4)	and (21) or (2)	and (35) or (6)	60.0 33.3			1.0
B3 A/S	and (1) or (0)	and (4) or (0)	and (5) or (0)	80.0 –			
B4 T/S	and (1) or (1)	and (1) or (0)	and (2) or (1)	50.0 0.0			
B5 S/S	and (7) or (17)	and (39) or (3)	and (46) or (20)	84.8 15.0			
C	XXXXX	147	147	100.0		1.1	
Totals	9,567	3,691	13,258	27.8		100.0	

Search Type Explanations: T–title keyword search; A–personal and corporate author search; K–corporate author keyword search; S–subject browse search; M–medical subject browse search; O–official LCSH subject search; W–series title browse search; X–official author/title series search; Y–series title keyword search; Z–corporate author series keyword search; B–Boolean search; B1–author/author Boolean search; B2–author/title Boolean search; B3–author/subject Boolean search; B4–titl e/subject Boolean search; B5–subject/subject Boolean search; C–call number browse search.

s-search (subject browse), m-search (medical subject browse), and w-search (series title browse). And c-searches (call number browse) always are recorded as null set searches, so the actual user zero-hit rate may be better represented if those types are excluded, and only those search types where it is possible to retrieve something or nothing are analyzed. If this is done, the percentage of searches that retrieved nothing rises from 27.9 percent, as noted in the totals at the foot of the table, to 40.5 percent. In other words, during unique data-entry searches where the possibility of retrieving either something or nothing exists, approximately 4 out of every 10 searches yield nothing. The user fails to gain access to the database, either an authority file or the file of bibliographic records. If the search sessions are analyzed with single data-entry search statements as the basic unit of measurement, 40 percent of the time the user fails to gain access to the catalog.

The same type of analysis by type of search can be done for dial access use of the system. The results of the present study of all dial access use at one campus of a four-campus university over an eleven-month period in 1988 and 1989 are presented in Table 10.2.

Discussion. Again, if the four BROWSE search options (s, m, w, c) are discounted, because they always drop the user into the database at the next closest match to the data entered—making a zero-hit search impossible—the zero-hit rate for dial access users rises from 47 percent to 50.8 percent (8,370 divided by 16,466). In other words, in instances of data-entry search statements where it is possible to retrieve a null set, over half the time dial access users retrieve nothing. If the data-entry stage of the search session is thought of as the point of the search when the user is required to fess-up, approximately half of the time dial access users are being rejected. It must be stressed, however, that these figures are based on a line-by-line analysis, after the unique data-entry searches have been isolated.

Compared to in-house use, these results show low use of controlled vocabulary subject access. Less than 10 percent of the unique data-entry searches utilized the controlled vocabulary subject headings. Only 0.5 percent of the unique data-entry searches were series searches. The "not" Boolean operation was not offered in menu-mode in the system studied. The "or" operation is not heavily used. When it is used, often the user seems to be confused between the "or" and "and" operations.

Other studies corroborate the evidence of low use of new and advanced system features. The amount of call number searching as a percentage of total searches on an installation of the VTLS system, where only author, title, subject, and call number searches were offered, was about 3–4 percent (Kaske, 1988A; 274). If the funding required to develop and offer advanced features is significant, low use cannot justify the cost.

There are several possible reasons why dial access users of this particular online catalog use the controlled vocabulary subject access much less than in-house public users. Kalin suggests that remote users are older

Table 10.2: Dial Access Use by Search Type
(Eleven Months in 1988–1989)
Unique Data-Entry Search Statements

Search Type	Searches with Hits	0-Hit Searches	Total Searches	0-Hit Searches as % of Type		Type of Search as % of Total	
T	6,126	7,310	13,436	54.4			74.1
A	1,545	753	2,298	32.8	33.2	12.7	13.8
K	120	76	196	38.8		1.1	
S	1,365	XXXXX	1,365	0.0		7.5	
M	117	XXXXX	117	0.0		0.6	9.5
O	155	81	236	34.3		1.3	
W	29	XXXXX	29	0.0		0.2	
X	10	6	16	37.5	44.6	0.1	0.5
Y	22	16	38	42.1		0.2	
Z	4	7	11	63.6		0.1	
B	and 90 / or 21	and 106 / or 15	and 196 / or 36	54.1 / 41.7	52.2		
B1 A/A	and (2) / or (0)	and (7) / or (0)	and (9) / or (0)	77.8 / –			
B2 A/T	and (80) / or (0)	and (70) / or (0)	and (150) / or (0)	46.7 / –			
B3 A/S	and (1) / or (0)	and (2) / or (0)	and (3) / or (0)	66.7 / –			1.3
B4 T/S	and (2) / or (6)	and (6) / or (0)	and (8) / or (6)	75.0 / 0.0			
B5 S/S	and (5) / or (15)	and (21) / or (15)	and (26) / or (30)	80.8 / 50.0			
C	XXXXX	165	165	100.0			0.9
ISBN	3	0	3	0.0			0.0
Totals	9,607	8,535	18,142	47.0			100.1

and more affluent than in-house users.[3] Remote access users are the cream of the crop in many ways. Kaske suggests that the difference can be explained by the simple fact that remote users know what they are looking for, while in-house users often do not.[4] A third possible explanation is that remote users are a relatively new user population, or they are using the online catalog much more than in the past. A fourth possibility is that remote users are a subset of the former monolithic group of in-house public users. That subset has quit or substantially reduced its amount of in-house searching of the online catalog.

The zero-hit rate for title keyword searches may be higher for dial access users than for in-house users of the public access terminals because dial access is used by other area libraries to check the library's holdings in preparation for interlibrary loan requests. Many of the titles searched are beyond the scope of an academic library. The zero-hit rate for the author search may be the lowest among the major access points because right-hand truncation automatically is supplied by the system to whatever data are entered by the user.

Tolle's (1983) study attempted to establish relationships between the various types of searches. Because it was performed manually, rather than electronically, this study could not provide firm figures on the patterns of search commands in relation to other search commands. During the manual analysis of the transaction log of remote access users, however, it was noticed that remote access users tend to stick with the same type of search (usually title or author) for a relatively large number of commands. They seem to jump less frequently than in-house users from one type of search to another. The remote access user often seems to be working from lists or bibliographies.

The significant variations of remote access searching behavior by search type continue from month to month. July 1989 was the month with the most concentrated title keyword searching. Title keyword searches accounted for nearly 83.7 percent of all unique data-entry searches recorded. The June 1989 zero-hit rate among title keyword searches alone was over 60 percent, another record for the months analyzed.

Has the privacy of remote access to online catalogs allowed users to search more for potentially embarrassing information? There is evidence that remote users occasionally will search for materials having to do with sex, dieting, and other aspects of the human body, almost always in what appears to be a unpremeditated fashion, often in the midst of other search topics.

Other studies of usage patterns by search type. Remote usage patterns by type of search have been studied in other library catalogs. A mailed survey of dial access users of MELVYL at the University of California–Berkeley found that 63 percent of the respondents indicated they had searched the title index, 56 percent the author index, 48 percent the periodical title index, and only 31 percent said they had searched by subject (Machovec, 1988; 2). A study of the Pica system in the Netherlands by Look Costers and J. Buys (1986; 352) in 1985 found that in menu-mode approximately 47 percent of the searches were for titles, while 35 percent were by author. In command-mode approximately 57 percent were title searches, compared to only 20 percent by author.

Use of the Scoping Option

Users have some control over advanced features that were not available in early catalog formats: scoping, truncation, and limiting. Transaction logs can be used to compare dial access usage of these options to in-house use. In the online catalog system studied, only scoping and truncation were offered as user-controlled advanced features.

Although the online catalog studied currently offers twelve types of searches in menu-mode (including title keyword, author, subject browse, Boolean, call number browse), these twelve access points boil down to four main types of system commands: TERM, BROWSE, FIND, and SELECT. The TERM and BROWSE searches provide access to the various authority files: author, subject, and series. The SELECT command is used to select an item from a numbered display, usually a retrieved set of bibliographic records. A recent modification to the catalog allows users to search for circulation information within the local holdings file.

The University of Missouri implemented campus scoping for FIND searches for bibliographic records within its online catalog (Clark, 1989; 149). Sharon Clark presents a detailed discussion of the design aspects of scoping options, but she does not report on the actual use of the scoping option. In menu mode only the FIND command can handle user-initiated scoping. The default scoping for the catalog is the local campus of the four-campus university. A distance of at least ninety miles separates each campus of the university. Users have the option during FIND searches to broaden the scope to search all four campus holdings simultaneously. Users also can choose to search any of the other three campuses' holdings individually, but these options are rarely mentioned on screen or in the documentation, so the options often are not utilized. During the study period nearly all of the scoping options were for union scoping. The user initiates union scoping by entering a two-character sequence ($u) at the end of data-entry or option-selection during a FIND search statement.

Most search sessions involve a combination of TERM, BROWSE, FIND, and SELECT commands. If users attempt to scope during a TERM, BROWSE, or SELECT command, their scoping attempts are considered untimely. They should have attempted to scope at an earlier or later stage of their search session. If they attempt to scope during a FIND search but enter the wrong character string, they merely flubbed the scope command.

Tables 10.3 and 10.4 indicate how much scoping is undertaken for both selected in-house terminals and dial access for selected months.

The total search figures are the sums of all searches (TERM, BROWSE, FIND, SELECT, and CIRCULATION) for the given month at the given location. The total searches for dial access search sessions do not include the command to log off and apparent attempts to log off.

A tentative conclusion drawn from the selected data is that dial access users utilize the union scoping option much more often than in-house public users. This conclusion is more amazing and significant when it is remembered that a sizable portion of dial access FIND searches are undertaken by other libraries in the Kansas City metropolitan area to verify local holdings before submitting interlibrary loan requests. These other libraries rarely if ever utilize the union scoping options, because they do not fit their needs. If these interlibrary loan searches could be categorically identified and removed from the analysis, the amount of union scoping during dial access use could approach the 50 percent range.

At the time of the study, dial access users were required to choose to union scope at each FIND search statement. They could not set the default to union scope at the beginning of their dial access sessions. The data also indicate that dial access users attempt union scoping at the wrong time in the search session (i.e., during a TERM, BROWSE, or SELECT statement) more often than that they enter the wrong character sequence. In other words, they know how to scope, but not exactly when.

The amount of scoping done by dial access users may indicate more than just the utilization of an advanced feature of the online catalog compared to the card catalog. It may also indicate a declining interest in (or allegiance to) the local collections. A significant portion of dial access users may be using the online catalog to identify items and confirm the bibliographic information about them, rather than to find a call number for an item held locally.

Use of the Truncation Option

Online catalogs do a good job of helping users move from topics to the identification and retrieval of specific items, but not such a good job of moving from specific items to other items on the topic. Many users do not know where the assigned headings are located in the bibliographic records. A tactic that could be taught during instructional sessions is one in which users choose the most important words from the known item and truncate them judiciously to retrieve other similar items, even during known item searching.

Only right-hand truncation is available in the online catalog studied. Truncation is not necessary during the BROWSE searches (s, m, w, c), and truncation is automatically supplied by the system during an author term (signified by "a") search. For all other searches, if the user wants to truncate during a search, the truncation must be initiated and executed by the user. Although it is potentially useful during title keyword, corporate author keyword, official subject term, official series term, series keyword, corporate author series keyword, and Boolean searches, truncation could be particularly useful during title keyword searches to retrieve singular, plural, and variant endings to basic word stems. As reported above, approximately 75 percent of all unique data-entry searches during the eleven months of dial access sessions studied were title keyword searches.

Month	Total Searches	Total FIND Searches	Correct Union Scoping	% of Total FIND	Flubbed Scoping Attempts	Untimely Scoping Attempts
1/88	1821	741	49	6.6	3	2
12/88	1270	512	13	2.5	1	0
2/89	2835	1065	33	3.1	5	1
Totals	5926	2318	95		9	3
Avg./Mon.	1975	773	32	4.1	3	1

Table 10.3: In-House Use of Scoping Option
(At Selected Individual Public Access Terminals)

Month	Total Searches	Total FIND Searches	Correct Union Scoping	% of Total FIND	Flubbed Scoping Attempts	Untimely Scoping Attempts
5/89	2640	1461	381	26.1	0	33
6/89	2393	1382	382	27.6	16	44
7/89	2136	1490	418	28.1	5	23
Totals	7169	4333	1181	27.3	21	100
Avg./Mon.	2390	1444	394	27.3	7	33

Table 10.4: Dial Access Use of Scoping Option

Neither group of public users, in-house or remote, seem to use truncation extensively. During the dial access searching activity of January 1989, there were 1,425 unique data-entry searches where user-initiated truncation could have been useful. Only 38 of those searches (2.7 percent) utilized the truncation function. One user-initiated truncation occurred during an a-search, which was redundant. A little more than half of the truncated searches (19 of 39) truncated only the last word entered. A maximum of 3 title keywords may be truncated during a single search statement. Only 3 of the 39 searches involved truncation of more than one word, and 35 of the user-initiated truncations occurred during a title keyword search. A total of 20 search sessions during the month contained all of the truncation attempts, 6.6 percent of all search sessions during January 1989.

For the February 1989 dial access activity, there were 1,486 unique data-entry searches where user-initiated truncation could have been useful. Only 51 of those searches (3.4 percent) utilized truncation. Over 35 percent (18 of 51) truncated more than 1 word in the search statement. The 51 truncation attempts occurred in just 25 search sessions, about 8 percent of all dial access search sessions in February 1989.

User-initiated truncation is almost nonexistent during in-house use of the online catalog. In January 1988 at a terminal in the main array of terminals in the reference section of the main library on campus, only 1 search of the 259 truncatable searches actually contained user-initiated truncation.

Although the scoping and truncation options are used more by dial access users than by in-house users, neither option is used extensively. The scoping option seems more popular than the truncation option. From a data processing point of view, truncated searches are inefficient for the system. They tend to slow down response time. From the user's point of view, however, truncation could be a powerful searching tool. It is regrettable that it is an underutilized option.

Amount of Data Entered During Title Keyword Searches

During an earlier study, Walker (1988; 24) determined that in online catalog search statements the average number of significant words is usually a little over two, and few searches contain more than three words. Walker did not substantiate this claim, even though this was a researchable and verifiable question. We can use transaction log analysis to determine the mean number of keywords entered in various types of searches, such as title keyword searches. We also can determine if the averages vary significantly between searches that produce hits and those that yield nothing.

The first 160 dial access, title keyword search statements in December 1988 contained 496 keywords, excluding stopwords—an average of 3.1 keywords per title keyword search. There were only 65 searches in that group that produced hits. They contained 164 keywords, an average of 2.52 keywords per search. The 95 searches that failed to produce hits contained 332 keywords, an average of 3.49 keywords per search. On average, a zero-hit title keyword search contains one more word than the average title keyword search with hits.

Failure (Zero-Hit) Rates

Failure can be interpreted as low precision, low or no recall, recall that is too high, or dissatisfaction with the system and/or the search results. For the purposes of this study, failure is defined as a search that produced no hits. The failure rates as measured and presented via this method of analysis do not include failures users have getting logged on to the system, failures of retrieval sets that are too large, and failures of irrelevant hits.

Failure rates should not be examined without speculating about the situations surrounding failures in the use of online catalogs, especially remote access use. This is where the microanalysis of transaction logs—where analysts look at the dynamics of individual search sessions rather than aggregate statistical patterns—can play a role. Christine Borgman has done significant research on the psychology of the online searching behavior of users.

One drawback of this method of study is that we almost must assume that users come to the search with correct information. Often it is difficult to determine if users bring correct citation information to their known-item searches. This is especially true of personal author searches. Sometimes the entered data captured on the logs indicates that a user knows that his or her spelling of a word, especially personal names, is questionable, so he or she tries various possible spellings until at least one hit is retrieved.

Some users of the online catalog have serious misconceptions about the scope of the catalog. Scoping misconceptions include overly optimistic assumptions about the status of retrospective conversion, misconceptions about the subject scope of the collection, including the scope of treatments of subjects (e.g., many users look for very popular materials), and misconceptions about the item formats available in the database.

When users express extreme frustration toward online catalogs, is it because the system simply failed to provide the expected or desired outcome, or because the user senses his or her own inadequacy in a new age in failing to exhibit an understanding of the bibliographic retrieval system via a satisfactory, successful search session? The inability to successfully operate a new technological device engenders a sense of human inadequacy.

Ercegovac (1989; 28) makes a useful distinction between the goal to minimize the incidence of errors and the goal to minimize the effect of the errors on the overall searching performance. Perhaps the desirable goal in this area is to minimize the effects of errors, but we must be careful not to adopt methods for achieving the goal that encourage counterproductive behavior or beliefs in the user population. For the definition of failure used in this study, it cannot be assumed that correcting the probable cause of zero hits necessarily will produce a search with hits.

Failure may be caused primarily by the user, the system, the database, or the collection, or a combination of any of them. The effects of collection size on failure rates have been little mentioned by writers on online catalogs, perhaps because most of the writers are American, used to large university collections (Walker, 1988; 22).

Other Studies of Failure Rates

The 1985 study by Costers and Buys (1986; 353) found that approximately 45 percent of primary search actions in menu-mode produced no hits. In command-mode the zero-hit rate fell to approximately 30 percent. From the Pikes Peak survey of 1988, 66 percent of the remote users, compared to 62 percent of the in-house users, responded that they usually found what they were searching for in the online catalog (Magrath, 1989; 535). There is a fundamental discrepancy, however, between how users assess success and failure and how failure is measured by the online catalog and this study. The system measures failure data entry by data entry, line by line. Most users do not define failure so instantaneously. They withhold judgment about their search until their search session is complete. Perhaps some users do not concede failure until several search sessions have been completed without satisfactory results.

Probable Causes of Usage Problems

Once the frequency and patterns of failure have been studied, the next step is to assign probable causes for the failed searches. Because it was not feasible to reenter all zero-hit searches to determine the exact cause of failure, in most instances the analyzers made an intelligent guess of the probable cause, based on a reading of the transaction. Fourteen types of probable causes were identified as the logs were examined. The analyzers did not try to establish categories of probable causes prior to examining the logs (see Table 10.5).

Table 10.5: Categories of Probable Causes of Zero Hits

1	MAL	Malicious entries, including both random strings of characters and obscene entries.

2	TYPO	Typographical errors, such that the word entered would not be considered a potential variant spelling by the average adult. If the analyzer could not determine whether the problem was a misspelling or a typographical error, it was considered a typo.
3	LINE	Failure to clear the remainder of the line. The online catalog studied reads all characters entered on the two lines reserved for data entry.
4	SPELL	If the entered word was a conceivable variant spelling, the problem was considered a spelling error. Included in this category are evident errors in the citation, usually in the title or the author's name. These searches usually are detected only if the search is replicated with slight modifications to the personal name or title keywords.
5	FIRST	The first name of a personal name was entered first. If the user had problems entering a foreign personal name, the problem was placed in category 11 below.
6	MI	The middle initial or name of a personal name was entered. If the user enters the last name, first initial, and middle initial, the middle initial gets right-truncated, but the first initial does not. This situation usually results in zero hits (i.e., the user is not even taken into the list of authors).
7	VOCAB	Basic misunderstanding of controlled vocabularies. If the string of characters was conceivable as a reasonable subject access point, it was not classified as a basic misunderstanding of controlled vocabularies. Entries such as "books about dogs" and "information for people considering opening a health club" were placed here.
8	FORMAT	The item sought, such as periodical articles and government documents, probably was in a format not supported by the online catalog studied.
9	SEARCH	Based on the data entered, the wrong type of search was used. The most frequent problem here was the attempt to add subheadings during a subject browse search.
10	BOOLE	Attempted a Boolean search in other than b-search routine. Often multiple authors were entered simultaneously, or titles and series titles.
11	LUMIN	Confusion about other rules and procedures, often involving punctuation, specific to the online catalog studied.
12	DB	Confusion about the general structure and logic of database searching. The classic example is the situation when the user enters a three-word title keyword search that produces zero hits, so the user adds a fouth keyword, evidently thinking that the revised search conceivably could produce hits.
13	OPACS	Confusion with other OPAC and software commands. Different OPACs in the metropolitan area create confusion for LUMIN users.
14	NOT	The item sought probably was not in the database. Sometimes users were looking for new items that were still on order or in process. The online catalog studied did not have an acquisitions module. These categories of probable

causes cannot easily detect and account for situations where the user brings incorrect citation information to the search.

The categories of probable cause are grouped into an ascending degree of difficulty, from basic user errors to basic collection inadequacies. Causes 2 through 4 deal with keying problems. Causes 5 through 7 focus on the problems with controlled vocabularies and authority files. Causes 8 through 11 address problems users have understanding the scope, rules, and procedures of the particular online catalog studied. Causes 12 through 14 point to problems users have relating the online catalog to other software and information systems (see Tables 10.6, 10.7).

Only one probable cause was assigned to any given problem search statement. If it appeared that a single search statement contained several errors, the lowest order probable cause was assigned. In this method of analysis, the fourteenth probable cause functions as the default. If no other probable cause for the zero-hit search could be detected, the assumption was made that the item or topic sought probably was not in the database. In an effort to determine probable cause, the analyzers replicated some of the search statements at the time of analysis, but replication was not systematic.

The distribution of probable causes of remote user problems indicates that they have better skills to access the online catalog system (Table 10.7). Their errors tend to push the limits of the system, particularly regarding the scope and quality of the collection. Actually, there is a fairly limited set of types of errors occurring during use of the online catalog studied.

The list of categories may be professionally biased. The probable causes listed first are problems for which the user is solely or primarily responsible. The failure of collection development is listed last. From the user's perspective, it seems natural to assume that a search that produced zero hits was caused first and foremost by the items' not being in the collection. Most users are not sufficiently introspective to look for typographical errors first. Most users will look for fault in the collections, the database, or the user interface before they will examine their own input.

Sometimes users are looking for new items that are on order or in process but have not yet been added to the online catalog. Sometimes when searches that produced zero hits on the recorded logs are replicated at a later date, the known item is found. The online catalog studied did not contain items that were on order or in process.

Category 11, dealing with specific problems with the user interface of the specific system, may be of particular interest to researchers. This category could be subdivided into problems entering foreign words and names, problems with grammatical punctuation, problems with punctuation specific to the system design, and problems with scoping.

The same analysis of probable causes of errors can be applied to the dial access activity on the same system. Three different months were analyzed.

Table 10.6: In-House Probable Causes of Problems
(Jan., Feb. 1988)

PROBLEM	T	A	K	S	M	O	W	X	Y	Z	B	C	OTH	TOTAL	%
1 MAL	4	6	0	2	0	4	0	0	0	0	3	0	0	19	1.0
2 TYPO	107	34	1	47	2	11	0	0	0	0	3	0	0	205	10.9
3 LINE	31	6	4	15	0	6	0	0	0	0	0	0	1	63	3.4
4 SPELL	69	62	2	43	1	7	0	0	1	0	0	0	0	185	9.9
5 FIRST	0	61	0	28	0	9	0	0	0	0	1	0	0	99	5.3
6 MI	0	89	0	1	0	1	0	0	0	0	0	0	0	91	4.9
7 VOCAB	0	2	0	51	1	31	0	0	0	0	1	0	0	86	4.6
8 FORMAT	29	0	0	0	0	0	1	0	0	0	0	0	0	30	1.6
9 SEARCH	36	11	3	108	0	4	3	2	2	0	8	4	1	182	9.7
10 BOOLE	1	13	1	2	0	0	0	0	0	0	0	0	0	17	0.9
11 LUMIN	34	30	0	8	4	15	0	0	0	0	0	49	5	145	7.7
12 DB	8	3	1	0	0	0	0	0	0	0	2	0	0	14	0.7
13 OPACS	5	0	0	0	0	0	0	0	0	0	0	0	0	5	0.3
14 NOT	500	120	2	1	0	85	0	0	6	1	17	0	0	732	39.0
Totals	824	437	14	306	8	173	4	2	9	1	35	53	7	1873	
Percent	44	23	1	16		9					2	3			100.0

Reprinted from Peters, 1989.

Comparison of probable causes of errors between in-house and dial access public users indicates that dial access users make fewer typographical and spelling errors. The dial access users seem to be exploring the limits of the database and the collection. Some of this is caused by other libraries' trying to verify local holdings prior to initiating an interlibrary loan request. Sometimes the items sought are clearly beyond the scope of an academic library collection, but they are searched as a matter of course. Other

Table 10.7: Dial Access Probable Causes of Problems (Apr., Dec. 1988, July 1989)

PROBLEM	T	A	K	S	M	O	W	X	Y	Z	B	C	OTH	TOTAL	%
1 MAL	3	0	0	0	0	0	0	0	0	0	0	0	0	3	0.1
2 TYPO	164	8	3	3	0	5	0	0	1	0	1	0	0	185	8.6
3 LINE	36	5	0	0	0	0	0	0	0	0	0	0	0	41	1.9
4 SPELL	53	2	0	1	0	1	0	0	0	0	0	0	0	57	2.6
5 FIRST	0	2	0	0	0	1	0	0	0	0	0	0	0	3	0.1
6 MI	0	11	0	0	0	0	0	0	0	0	0	0	0	11	0.5
7 VOCAB	0	7	0	2	0	0	0	0	0	0	0	0	0	9	0.4
8 FORMAT	0	0	0	0	0	0	0	'O	0	0	0	0	0	0	0.0
9 SEARCH	5	3	0	14	0	1	0	0	0	0	1	0	0	24	1.1
10 BOOLE	2	1	0	0	0	0	0	0	0	0	0	0	0	3	0.1
11 LUMIN	24	38	1	3	0	2	0	0	1	0	1	2	0	72	3.3
12 DB	13	0	0	0	0	0	0	0	0	0	0	0	0	13	0.6
13 OPACS	0	1	0	0	0	0	0	0	0	0	0	0	0	1	0.0
14 NOT	1591	114	1	0	0	10	0	3	3	0	11	0	0	1733	80.4
Totals	1891	192	5	23	0	20	0	3	5	0	14	2	0	2155	
Percent	88	9		1		1					1				100.0

items evidently not in the database seem to be likely candidates for inclusion in the collection.

Other Studies of Probable Cause

Other researchers have studied the frequency of spelling errors, but few have made the distinction between typographical errors and evident spelling errors. A transaction analysis project by Costers and Buys (1986; 346) in 1985 revealed that typographic errors were common. During another study it was discovered that approximately 10 percent of the searches of the OKAPI online catalog system (of the Polytechnic of Central London) contained at least one dubious spelling (Walker, 1988; 25). In-house public access users of the online catalog studied here have a higher misspelling/typographical error rate than that, but remote use failures where the probable cause is either a typing or spelling error also average about 10 percent. Walker based his percentage on the total number of searches, while the percentages presented in this study are based on the subset of unique data-entry search statements that produced no hits. Incomplete or dysfunctional conceptual models of the online catalog system also can cause errors and null sets. In a protocol analysis study of thirty first-time users of the LCS system at Ohio State University, many user errors resulted from the development or activation of inappropriate mental representations of the system (Smith, 1985; 274).

Borgman (1986; 387) bisects user problems into the mechanical and the conceptual. Is the problem within the automated system or within the user? Problems may be inherent to a specific type of system, to a specific type of user, or inherent in the task of information retrieval. Is the solution to be found by changing the system or by educating the users? Once the problems have been identified, some researchers want to fix the online system, while others want to educate the users.

Margaret Henty also classified the reasons for failure, and found that 32.7 percent were due to spelling errors, 13.6 percent due to improper use of punctuation, 4.3 percent due to omitted spaces between words, and 1.2 percent due to the inappropriate use of acronyms and abbreviations. Only 14.1 percent of the search statements appeared to simply not match any bibliographic records in the catalog (Tague, 1989; 54).

Conclusion

If dial access users perform more known-item searches and less subject searches than in-house users, and if dial access is the wave of the future in access to online catalogs, and if the current dial access users are a relatively representative sample of future dial access users, perhaps the profession is not wise to spend so much time and money to improve controlled vocabulary subjecct access. There is strong evidence that some title keyword searches performed by remote access users are uncontrolled vocabulary subject searches. The users seem to favor this type of subject search, preferring high precision rather than high recall. There is little indication, however, that remote access users know how to interpret the information contained in the records of a highly precise, title keyword uncontrolled vocabulary subject search, or to go on and use official subject searches to increase the recall of relevant items.

On almost all counts dial access searching behavior is distinctly different than in-house public access use of the online catalog. The key findings are the dominance of title keyword searching and the low incidence of zero-hit searches caused by user errors. The next chapter will examine some of the temporal aspects of dial access use.

Notes

1. Table 10.1 is a slightly revised and corrected version of one originally printed in Peters, 1989.

2. The menu-mode search options are listed in the order given in Table 9.1.

3. The ISBN number cannot be used as an access point in menu-mode either in-house or through dial access. Command-mode searches, however, can be entered directly from menu-mode screens. At least one dial access user knew how to do this.

4. Personal BITNET correspondence, March 1990.

5. Personal BITNET correspondence, March 1990.

Chapter 11

Temporal Aspects
of Dial Access

Introduction

One of the arguments often presented in favor of remote access to online catalogs and other library databases is that remote access frees the users from the limited hours when the libraries are open. Remote access to online catalogs, it is argued, will help distribute the searching load on the system over a greater period of time, thus lessening peak demand and improving response time. On some systems remote searchers can search anytime of the day or night. During the period of this study, the online catalog studied was available by remote access six days a week from 7 A.M. until midnight, and Sundays from noon to midnight.

Dial access use can be divided into segments using the usual divisions of time—months, weeks, days, and hours. This method ignores the lived temporal experience of using the online catalog, but it has advantages in allowing comparisons to other bibliographic storage and retrieval systems. This chapter will study the temporal aspects of dial access—by hour of day, day of week, week of year, and month of year. Comparisons will be made to in-house and total use of the same system. In general, the claim often made in favor of offering dial access to an online catalog system—that dial access will increase use of the system during off-days and off-hours—was not supported by the dial access searching patterns observed at the study site.

Dial Access Session Lengths

The first task is to determine the length of dial access sessions. It is difficult to get accurate figures on the length of catalog search sessions by in-house users. Remote access, however, offers some new possibilities. One of the drawbacks of using transaction logs to analyze in-house users is that on most systems the users are not required to log-on, so it is difficult to tell when one user leaves the terminal and another approaches. Transaction logs of remote access users can at least indicate when discrete dial access sessions begin and end. Each dial access port is identified. The command to log-off is recorded on the log. If the user fails to officially log-off, the system bumps the user off the line after approximately ten minutes of inactivity.

There are at least two ways to measure the length of a search session. The first is to use standard measures of time, such as minutes and seconds. One disadvantage of this method of measurement is that the rate of searching is discounted. For example, a ten-minute search session may contain only three subject browse searches or it may contain over thirty title keyword searches. Both searches lasted ten minutes, but that does not mean that the same amount of searching was done during each search session.

The other method of measurement is to count the number of searches attempted, regardless of the amount of time taken to enter the search statements. One drawback of this approach is arriving at a fair and acceptable definition of a search. Most online catalogs have more than one search state, and each search state could be given a relative weight. For example, is a user browsing through the list of controlled vocabulary subject headings, doing as much searching as a user performing a complex Boolean query? A subject browse search, for example, could be given more weight than a series title keyword search, because the first search conceivably provides access to many more bibliographic records. Again, professional biases concerning the purpose of an online catalog could affect the analysis.

Through the use of this technique to identify discrete search sessions, four months of dial access search sessions were analyzed for length. During visual analysis of the logs, the length of each search session was rounded off to the nearest minute. If the user failed to officially log-off, the ten-minute interval between the last recorded searching activity and the moment of disconnection was not included in the session length. The results are presented in Table 11.1.

Overall, 14.6 percent of all search sessions were no-log-off sessions. This percentage is high enough to justify the continuation of automatically bumping inactive search sessions, but it is not so high that the fears of computing center personnel that remote access users of online catalogs are irresponsible or inconsiderate users of the dial access ports into the campus computer network. There is no firmly established trend in the growth or decline in the number or percentage of search sessions where no-log-off command is recorded. Although the average length of no-log-off sessions was higher than the average length of all search sessions for three of the four months, the difference does not justify procedural or system changes. We cannot conclude that searchers who, during individual search sessions, spend more time connected to the online catalog tend to fail to log-off.

Other studies of search session length found shorter sessions. Tolle (1983; 105) found that most remote access search sessions lasted less than ten minutes. Carole Moore (1981; 298) found through surveys that the median search session length at four universities' libraries ranged from two to eight minutes. Borgman's (1983; 166) study of in-house use found that search sessions had a median of five to six transactions, with elapsed times of two to four minutes. The survey of ARL libraries by Abbott and Davis (1988) discovered that the average dial access session lasts four to six minutes. Lipetz and Paulson (1987; 615) speculate that the duration of catalog searches is much more dpendent on unknown characteristics of the user population, perhaps a mixture of physiological and educational attributes, than on the physical or informational features of catalog systems. Brownrigg (1983; 111) suggests that, as more services and information become available through the online catalog, and as more users are able to use the online catalog from more comfortable locations, the average length of search sessions will increase.

A brief analysis was done using the other method for measuring session lengths. Considering the eleven months of the study as a whole, an average dial access search session consisted of less than twelve total searches, and less than seven unique data-entry searches.

By Hour of the Day

The next task is to determine the hours of the day when remote access is heaviest. In general, the remote access users of the online catalog studied do not use the system much in the evenings and on weekends. Late mornings and early afternoons on weekdays tend to be the periods of peak use. This probably also parallels the peak demand periods for in-house users, including library staff. It would seem, then, at least at present and at this particular location, the hope that offering remote access to the online catalog would spread the demand on the system over more hours of the day is not being realized. Users tend to search the online catalog during normal business hours, regardless of their location and mode of access (see Table 11.2).

Data collected from questionnaires at other libraries offering remote access indicate otherwise. The majority of the respondents to a survey of remote access users conducted by the Pikes Peak Library District in 1988 reported that they remotely access the library's databases between 4 P.M. and midnight (Magrath, 1989; 535). A study of remote access use by hour of the day at Penn State in 1984 found that the heaviest period of use occurred between 3 P.M. and 5 P.M., with a smaller peak between 7 P.M. and 9 P.M. (Sarah Kalin, 1984; 209). Evidently each site exhibits different remote searching peaks by hour of day.

If remote access users have problems logging on, they should be able to contact a member of the reference staff by telephone for assistance. Periods of peak demand at the reference desk of the main library on campus are in the late morning and early afternoon. Thus the reference desk is

Month	Total Search Sessions	Total Min.	Avg. Min. All Sessions	No Log off Sessions	Percent of all Sessions	Avg. Min. No Log off Sessions
Apr 88	177	1809	10.2	20	11.3	11.2
May 88	151	1823	12.1	28	18.5	8.3
Nov 88	276	2818	10.2	46	16.7	15.3
Dec 88	210	2172	10.3	25	11.9	18.6
Totals	814	8622		119		
Avg./Mon.	204	2156	10.6	30	14.6	13.6

Table 11.1: Dial Access Session Lengths

staffed while most dial access users are trying to log-on, but the hours of peak dial access activity also are the peak periods of in-house and telephone and reference service at the main library on campus.

Table 11.2: Dial Access by Hour of Day
(All Eleven Months)
293 Days of Recorded Searching Activity

Hour of Day	Total Searches	TS Avg/Day	Unique Data-Entry Searches	UDES Avg/Day	Search Session Starts	SSS Avg/Day
7	271	0.92	162	0.55	25	0.09
8	1,668	5.69	1,000	3.41	164	0.56
9	2,481	8.47	1,289	4.40	211	0.72
10	2,458	8.39	1,321	4.51	253	0.86
11	3,398	11.60	2,383	8.13	285	0.97
12	2,817	9.61	1,868	6.38	200	0.68
13	4,149	14.16	2,711	9.25	366	1.25
14	4,228	14.43	2,787	9.51	329	1.12
15	3,217	10.98	1,913	6.53	302	1.03
16	2,240	7.65	1,171	4.00	244	0.83
17	1,127	3.85	576	1.97	113	0.39
18	553	1.89	194	0.66	36	0.12
19	713	2.43	235	0.80	37	0.13
20	623	2.13	230	0.78	36	0.12
21	473	1.61	117	0.40	26	0.09
22	274	0.94	117	0.40	34	0.12
23	246	0.84	68	0.23	14	0.05
Totals	30,936	105.58	18,142	61.89	2,675	9.13

The patterns of dial access use by hour of the day during the study period become more self-evident if the figures are plotted on a graph (see Graph 11.1).

A research policy question involves which of the three measures of search sessions—search session starts, total searches, or unique data-entry searches—should be given the most weight in determining dial access usage by hour of the day. The correlation between total searches and unique data-entry searches seems to be stronger than the relationships between either of those dependent variables and search session starts. If we assume that search session starts is the key dependent variable in determining demands of remote access users on the library's public services points, it is significant

Graph 11.1: Dial Access by Hour of Day
(All Eleven Months)

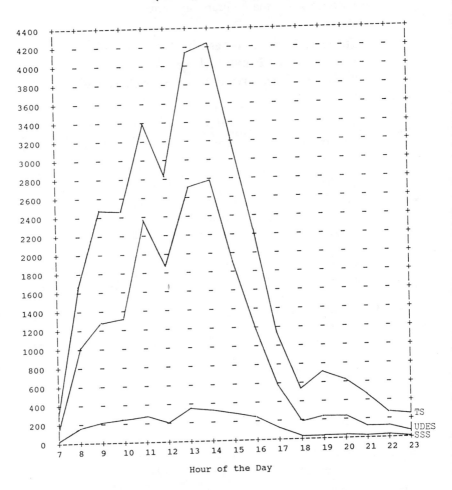

Hour of the Day

to note that peak times for search session starts do not always correspond to peaks for total searches and unique data-entry searches.

By Day of the Week

Dial access use by day of the week also can be studied. During the eleven months of the study, there were 293 days of recorded dial access activity: 23 Sundays, 44 Mondays, 47 Tuesdays, Wednesdays, Thursdays, and Fridays, and 38 Saturdays (see Table 11.3 and Graph 11.2).

Days of the week when no activity was recorded, for whatever reason, were not counted when the averages were figured. It is impossible to determine whether the system was available and no searching occurred, or whether the system was unavailable. For example, in May 1988 only two Sundays of activity were contained on the transaction log, although there were four Sundays in the month. To get the average amount of activity for that day of the week during May, 1988, the total searches, unique data-entry searches, and search session starts were divided by two, not four.

For all three variables, Wednesday is the day of the week when dial access usage is the heaviest. Although Wednesday is clearly the heaviest day of use in terms of total searches, almost every weekday has approximately eleven search session starts on average. If Sarah Kalin is correct that users ask for assistance primarily when they are trying to log-on, just as planes tend to be in most danger just before and after takeoff, the balance of search session starts during the weekdays seems to indicate that additional reference help on evenings and weekends is not necessary, at least at the site studied.

Relationships between the three variables are not uniform and predictable. For example, Friday is the third heaviest day of the week in terms of average number of total searches, second in terms of average number of unique data-entry searches, and fifth in terms of average number of search sessions.

Comparison with In-House Public Terminal Use

The Office of Library Systems of the University of Missouri maintains usage data for the entire online catalog system. It must be noted that the Office of Library Systems' definition of a transaction is different than the definition used in this report. The system support staff defines a transaction as an individual request sent to the main CPU of the system. These "internal transactions" usually are more numerous than the count of individual search statements. Moreover, there is not a stable proportional relationship between the two definitions of transactions. An inefficient search request from the perspective of the system (such as a title keyword search on "American History") requires more requests sent to the central processing unit than a more efficient search, such as a search by ISBN.

Terminals are divided into four types: public, staff, circulation, and remote. Some system-wide statistics on remote use have been generated. Remote terminals include any terminals located outside the libraries used to access the online catalog, and all dial access use, regardless of location. When all remote access use system-wide was isolated and studied, Tuesday was the day of peak use, slightly ahead of the other four weekdays. Thursday was the weekday with the least amount of remote access activity system-wide (*LSO Update* [October 20, 1989], 2).

During a one-week study of remote access activity into the LIAS online

Day of Week	(n)	Total Searches	TS Avg/Day	Unique Data-Entry Searches	UDES Avg/Day	Search Session Starts	SSS Avg/Day
Sun.	(23)	975	42.39	368	16.00	44	1.91
Mon.	(44)	4754	108.05	2760	62.73	485	11.02
Tues.	(47)	6105	129.89	3483	74.11	533	11.34
Wed.	(47)	6787	144.40	3952	84.09	547	11.64
Thurs.	(47)	5300	112.77	3156	67.15	532	11.32
Fri.	(47)	5477	116.53	3616	76.74	443	9.43
Sat.	(38)	1538	40.47	807	21.24	91	2.39
Totals	(293)	30,936	105.58	18,142	61.89	2,675	9.13

Table 11.3: Dial Access by Day of Week (All Eleven Months) 293 Days of Recorded Searching Activity

Graph 11.2: Dial Access by Day of Week
(All Eleven Months)

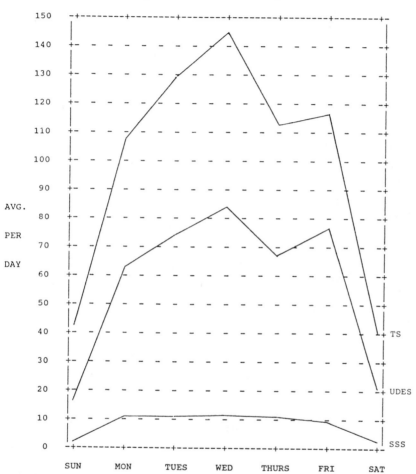

catalog at Penn State in April 1984, Sarah Kalin (1984; 209) found that Wednesday was the period of heaviest activity, with Tuesday and Friday almost tied for second.

Comparisons also can be made to all use of the system (i.e., all types of terminals at all four campuses). During September 1989, Tuesday was the busiest day at all terminals, with Wednesday and Thursday a close second and third. Monday and Friday had less terminal activity, and Saturday and Sunday approximately one-third the activity of the peak days in midweek (*LSO Update* [October 13, 1989], 4). In the last four months of 1989 overall, the first two workdays of the week contained the most transactions system-wide.

The Online Catalog

Table 11.4: Dial Access by Week of Year

Week	Start Date	Total Searches	Unique Data-Entry Searches	Search Sessions
⋆ 14	04/03/88	551	394	51
⋆ 15	04/10/88	549	355	41
⋆ 16	04/17/88	456	297	35
⋆ 17	04/24/88	461	280	39
+ 18	05/01/88	486	322	29
19	05/08/88	1346	586	49
20	05/15/88	380	202	39
21	05/22/88	443	242	31
⋆ 45	11/06/88	791	492	67
⋆ 46	11/13/88	990	759	74
⋆ 47	11/20/88	662	475	47
⋆ 48	11/27/88	626	425	66
⋆ 49	12/04/88	723	421	51
+ 50	12/11/88	683	477	67
51	12/18/88	497	229	42
52	12/25/88	301	202	23
1	1/01/89	729	330	45
2	1/08/89	541	362	58
⋆ 3	1/15/89	691	345	73
⋆ 4	1/22/89	1027	628	96
⋆ 5	1/29/89	859	461	86
⋆ 6	2/05/89	1128	568	84
⋆ 7	2/12/89	985	564	72
⋆ 8	2/19/89	614	393	69
⋆ 9	2/26/89	688	390	68
⋆ 10	3/05/89	776	430	75
11	3/12/89	669	414	70
⋆ 12	3/19/89	740	459	68
⋆ 13	3/26/89	638	366	60
⋆ 14	4/02/89	712	365	59
⋆ 15	4/09 89	686	345	62
⋆ 16	4/16/89	931	619	60
⋆ 17	4/23/89	678	362	69
⋆ 18	4/30/89	572	288	60
+ 19	5/07/89	471	255	46
20	5/14/89	513	308	49
21	5/21/89	729	371	53
22	5/28/89	580	291	58

Week	Start Date	Total Searches	Unique Data-Entry Searches	Search Sessions
* 23	6/04/89	621	337	76
* 24	6/11/89	326	225	47
* 25	6/18/89	650	353	50
* 26	6/25/89	630	283	45
* 27	7/02/89	402	290	42
* 28	7/09/89	589	431	49
* 29	7/16/89	476	345	54
+ 30	7/23/89	615	382	58
In-Session Subtotals		23,483	14,181	2,095
In-Session Avg/Week		670.94	405.17	59.86
Intersession Subtotals		6,728	3,537	517
Intersession Avg/Week		611.64	321.55	47.00
Totals		30,211	17,718	2,612
Avg/Week		656.76	385.17	56.78

* = weeks when classes were in session.

+ = weeks when final exams were being taken.

By Week of Year

The week of the year is important in many academic service functions, so it may be useful to study dial access activity during the weeks of the year. Comparisons can be made between weeks when classes are in session and intersession weeks, to test the hypothesis that dial access users of the online catalog exhibit the typical cyclical patterns of in-house users based on the progress of the semester (see Table 11.4 and Graph 11.3).

There were forty-six full weeks of recorded dial access searching activities during the study period.[1] Classes were in session (or finals were being given) during thirty-five of the weeks of the study. The other eleven weeks were intersession periods (including one week of spring break). In general, there is more dial access searching activity across all three variables when classes are in session than during intersession periods. If the results are placed on a graph, however, no clear pattern of use by week of year emerges. The first week of intersession after spring semester 1988 was the heaviest week of dial access activity (in terms of total searches) during

Graph 11.3: Dial Access by Week of Year

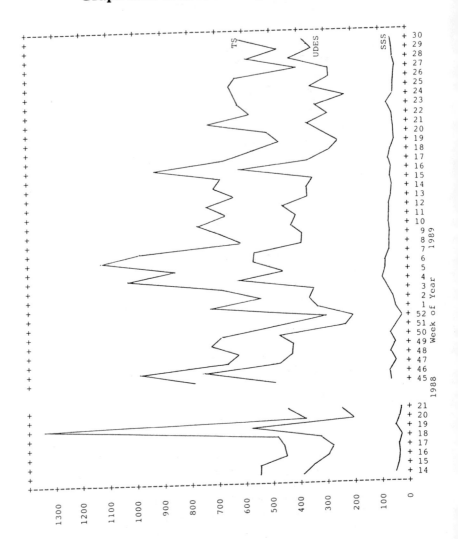

the study period, yet the first week of intersession after spring semester 1989 reveals only a small increase in dial access activity.

By Month of Year

Studies of remote use activity by months of the year can help determine if the total use of remote access to the online catalog is increasing over time (see Table 11.5 and Graph 11.4). Cycles of use based on the academic semester, the month, or the season also may appear. Again, in-house use of the system can serve as a basis for comparison. For the total use of the online catalog system, including all four campuses of the university and all types of users (staff, circulation, in-house public, and remote), the peak months of usage are October and November (*LSO Update* [January 12, 1990], 4).

Table 11.5: Dial Access by Month

Month	Total Searches	Unique Data-Entry Searches	Search Session Starts
4/88	2,166	1,400	177
5/88	2,703	1,368	151
11/88	3,274	2,299	276
12/88	2,527	1,515	210
1/89	3,399	1,872	305
2/89	3,597	1,983	314
3/89	3,049	1,825	303
4/89	3,052	1,721	252
5/89	2,640	1,360	237
6/89	2,393	1,330	244
7/89	2,136	1,469	206
Totals	30,936	18,142	2,675

Total Session—the total number of searches, excluding the log-off command and apparent log-off attempts.
Unique Data-Entry Sessions—the total number of unique data-entry searches, where the user is required to actually enter data, rather than an alphanumeric option listed on the screen.
Search Session Starts—the number of dial access search sessions begun.

Graph 11.4: Dial Access by Month

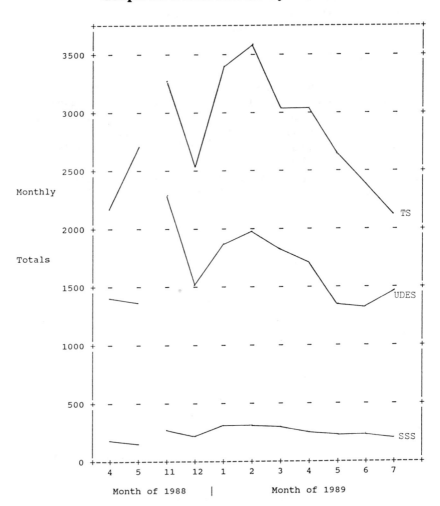

Comparison with Total System Use

During the summer months of May, June, July, and August, total use of the online catalog throughout the entire system (i.e., all four campuses and all types of users—staff, in-house public users, and remote users) falls to less than two-thirds of the use during the peak academic months, such as February, March, April, and September (*LSO Update* [October 13, 1989], 4). Summertime lulls in dial access activity at the one campus studied were evident but not as pronounced.

The peak month for internal transactions from remote terminals system-wide during the spring semester of 1989 was February, when nearly

60,000 internal transactions were recorded (*LSO Update* [October 27, 1987], 2). February was also the peak month for all three variables—total searches, unique data-entry searches, and search sessions—of this study of dial access activity at one campus.

Overall (i.e., system-wide for all types of terminals) the three core months of the fall semester of 1989 (September, October, and November) contained more internal transaction activity than the three core months of the spring 1989 semester (February, March, and April) (*LSO Update* [December 15, 1989], 4).

The dial access users of the online catalog at the site studied are not night owls or weekend searchers. Dial access activity seems to be influenced by the typical workweek. The cycles of the academic year have some effect on patterns of dial access searching. Dial access activity seems to be increasing at the study site, but not exponentially.

Notes

1. The totals given here do not match the totals provided elsewhere in this book, because there were isolated days of activity in early April 1988, late May 1988, and early November 1988 that did not occur during weeks fully within the period of study. If the 725 total searches, 424 unique data-entry searches, and 63 search sessions are added to the totals given in this table, the same grand totals for each variable studied are achieved.

Chapter 12
Remote Subject Searching

Introduction

The subject searching behavior and success of online catalog users is of perennial interest to the library profession. Although the results presented in previous chapters indicate that subject searching is not utilized as much by dial access users as by in-house users of the online catalog studied, remote access subject searching behavior still warrants further examination.

A subject search is difficult to define. A first difficulty is deciding which search options provide subject access. Of the twelve search options offered by the online catalog studied, at least six could provide subject access: title keyword find, subject browse, medical subject browse, official subject term, Boolean find, and call number browse. The distinction between a known-item search and a subject search, never extremely clear, really becomes fuzzy in the online environment. For example, a call number search can be either a known-item search or a subject search, depending on what the user brings to the search and what she or he expects to get out of the search. Title keyword searching is particularly powerful both for known-item searching and for uncontrolled vocabulary subject searches (Peters and Kurth, 1990). The latent conflict between producers of information and those who store and retrieve it is evident in the tendency of the storers and retrievers to refer to title keyword searches as uncontrolled vocabulary subject searches, when actually the authors (the producers) control the vocabulary.

A second difficulty is that subject search sessions (as tentatively identified by analyzers of transaction logs) and dial access search sessions do not always coincide. Sometimes a single dial access search session will contain several subject search sessions, identified by abrupt, decisive changes in topic, and, conversely, sometimes a single subject search session will spread over several dial access sessions.

A common perception about subject access is that most subject search sessions contain mostly controlled vocabulary subject search statements. The results presented below suggest that subject search sessions are not as intensely dependent on controlled vocabulary subject search statements as is commonly believed.

Neal Kaske (1988A, 1988B) has done some research on the use of

212

transaction logs to study subject searching behavior. The work presented in this chapter attempts to build on his earlier research.

Subject Search Methods in the Online Catalog Studied

For the purposes of this study, a subject search session was defined as any dial access session containing at least one controlled vocabulary subject search statement. Three controlled vocabulary subject searches are available in the online catalog studied: subject browse, medical subject browse, and an official LCSH term search. The two browse searches simply drop the user into the controlled vocabulary subject lists at the subsequent closest match to the characters entered by the user. The official subject term search requires users to enter headings and subheadings for utilized LCSH headings, separated by double dashes. The online catalog studied allows users of the official subject headings to treat main headings and subdivisions as separate phrases combined with an implicit Boolean "and," although most users seem unaware of this.

Other access points to subject-rich fields include a title keyword search, a call number browse search, and Boolean searches involving controlled vocabulary subject lists. For the purposes of this study, these search options were considered to be ancillary subject access points. Technically, the fifth type of Boolean search is able to combine two controlled vocabulary subject search sets, but Boolean searching offers enough unique challenges to warrant exlcuding it from normal or pure subject searches. Arguments could be made that the call number browse search is a controlled vocabulary subject search, with the classification scheme as the controlled vocabulary, but it too presents enough unique problems to warrant being bracketed for the purposes of this phase of the research. Call number browsing and Boolean searching are not heavily used by either in-house or remote users.[1]

Subject Search Session Lengths

One hypothesis to be tested is whether the set of dial access sessions containing at least one controlled vocabulary subject search statement lasts longer on average than the average length of all dial access search sessions. As was noted in Chapter 11, both the number of unique data-entry search statements and time can be used to measure the lengths of search sessions.

Although the percentage of subject search statements is small compared to in-house use of the online catalog, the percentage of remote access search sessions containing at least one subject search is significant and worthy of consideration. The decision concerning the basic unit of measurement—the

Month	n	Min	S	M	O	S/M/O	Non-Subj	T	A/K	W/X Y/Z	B	C	Total
Nov 1988	43	681	80	3	4	87	173	62	83	10	2	16	260
Dec 1988	49	783	82	2	40	124	121	88	14	9	5	5	245
May 1989	59	949	120	31	28	179	135	85	42	2	5	1	314
Jun 1989	48	638	108	9	5	122	132	88	34	1	5	4	254
Totals	199	3051	390	45	77	512	561	323	173	22	17	26	1073
Percent			36	4	7	48	52	30	16	2	2	2	100

Table 12.1: Controlled Vocabulary Subject Search Sessions

individual search statements or the entire search sessions—influences the perception of the frequency and intensity of subject searching. For example, in the dial access activity during December 1988, although only 8.2 percent of the unique data-entry search statements were controlled vocabulary subject statements, 49 of the 210 dial access search sessions (23.3 percent) contained at least one controlled vocabulary subject search statement.

In November 1988 the 87 controlled vocabulary subject search statements recorded in the dial access log occurred during 43 search sessions, an average of only 2 controlled vocabulary subject search statements per subject search session. Only 15.6 percent of all dial access search sessions involved some controlled vocabulary subject searching. The subject search sessions averaged 15.8 minutes in length, compared to an overall average of 10.4 minutes for the month.

The 124 controlled vocabulary subject search statements found in the dial access log for December 1988 were contained in 49 search sessions, for an average of slightly more than 2.5 subject searches per session. Nearly all of those 49 sessions contained other types of searches as well. Pure controlled vocabulary subject search sessions are rare occurrences in remote sessions, and probably in in-house sessions as well. The 49 search sessions containing at least one controlled vocabulary subject search lasted 783 minutes, an average of approximately 16 minutes per session. This is significantly longer than the average for all search sessions for the month, 10.3 minutes per search session.

Although it can be tentatively concluded that search sessions containing controlled vocabulary subject search statements last longer than the average search session, the increased length may not be caused by the subject search statements themselves, because most of the subject search sessions were not exclusively controlled vocabulary subject search sessions.

Controlled Vocabulary Subject Search Sessions

During discussions of subject searching behavior using online catalogs, it is easy to be lulled into the assumption that subject search sessions are discrete, identifiable search sessions, almost completely separated from known-item search sessions. In the next stage of the analysis, the dial access sessions for four months that contained at least one controlled vocabulary subject search statement were isolated for further analysis. The evidence indicates that subject search sessions do not make intensive use of the controlled vocabulary subject access points (see Table 12.1).

The "number" column indicates the number of dial access sessions for the month containing at least one controlled vocabulary subject search statement. The "minutes" column indicates the cumulative length of the subject search sessions, when each individual session is rounded to the nearest minute. For purposes of easy comparison, the total number of controlled vocabulary subject searches (s/m/o) and the total number of other searches (labeled "nonsubject" for convenience) are aligned next to each other in the center of the table.

Less than 21 percent (199 out of 968) of the dial access sessions during the four months contained at least once controlled vocabulary subject search statement. This may be a better indication of how much subject searching is being done than the 8.2 percent figure for s/m/o searches in the breakdown of searching activity by type in the tables in Chapter 10. For purposes of comparison, Borgman's (1983; 167) study of in-house use of an academic online catalog found that about 34 percent of all sessions contained at least one attempt at a controlled vocabulary subject search.

If a pure subject search session is defined as a dial access session containing only controlled vocabulary subject search statements, approximately 34.7 percent (69 of the 199) of the subject sessions were pure. Only about 11.6 percent of the subject sessions (23 of 199) contained more than one type of controlled vocabulary subject search statement. Thus there is some evidence indicating that dial access users only infrequently try several types of controlled vocabulary subject search types within any individual search sessions.

The average length in minutes of the subject search sessions was 15.33 minutes. Over half (52 percent) of the search statements entered during dial access subject search sessions are not controlled vocabulary subject search statements. On average, only a little over 2.5 controlled vocabulary subject search statements are entered during a dial access subject search session. Overall, an average of approximately 5.4 unique data-entry search statements of all types are entered during a dial access subject search session.

Several factors mitigate against the findings of this stage of the analysis. First, what were isolated and studied were dial access sessions, not necessarily subject search sessions. As pointed out in Chapter 9, often there is not an exact correspondence between dial access sessions and subject search sessions. Sometimes the subject search is a subset of a larger dial access session. Other times a single subject search session spreads over two or more dial access sessions. Based on the current state of transaction logging and analysis, however, we can identify dial access sessions with confidence, but not subject search sessions.

Second, this analysis assumes that a controlled vocabulary unique data-entry subject search statement has equal value to other types of unique data-entry searches. The argument could be made that, by providing access to the subject authority file, not to bibliographic records, the controlled vocabulary subject searches, particulary the two browse searches, potentially provide access to more bibliographic records than the average non-controlled vocabulary unique data-entry search.

Subject Searching (S, M, O) by Hour of Day and Day of week

Much more research and speculative interest has been paid by the profession to subject searching than to other types of searches. If we assume that subject searching presents the most problems for remote access users, it would be helpful to know if there are peak times during the hours of the day and the days of the week for dial access subject searching. Table 12.2 plots the incidence of controlled vocabulary subject search statements by hour of the day and day of the week for three selected months.

Table 12.2: Dial Access Subject Searching (May, Nov., Dec. 1988)

Hour	Sun.	Mon.	Tues.	Wed.	Thurs.	Fri.	Sat.	Totals	Percent
7		1						1	0
8		2	1	3	3	2		11	3
9		5	16	2	5	6	1	35	10
10		6	5	2	9	7		29	9
11		1			2	2		5	1
12		1		1	15	3	1	21	6
13		2	1	18	5	3	12	41	12
14		5	6	5	23	1	1	41	12
15		5	4	5	1	5	6	26	8
16		14	1	1	1		7	24	7
17	1	1	4		3		10	19	6
18	5		3		2			10	3
19		3	2		11	1	2	19	6
20	12		8		2	1	5	28	8
21	3							3	1
22	4	1	3	13		1	1	23	7
23								0	0
Totals	25	47	54	50	82	32	46	336	
Percent	7	14	16	15	24	10	14		100

The Online Catalog

The results presented in Table 12.2 can then be plotted on a graph to indicate the shape of dial access subject searching by hour of the day. The individual unique data-entry subject search statements, rather than the subject search sessions, are being analyzed here (see Graphs 12.1, 12.2).

Graph 12.1: Dial Access Subject Searches by Hour of Day (May, Nov., Dec. 1988)

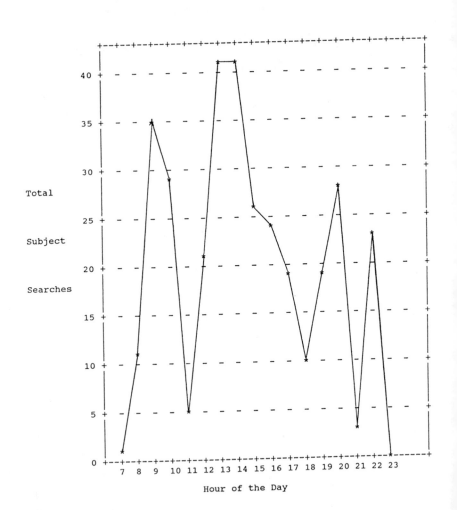

Graph 12.2: Dial Access Subject Searches by Day of Week (May, Nov., Dec. 1988)

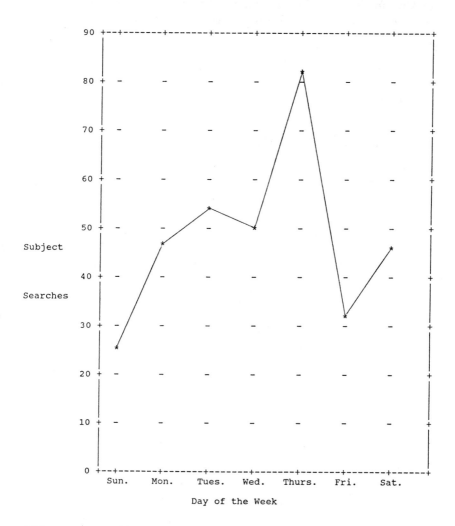

Discussion of Dial Access Subject Searching

It is incorrect to assume that using controlled vocabulary to find information on a topic is the correct and proper way, while uncontrolled vocabulary subject searching is cheating or second-rate. We need to rethink the value of uncontrolled vocabulary subject searching. In the older information storage and retrieval systems, uncontrolled vocabulary subject searching may have been less efficient and productive than using the controlled vocabulary only, because the designers of the systems intended it that way. It should be kept in mind that, although user behavior when looking for information on a topic may be more interesting than user behavior when looking for known items, subject searching still constitutes a small portion of all remote access use.

Notes

1. Refer to the tables in Chapter 10.

Chapter 13

Remote Access and Academic Communications

Introduction

The development of remote access is somewhat inexplicable. Similar to the development of online catalog themselves, there did not seem to be strong user demand for remote access. The technological ability to provide remote access was available, and the costs of providing the service were not prohibitive, so remote access was revived. Earlier forms of the library catalog, particularly the book catalog, provided convenient remote access (assuming copies of the book catalog were plentiful and cheap), but these catalogs were difficult to maintain, and remote users could not do much with the bibliographic records they retrieved from remote locations. A book catalog provides remote access, but it is not current, does not contain circulation information, and the bibliographic records cannot be easily manipulated.

Remote access to online catalogs makes distance less important in the process of identifying, locating, and retrieving information. As such, it joins a distinguished list of technological advances that have helped humans overcome distance—the railroad, the telegraph, the telephone, and television. If we state the fact a little differently, however, and say that remote access to online catalogs has removed much of the value and importance of location, the implications for libraries and library catalogs are more foreboding. This revaluation will have far-reaching implications for the customary mission and primary activities of the academic library. The positive correlation between the geographic proximity of an item of recorded scholarly information and its accessibility is gradually dissolving.

The Transmission of Information

Libraries are just beginning to provide major services in the areas of information transportation and transmission. In the past, middlemen relegated this function to the producers and consumers, as outlined in

221

Chapter 3. The publisher or jobber ships the book to the library premises, and the user retrieves the item from the shelves and transports it home. Cataloging, classification, and intellectual retrieval historically have been the librarians' areas of expertise. The popular image of the library as the mind or collective memory of the institution (or, if you are more ambitious, the society) is revealing in this context. The library is like a mind, rather than a nervous system. It is seen as a storehouse of information—gray matter—not as a communications medium.

Remote access to online catalogs, however, is getting libraries more involved in the transmission of information. Although services like remote access to online catalogs build on communications systems already in place, such as telephone service and campus computing networks, libraries are making major commitments to providing services via telecommunications. With interlibrary loan, libraries relied heavily on governmental and commercial courier services. Database searching relied on commercial telecommunications. Now libraries are working independently or with local campus computing centers to create local area networks, gateways, and electronic mail scholarly conferences and journals.

Conceptualization Problems

With the introduction of online catalogs the user lost most of her or his spatial orientation with the bibliographic database being searched. Book and card catalogs stressed this spatial orientation. The card catalog was a physical presence in the reference room. To pull open a drawer was to gain direct spatial orientation with the portion of the database of interest. The physical presence of the entire online catalog database on some mainframe computer, optical disk, or hard disk no longer matters to the average use of the online catalog, because in essence an individualized database is created for users with each search. The organization of the entire database on its storage medium is now of little or no interest to librarians and patrons alike.

Remote access is a type of access that is not physical. This fact grates against a basic underlying assumption in librarianship. Historically, the dominant interpretation of the charge to facilitate access to documents has been the judicious assembling of local collections as the only effective means of providing convenient physical access to documents (Buckland, 1989B; 389). In the coming years physical access to documents will decline in importance. This fundamental change in the way users access information will shatter the equation between documents and texts. Texts will cease to be rigid, static things under the control of the author and publisher. Already with the advent of word processing the concept of logical, discrete versions of texts has lost much practical application and meaning. Texts have become much more unstable and fluid. The ability of online catalogs and other library systems to handle this new type of text is inadequate. Libraries have assumed that intellectual texts would always be relatively stable entities tied to tangible carriers.

It was suggested in Chapter 2 that the introduction of online catalogs made the physical presence of the catalog no longer relevant. Remote access now threatens the user's spatial orientation with the library as a whole. Some librarians have nurtured this new perception of the library as something akin to a database vendor, seeing nothing wrong or lamentable in having most users perceive the library as a service, not an edifice. Perhaps many librarians would like to see libraries achieve the same type of high-tech aura, premised on a physical intangibility, achieved by DIALOG, OCLC, BRS, and RLIN.

In the past libraries provided fragmented access to materials and services. One room contained the periodicals. Another room contained the nonfiction books. One desk was for finding information. Another desk was for checking out materials. With remote access to online catalogs, remote users have only one access point to the library—through the terminal monitor. This is one sense in which the catalog is becoming the library. If a remote user has a question during a search session, even her or his telephone will not be available unless the user logs-off.

Referring to this type of access as "remote access" reveals the dominant professional orientation to the issue. From the user's point of view, this new type of access is not remote at all. In fact, it is much closer to the project site than previous forms of access. Remote access is at once also close access, depending on the point of view taken.

Manipulating Downloaded Information

So far this chapter has examined changes in methods of access. The advent of personal computers, modems, and remote access also has opened up possibilities for new uses or applications of library information. Anything that is captured and downloaded in machine-readable form can be manipulated. The new information technology is transforming the use of library materials with computer-based techniques for identifying, locating, accessing, transferring, analyzing, manipulating, comparing, and revising texts (Buckland, 1989B; 394). Remote access to online catalogs has made the downloading and machine manipulation of bibliographic information easier, but this trend is not an essential or inevitable apsect of remote access development.

James Rice (1987, 1989B) has written several articles on the possible uses of bibliographic information downloaded into personal computers. What is new is the technical and economic feasibility to capture large quantities of bibliographic, textual, and numeric data in machine-readable form and to manipulate it, replicate it, and make it easily accessible on personal computers (De Gennaro, 1987; 32). Are there differences (behaviorially, practically, economically, and ethically) in the way users download and manipulate information from online database search services and online catalogs? Owners of online catalog databases tend to be less resistant than owners of other online bibliographic databases to end-user downloading and manipulation of bibliographic records.

Management of information by end-users is currently going through a transition from the maintenance of paper files to electronic files (Rice, 1987; 303). Should libraries do as much as possible or feasible to facilitate end-user management and manipulation of information, or should we assume a hands-off attitude? If we do not provide the information in a way that best helps the user, do we run the risk of losing portions of our clientele? As the power, speed, and capacity of personal information management improves, will individual scholars find less use for communal information management systems, commonly called libraries?

As a user builds a personal information system near a project or work site (e.g., home, office, or lab), the challenge is to integrate into the local system the information gained from diverse sources. Access to large amounts of information in electronic format creates as many problems as it solves. The central problem for scholars engaged in electronic research has gone through three distinct phases. The first problem was that of simply gaining access to the new automated databases. The second problem was controlling the massive amounts of downloaded information and data. Now the challenge is to integrate the diverse record formats of information gleaned from diverse remote databases (Weiskel, 1988; 9–10). If the format of the imported information is incompatible with the project information system, determining the intellectual compatibility and applicability of the incoming information requires more work.

The Purpose of Remote Access

Throughout this book it has been suggested that online catalogs need to be considered in a context larger than that of library catalogs. Specifically, in order to adequately understand online catalog development, an awareness of the basic concerns of the philosophy of technology and the unique characteristics of technological devices is necessary. This broadening of horizons also is necessary when considering the purpose of remote access to online catalogs. For example, Dow (1988; 83) suggests that remote access to an online catalog is not really about libraries and library catalogs, but about scholars gathering and reformatting information.

Remote access to online catalogs has brought actual use of online catalog systems much closer to their promise and potential. Ironically, remote access also has dealt a serious blow to the viability of the online library catalog. We now must ask whether the library catalog ever really was intended to serve the needs of serious scholars. Is remote access to online catalogs an attempt to make serious scholars frequent users of online catalogs? Is remote access a way of courting high-end-users?

Remote Access to What?

A distinction needs to be made between remote access to bibliographic records and remote access to the texts themselves. Some commentators may see remote access to bibliographic records as just the first step toward the ultimate goal of remote access to the texts themselves. Online remote access to full texts is the final goal of this line of technological development. This book has suggested, however, that some remote users seem to value the bibliographic records themselves as texts. There is some cause to worry, furthermore, that once widespread access to full texts of scholarly works online becomes technologically and economically feasible, libraries and online catalogs as middlemen will be bypassed by the producers of the texts. The publishers (or even the authors themselves) may evolve into institutional file servers, rather than relying on university libraries to fulfill that function.

New Users or New Delivery Method?

It remains to be confirmed whether, by and large, remote users are new users of the library catalog, or whether remote access is just a new way to access and deliver the same product. If the latter hypothesis is confirmed, perhaps remote access should not be seen as a threat to in-house use, but rather as a complement. Perhaps the economics of offering the same product in different formats is changing. To attract the entire potential market for a product or service, suppliers may need to offer their product in several formats. For example, just as *Psychological Abstracts* is available as a paper product, a CD-ROM package, a commercially vended database, and a locally mounted database, the online library catalog may be available in-house, through dial access, from a local area network, and via the regional and national computer networks. Each format would serve a different segment of the set of potential users of the online catalog. As library services are designed for specific user groups, however, libraries may discover that they do not have the resources to support all these specialized services. A crisis in the definition of the library's primary clientele may ensue.

Administrative Concerns About Remote Access

The prospect of widespread remote access to many library services raises several administrative concerns. Charles Bailey (1990; 91) identifies four reasons for administrative concerns about remote access, particularly remote access via the Internet: providing technical support is not a normal library function; the library owes allegiance to its primary clientele; remote access presents security risks to the automated system; and locally mounted proprietary databases often cannot be used by unaffiliated users. Brownrigg (1983; 111) sees remote access primarily as a policy issue. Remote access is a unique experiment with almost uncontrolled public access to computer utilities. The problem is to provide as much access as possible while still permitting fair and wide distribution of limited resources among as many people as possible.

Many library administrators fear that other libraries will use free remote access to an online catalog to download and clone the database, thus realizing considerable cost savings in the creation of a second library catalog. The distinction between a personal information system consisting largely of downloaded bibliographic records and a bona fide public access library will be difficult to make in the future as distributed processing and distributed access continue to expand. On the whole, however, most library administrators seem more concerned about the service demands surrounding the provision of remote access (especially to unaffiliated user groups) than the prospects of remote users pirating the database.

An academic library usually considers its campus users (faculty, staff and students) to be its primary clientele. This primary clientele really is the intersection of a specific geographic location (the campus) and a multitude of scholarly interests. The purpose of the library is to support those scholarly interests. In the new era of remote access to information, it may make more sense to define the library's mission along the axis of scholarly interests than along the axis of geographic location. Remote access of all types, especially access via the Internet and other national networks, may attract scholars with similar interests yet distant geographic locations to the same library catalog. The valiant attempt to build a library with at least some information on all topics may give way to libraries with closely defined subject parameters. Most of the users of the library will be those people interested in that closely defined subject. The users will access the library's information from diverse, remote locations. If this scenario begins to materialize, the possibility of allowing the users to act as gatekeepers or referees of the information in the system becomes more feasible. A university should be interested in increasing the productivity of faculty, students, and staff. But many universities, particularly private institutions, may be reluctant to support remote access if most access users are not part of the traditional primary clientele.

Remote Access as Experienced by Remote Users

We have examined the implications of remote access for the library and the parent institution, but what are the implications for the remote user? When users are confronted with a smorgasbord of more than one hundred online catalogs available through the Internet, how will they react? When a user in Iowa is connected to a computer in Colorado, does the user have any sense of being in Colorado? The gradual weakening of the human sense of reality is the direct result of modern technology (Hardison, 1989; 321). Is remote access to online catalogs creating a new sense of bibliographic reality? Before that can be answered, more theoretical and research work needs to be done on the established sense of bibliographic reality. An interesting research project would be to follow remote access from the perspective of a single user, rather than from the perspective of a single automated system. Remote access to online catalogs certainly alters the user's relationship to space and time. Space is devalued, and time spent in front of a terminal often is perceived differently than time spent in other pursuits. Perhaps what needs to be studied, however, are the changes that occur to the remote user's sense of bibliography and the flow of information. Perhaps remote access results in subtle changes in the user's sense of ownership, intellectual property, and the relationship between bibliographic records and intellectual texts.

Remote access to online catalogs seems to empower users to be more productive and to better control the means of production. What sense of power do users develop when they are able to access a significant amount of information from their work areas, and are able to manipulate the information once it has been downloaded? Heidegger wrote that "technology . . . develops in itself a specific kind of discipline and a unique kind of consciousness of conquest" (quoted in Zimmerman, 1990; 214).

New Experiences of Redundancies

The redundancy of information contained in many online catalogs quickly will become a nuisance to remote users. They may long for access to a true union catalog, such as OCLC or RLIN, where the emphasis (ideally) is on unique bibliographic items, not local holdings. One goal of information dissemination (and education in general, for that matter) is absolute redundancy, in the sense that all people would know (or at least have easy access to) all recorded information. In this sense redundancy is a pure good. In a practical sense, however, redundancy can be bad, especially when the redundancies occur across online catalog databases. For example, if 75 percent of the bibliographic records on a topic in a second online catalog are the same as the records in a first, it is inefficient for the user to wade through the retrieved set of items in the second catalog just to identify the unique items. When a user has access to fifty or more online catalogs, the search for new, unique items in each online catalog will be very tedious and frustrating. The current system of online catalogs as a group does not help the individual user identify unique texts that may be useful during a project. Shared cataloging has advanced much more rapidly than shared catalogs.

The Future of Remote Access

In the past, assuming the desired item had been identified, distance was the principal barrier to access. Now time, money, and procedural knowledge about remote access are the main barriers. What remains to be seen is whether, as the size of remote user groups grow, their unique characteristics, compared to in-house users, will evaporate. Economics may inhibit the growth of remote access, because telecommunications costs have not fallen as dramatically as costs for computer processing power and machine-readable data storage (Arms, 1990; 25). Perhaps most remote users really want remote access to the collection itself, rather than to the catalog. The question of the information really desired and sought by most remote users remains unresolved.

Distance between information storage and retrieval systems and users is not an entirely bad thing—not something to be overcome at almost any cost. A user working on a project does not want texts and information intruding into the work area unannounced and uninvited. As databases proliferate, grow in size, offer easier access from almost any location, the real growth sector in the information industry may not be in helping people find information, but rather in helping them keep unwanted inMolformation at a distance.

Merging Libraries and Computing Centers

Remote access to online catalogs raises several institutional issues. The development has generated increased campus interest in the library catalog as a resource. Where do online library catalogs function within the broader mission of the nation's system of universities and research centers? Librarians finally are accepting the fact that there will be close ties between the concerns of librarianship and the concerns of computing and telecommunications providers for the foreseeable future. It is undeniable that there is some convergence between library services, computing services, and telecommunications services (Buckland, 1989B; 391). Columbia University's announced intentions of integrating many of the library and computer center functions through a mutually accessible computer communications network known as the Doughnut may serve as a national model for cooperation between libraries and computing centers (Weiskel, 1986; 561). Areas where close cooperation between libraries and computing centers could be beneficial include new and expanded indexing structures, retrospective conversion of materials to machine-readable form, improved access to information, security precautions, and cost containment (Molholt, 1985; 286).

The real issue behind the possibility of merging libraries and computing centers is the admission that the library cannot respond alone to the new information environment on campus. Librarians simply lack the expertise in certain areas to do what is needed. The library often is considered the heart of a campus, but it has tended to be (perhaps even preferred to be) a lonely heart. A secret fear of many librarians is that the library is actually the liver of the campus—the old seat of the emotions—while the computing center has become the true heart.

Missions of Libraries and Computing Centers

The ultimate immediate challenge for libraries and computing centers is to enhance the organization and accessibility of information that already exists within the university environment, including library-owned materials (Molholt, 1989; 96B). Perhaps libraries should focus on published information that was produced outside the university, while computing centers should focus on raw data and unpublished information produced within the university. Libraries tend to deal with textual information, whereas computing centers tend to deal with databased information. Libraries, as the name implies, have traditionally been places with a special interest in books. Computing centers, as the name also implies, have a special interest in another communication vehicle.

Kilgour thinks combining the two institutions would be a bad move, because the interests of the two groups are fundamentally different. The most important difference to note regarding remote access to online catalogs is whether remote access to the online catalog is routed through the university's central, shared computer or directly to the library's dedicated computer (Jamieson and Dolan, 1985; 4). The library should become an information support center (Molholt, 1985; 285). Computing centers also are drifting toward information management. They used to be involved primarily in number manipulations and hardware support, but now the focus of computing center activities is on information management—manifested in the provision of word processing stations, courseware support, and data file interpretation (Molholt, 1989; 96a).

As noted in Chapter 3, academic libraries are relative newcomers in being responsible for the transmission of information, and uncertainty about the library's role in that function is pertinent to this discussion. Part of the uncertainty stems from suggestions that emphasis on the transmission of bibliographic information comes at the cost of an older commitment to educating the primary clientele in the retrieval of published information. Subordinating the university library within an information technology group may be emphasizing a process (automation and telecommunications) over a program (educational resources and services) (Weber, 1988; 16).

Images of Libraries and Computing Centers

Another benefit of closer working relationships between libraries and computing centers is a melding of the images of both groups. The image of the librarian as a conservative bibliophile is waning as the image of the computing service staff's lack of commitment to service diminshes (Woodsworth, 1988; 29). A merging of the two units could result in an image of the staff that is both service-oriented and technologically apt.

Libraries are beginning to look to computing centers to supply them the computing power and technical expertise needed to support the acquisition and operation of local online electronic data files (De Gennaro, 1987; 40). Computing centers always have been interested most in access to, and manipulation of, information and data. They have never been too interested in the acquistion of information for future use. They have been pioneers in exploring ways to store more information as cheaply as possible, and they possess a high degree of technical expertise (Molholt, 1985; 286).

Libraries have become very user-friendly, service-oriented organizations. They have long familiarity with complex, highly structured files and collections. They strive to make access easy and egalitarian. Librarians tend to possess some subject expertise. They have an appreciation for standards and cooperation.

David Weber (1988; 6–7) suggests, however, that there are fundamental differences between academic libraries and academic information technology centers (ITCs), primarily because libraries have an established function within the university, while ITCs are relatively recent phenomena. The academic library has a distinctive scholarly professional culture, while the newer ITCs on campuses have the characteristics of dynamic international growth industries. The political tensions are grounded in the library's fear of losing its professional status, institutional role, and funding. Because the services provided by the two centers tend to overlap, they tend to chase the same dollars (Weiskel, 1986; 551). University administrators take a dim view of two similar services on campus that lead to duplication and waste. Administrators will not tolerate battles for competitive exclusion between libraries and computing centers (Weiskel, 1986; 554).

Katharina Klemperer (1989; 144) reports that the relationship and division of turf between the computer center and the library's automation department has been good. Both service points are based on a library model of service. The computer center provides facilities management, including operator services, management of hardware maintenance contracts, system administration, and backup services. The automation department within the library system concentrates on systems analysis and application programming.

Institutional Valuation of Information

All of this activity and struggle suggests that institutional interest in information storage, retrieval, and dissemination is increasing. It is unclear whether the value of information and information access has risen on academic campuses, resulting in a shift of information control away from relatively autonomous libraries and computing centers, or if the technological development has made realization possible of a long dormant institutional interest in the control of access to information.

In the coming years the library will be just one of several available nodes in the new information web. The library will be used only to the extent that it offers either unique kinds of information or commonly available forms of information that are less expensive and/or more convenient than those offered elsewhere (Weiskel, 1986; 550). Networking and related technology is the challenge and goal that will draw libraries and computing centers ever closer (Molholt, 1989, 96B).

In certain instances the network providing access to the online catalog from multiple sites will become more valuable to the university than the online catalog it was designed to provide access to. Lynch (1989B; 62) suggests that the thinking at the University of California has evolved from perceiving the MELVYL online catalog as a single resource requiring a remote access network to recognizing the necessity of a general purpose network providing access to many information resources, including MELVYL.

De Gennaro (1987; 41) thinks that full-scale mergers are neither necessary nor imminent, but greater voluntary cooperation, perhaps including some administrative reorganization such as occurred at Columbia in 1986, may be necessary. The predicted merger between libraries and computing centers—perhaps never a comfortable idea to either side— has instead evolved into a kind of functional cooperation (Molholt, 1989; 96a).

Academic Networks

The growth of local, regional, national, and international networks for electronic scholarly communication in the last half of the 1980s has been phenomenal. Lynch (1989B) provides a good overview of the history of this growth in California. Remote access to library catalogs could become increasingly popular as more scholars incorporate network communication into their scholarly styles. The predominant academic network applications have been remote access and electronic mail, with file transfer a distant third, and all other applications negligible compared to the top three (1989B; 73). If traffic for applications such as online catalogs, which are operationally critical to an organization, are carried over to general purpose networks, provision must be made to protect the integrity of these services in the face of resource constraints or unexpected resource demands (1989B; 75). The prospect of providing service to many unaffiliated remote users remains politically troublesome at the institutional level. Libraries with online catalogs now are able to encourage both formal and informal scholarly communication, whereas in the past the library was associated with formal, published scholarly communication only.

Shifting Funding Structures

The basis of most funding of libraries is geographic. The citizens of the community, school district, corporation, institution, or state fund the materials and services available in the local library. Susan Baerg Epstein believes that the growth of remote access to machine-readable databases will undermine the concept of a user's home or local library (Drabenstott, 1985; 110). As remote access to library databases becomes prevalent, usage patterns will change much sooner than the politics and economics of funding structures for libraries. If it is true that the library's primary clientele is not the group taking advantage of remote access, either the library can consider the service a secondary service, one of the first to be cut during eras of fiscal constraint, or it can redefine its notion of primary clientele.

Total University Information Systems

While libraries and computing centers have been engaged in skir-mishes over turf, the demands for efficient university-wide data transmis-sion may have swallowed both combatants. In this area librarians may not have been able to see the forest for the trees. In general, librarians have not been leaders in formulating campus-wide information policies and plans for the university (Weiskel, 1989; 12).

If teaching and research are the two principal functions of the univers-ity, Weiskel has serious doubts about the survival of the university as a forum for these activities. If university communication systems do not keep up with off-campus developments in business, industry, and retail enter-prises, researchers gradually will dissociate themselves from the university environment. Weiskel (1988) also believes that the new concepts and skills surrounding integrated scholarly information systems (ISIS) are not being taught in the traditional academic classrooms, and that they probably would be taught better by librarians and computing center personnel.

During discussions of all these possibilities and political battles, the needs of the academic user trying to pursue an information need or advance a project should not be lost. Because most users want computing to support their professional projects, the traditional separation of types of academic computing (e.g., academic, administrative, and library) becomes a hin-drance to the efficient advancement of the project (Buckland, 1987; 267). Even the distinction between personal and institutional computing blurs when an information need or project constitutes a cognitive clearing of required work and perceived possibilities. As online catalog systems move beyond traditional library catalog functions and goals toward becoming a vital tool in an era of enhanced electronic scholarly communication, the distance and formality that used to exist between the creator and the end-user may diminish. The barriers to direct communication between the producer and the consumer of intellectual works are falling down. This probably will affect both production and consumption behaviors. Middlemen, who pay close attention to storage and retrieval practices and behaviors, should be aware of changes taking place in other areas of the flow of information.

Chapter 14
Future Prospects

Decline and Fall of the Library Catalog

Perhaps the library catalog as we know it is dying, but the information profession simply has not realized it, or admitted it. Whatever assumes the name of library catalog in the future will not serve the same purpose as did the library catalogs in the late nineteenth century and most of the twentieth century. New production, storage, retrieval, and manipulation methods will place new demands on library catalogs. Users will search the online catalog in new ways.

If the online catalog is like an aging empire, the forces of internal and external decay are numerous. The decline of the importance of ownership of information, including the slipping positive correlation between what a library owns and what the user has easy access to, will cause a fundamental reexamination of the importance of library collections and the intent of the library catalog to provide access to a collection. The major premise of any library catalog—that physical location of the item is a primary factor in the easy accessibility to it—is slowly losing its truth value. Remote access to online catalogs is one cause of this fundamental shift. In the future many users of information stored electronically will neither know nor care where the information is physically stored. This certainly does not imply that users should not or will not care about the ultimate intellectual source of the information—the creator of the intellectual work. The maintainers of online catalogs have been tardy in confronting this trend and its implications.

The declining importance of the book as an information vehicle will force the catalog to include new formats. The composition of library collections is changing faster than the catalogs that supposedly provide access to the items in the collection. The principal causes of this diminution in value are the internal slipping of the bonds between the physical item and the intellectual work and the external rise in value of other information-carrying physical items, with journal articles in the vanguard. Those who design and maintain online catalog systems realize this and are taking steps to shift the emphasis and content of online catalogs to other media.

The crisis of the concept of a library catalog, wrought by technological

234

advances, may lead to the complete obsolescence of the library catalog. The demands and expectations of users, as their needs and interests slowly move away from information normally contained in a library catalog, may lead to a redefinition of a library's primary clientele along subject interest lines, rather than political and/or geographic lines. And the increasing malleability of information, causing users to want to deconstruct and reconstruct information to meet their demands with little regard for the original structure and format of the information, will lead to a crisis of the text.

Declining Importance of Books

What are called online catalogs must move away from being thought of primarily as the principal access to the book collection of a library or system of libraries. Research libraries now spend approximately 70 percent of their materials budgets on serials (Pitkin, 1988; 769). The demand can only grow louder that libraries quit spending so much money on online catalogs to provide access to a minor portion of their collections.

The book is beleaguered. Books may disappear both as physical objects and as a forum for extended argument or discussion (Lacey, 1982; 111). They probably will disintegrate rather than disappear. This disintegration will not involve a physical disintegration of the materials comprising books (although this is a severe problem), but rather the disintegration of the economic and intellectual advantages of organizing information in a book format. As interest in documents wanes, because documents no longer are important to intellectual access to works, researchers can channel their interests toward the cognitive aspects of the users or seekers of information, or to the intellectual works themselves and the structures of areas of knowledge. Cognitive mapping and diagrams of externally stored intellectual works will become much more important than the storage of documents.

Declining In-House Use of the Library

Throughout the history of libraries, librarians have assumed not only that libraries need to own and warehouse the materials, but also that libraries needs to provide space and a congenial environment for users. Remote use of online catalogs today may force a rethinking of that assumption in the near future. Users may soon perform many basic library transactions from remote locations (Drabenstott, 1988; 106). For a long time many librarians have bemoaned the fact that many people perceive the library as a warehouse for materials. In school and academic settings, many students perceive the library as a relatively quiet place to study. Online catalogs, remote access, and full text databases will allow the library to overcome the image of a study space with attached warehousing; yet, now that the possibilities can be realized, many librarians in the profession are reluctant to proceed.

Less Subject Access

An era characterized by a long-term decline in controlled vocabulary subject searching may be underway. It appears to have been preceded by a brief period of high interest in subject access. Markey and other researchers have found that the introduction of online catalogs seemed to increase the amount of subject searching being done, compared to subject searching in the card catalog. One study found that the introduction of the online subject catalog increased the proportion of subject searches performed at the public catalog from 27 percent to 49 percent (Lipetz and Paulson, 1987; 610). The subtle encouragements from the new devices to engage in controlled vocabulary subject searching behavior may have contributed to this rise in subject searching.

The research summarized earlier indicates that current dial access users of at least one online catalog search more by author and title than by subject. It remains to be seen whether this trend away from subject access will continue, as more patrons and more diverse patron groups gain remote access to the online catalog. As the profession is poised to begin major efforts to improve subject access to bibliographic records, we need to ask if the era of controlled vocabulary subject access is waning.

Always Full Text Retrieval?

Another basic assumption in need of examination is the tenet that most or nearly all users of online catalogs wish to ultimately retrieve the full text of the documents found. Is it correct to assume, as Arms (1990B; 314) and others do, that bibliographic information always is secondary information, mere information about texts? Is the retrieval of the full text the final object of most searches of online catalogs? Should the online catalog, as Buckland suggests, move toward becoming an online bibliography? Access is more important than ownership in the new online environment. As complete access to the full text becomes less valued and practiced, the integrity of texts and the validity of applications of texts becomes more suspect. It no longer can be assumed that most users of texts intend to, and actually do, read the entire text, from beginning to end in a linear fashion.

Library's Image

A deterioration of the image of the library will result as libraries shift from physical presence and ownership to remote access. The deterioration probably will not result so much in a shift from generally favorable user reactions toward the library to generally unfavorable reactions, but rather in a steady erosion of the user's mental model of the mission and organization of the library system. The idea of the library is being transformed from a collection of materials with requisite supporting services to a diffuse, perhaps even amorphous, information access and support system (Molholt, 1985; 287). Libraries may become communication networks and file servers with little or no real physical presence on campus. Libraries my be going the way of Dialog and BRS. The future will be characterized by distributed processing as well as distributed access.

This gradual erosion in the usual spatial and temporal modes of familiarity will create user confusion and alienation. Perhaps users accept their initial search results, rather than manipulate them to increase recall or precision, because they do not quite know where they are. They cannot conceptualize the content and structure of the online catalog in the same way they can see and imagine the content and structure of a card or book catalog. Remote access to online catalogs will only exacerbate this problem. Remote users of the library may have no physical entity to which they can relate. The library becomes just a phone number (or a telnet address) and an interface.

Libraries and Society

Today the U.S. information environment is cluttered and fragmented. Technology is ushering in a profusion of new players and relationships into the library and information industry. Before the new technology arrived, libraries were the major or sole source of scholarly information. Now they are losing their market share (De Gennaro, 1987; 17). Librarians need to be fully cognizant of the intents and actual uses of the systems and services offered through the library. The effects of our beliefs and biases on both system design and user behavior must become a subject of study.

Costs

Cost efficiencies, as well as technological efficiencies, have a way of presenting themselves as problems, then resolving themselves, so there are relatively few policy decisions to make about costs. In the past, discussions of costs and technological advances have precluded discussions of pedagogical, philosophical, and ethical issues about online catalogs. Nevertheless, costs and technological possibilities will continue to influence information storage and retrieval procedures.

Online catalogs have proven to be much more costly than originally anticipated. Early arguments supporting the development of online catalogs promised cost savings, primarily through reductions in staff. When all of the hidden and ongoing costs are taken into consideration, just the opposite seems to be the case. Joseph Matthews provides a useful overview of cost elements, both start-up and ongoing (Matthews, 1985; 83–88).

Questions about the real costs of online catalog systems remain unanswered. To what extent should cost considerations be admitted into the online catalog debate? Is the online catalog one of the essential functions of the library? What is the best cost ratio between access mechanisms and the acquisition of materials? What are the basic elements of cost in an online catlog system, and which cost area (for example, telecommunications) is rising the fastest? Could a system be designed that could be modified as the cost structure fluctuates over time, just as some power generators can use different materials, depending on which is cheaper at any given time? Many information systems ignore or downplay the cost efficiencies to be realized by the eventual end-user of the system. Remote access to online catalogs, and perhaps eventually to online libraries, allows end-users to realize significant cost and productive efficiencies, but remote access is not being supported on the wave of that argument.

Rather than own their catalogs and database delivery systems, libraries in the future may purchase such services from commercial and semi-commercial vendors, just as they now purchase indexing and shared cataloging services (Drabenstott, 1988; 111). Perhaps more and more of the costs and responsibilities of catalog maintenance will pass from the library to other participants in the flow of information.

The costs of storing printed material on-site may be higher than developing better remote access mechanisms to other sites. Some commentators are predicting that the costs of storing information on paper will become prohibitive in the twenty-first century (Drake, 1989; 117). As noted earlier, however, there is a large psychological hurdle to get over before a library will be ready to rely heavily or exclusively on remote access to information. Locally stored and locally controlled intellectual materials are still very attractive. The desire for control over materials is common to both middlemen and consumers.

Libraries should be encouraging readers and users to use the library without actually coming into the building. Many institutions, from banks to libraries, are reluctant to encourage remote access and remote transactions because a loss of institutional identity is feared. The feeling that the library is (or at least should be) the center of academic life on campus is still strong, and extensive remote access threatens that image of the library. Traditional primary patron groups probably will visit the library less often, and secondary, unaffiliated patron groups will have equal access to many library services and materials.

Unfulfilled Elitism?

As more emphasis is placed on online catalogs and more databases are made available through a single system, they may become just another type of overburdened library system, similar to interlibrary loan and reference service. Nielsen (1988) has argued that traditional reference service is fundamentally flawed and elitist, because if all users of the library who have a need for reference assistance actually used the reference service, the service would be vastly overburdened.[1] The same elitism may lurk in the idea of remote access to online library catalogs. Such a configuration is able to provide only a highly selective (and costly) amount of information about a highly selected subset of the library's collection (and an even more elective subset of the information readily available to the user) to a highly selective group of users. As the size of the databases grow, along with the number of users of online catalogs, will the systems be able to keep up with demand? Response time will be the first thing to suffer. Minimal standards for catalog users continue to rise. Card catalog users had to be able to alphabetize. Online catalog users had to be able to type without errors. Now remote users of online catalogs are expected to have access to computers in the home or workplace. The one skill we do not encourage users to develop is a basic knowledge of the methods of producing, storing, retrieving, and interpreting scholarly information.

Machine Readability

As optical scanning becomes more economically feasible, the horizons of machine-readable data are expanding. There may come a time when all textual information, including handwritten matter, becomes machine-readable. The dichotomy between printed and machine-readable information will become an historical curiosity. The ability to transfer information from printed form to machine-readable form and back will be achievable so easily and economically that it no longer will be an issue and major concern.

Futures for the Online Library Catalog

The library catalog, particularly the online version, has outgrown its original purpose—to provide access to items owned by an individual library. For all the published information about online catalogs, there has been remarkably little discussion about what online catalogs should become. Nevertheless, the outlines of the main options are beginning to emerge.

Buckland, for example, suggests that the catalog should become a bibliography, where location information and ownership records are occasionally attached, but are not an essential aspect of the system. This direction would bring online library catalogs closer to the databases maintained by the major bibliographic utilities, where the goal and emphasis is on providing bibliographic records for unique intellectual works, with holdings information a secondary consideration.

Another possible future for the online catalog is to have it become an online library, where full texts are available online. Kilgour and Pfaffenberger are two commentators who seem to advocate this scenario. The development challenges are to be able to store and retrieve vast amounts of full text. If such a direction of development is pursued, the value of the bibliographic record as a value-added surrogate for the full text of the intellectual item would lose merit as more full text becomes available through the online catalog. The current debate about how much (and what) information from the full text should be included in the bibliographic record would become moot.

Current online catalogs function more as access mechanisms than as true service points. The online catalog could become a new type of bona fide service point within the library, similar to the way automated teller machines have become service points in the banking industry. For example, a recent project at the University of Kansas libraries sought to provide a number of self-service circulation functions through the online catalog.[2]

The online catalog could become a venue for truly interactive scholarly information exchanges. Scholars would be able to attach comments or abstracts to bibliographic records for intellectual items. They would be able to download retrieved sets, manipulate them, and send them to students and colleagues. The online catalog would be subsumed under the development of a bigger system for scholarly information exchange. If this development path is pursued, the distinctions between the formal and informal colleges will become blurred. Electronic mail conferences provide a glimpse of the social aspects of the new era of scholarly communication.

The online catalog may become more like a commercial vendor of databases, not only in the search mechanics and options, but also as a database vendor/provider, file server, and gateway to other catalogs and vendors. This development option has received considerable funding and interest in the last decade.

Research Trends

In some respects this book has focused on meta-research—the conditions under which online catalog research can be possible and fruitful. Much more meta-analysis of the research activity surrounding online catalogs and their use is needed.

Regardless of the direction of future online catalog development, research into online catalogs must continue to develop as well. The research agenda for the first generation of online catalogs has spent itself. The next generation of research needs to be formulated. There is no more debate on whether online catalogs are technologically possible, desirable, economically viable, or acceptable to users. It is simply accepted by librarians, users, and governing bodies that library catalogs must and will go online (De Gennaro, 1987; 19). An expanded program of research in library and information science will require changes in institutional structures, graduate curricula, and professional philosophies (Molholt, 1988; 93). This book has focused on suggested changes to the professional philosophies.

Everyone assumes that all research into online catalogs is prescriptive. The assumption seems to be that, if research does not offer ways to improve the sytems, the value of the research is highly suspect. A major thesis of this book has been that the nature of the online catalog as a modern technological device may preclude the possibility of prescriptive research.

A reasonable fear, from the standpoint of library educators, if not designers, is that if certain trends in online catalog design continue, in the long term we will simply circumvent library literacy in much the same way fast food restaurants circumvent literacy by using pictures of food as key caps. Systems need to be designed so that the long-term educational effects on users are maximized.

The next generation of research into online catalog use should be characterized by an investigation into user behavior as well as attitudes, conducted by a generally disinterested group of rsearchers, using methods that build on previous research and are easily replicated, with results that are applicable. The research agenda should be designed to move away from massive, costly, one-time studies toward small-scale, efficient, easily replicated studies. The limitations of single-site studies need to be overcome. A better balance must be found between local studies that are easily applicable to the specific situation (and easily justified to the funding body) and broad studies that add to the collective knowledge of the profession. Hancock-Beaulieu (1989; 42) thinks that more qualitative research oriented toward the user's task is needed. Users' projects and the behavior undertaken to complete those projects, rather than impact studies of user attitudes, should become the focus of research.

Much more study needs to be done on institutional policies and individual attitudes toward dismantling texts. Scholarship is based on the dismantling of texts by readers, and a library catalog can be seen as a distillation of texts. This appears to be a situation where the prevailing drive in information technological development to make the machine perform more tasks has been reversed. It is acceptable for humans, but not computers, to deconstruct texts.

Why has research into online catalogs failed to draw on information from other pertinent fields? The areas of psychology, communication studies, philosophy, technology, computer science, and information science all are pertinent, yet most research has become inbred, citing the same books, articles, and studies.

Lynne Brindley (1989; 63) suggests that the focus of research will turn away from systems and bibliographic records toward users and their information-gathering habits, studied at the individual level. The focus of attention may shift from the functioning of the system, including the interface projected by the system, to the users of the system, their lived experience of using the system, and their needs. Currently this is the missing link in understanding online library catalogs and their use.

Design Trends

The dominant trend in the design of online catalogs is to make system functions as transparent to the user as possible. Transparency has been equated with user-friendliness. As connections between different catalogs are established, this desire to make online catalogs transparent remains a goal of design and implementation.

Perhaps the designers of online catalogs have been too preoccupied with ensuring that the results of each search statement are maximized, especially regarding recall, like a business corporation overly attentive to its profitability at the end of each quarter. Far less attention has been given to the long-term learning and retention of searching principles and skills by the users of the system. The needs of students and faculty engaged in learning and research should guide online catalog development (Bechtel, 1988; 32). Although this is true, the forces of economic and technological development have too much inertia to be swayed. A fundamental decision made when designing an online catalog is whether the system will be designed to satisfy the information needs of the projected user population as quickly and as easily as possible, or whether the system will try to encourage the user to be a better retriever of information over a longer period of time, after the immediate information need has been satisfied.

Conceptual Orientation

There are three major design questions to answer when designing a bibliographical retrieval tool: What will count as one item, and which items are to be included (the question of unit and scope); what information is to be supplied about each item; and what information, including organization, indexing, and arrangement, is necessary to allow one to find an item (the question of access) (Wilson, 1983; 9). For better or worse, library catalogs cast their lot with the locally owned physical item as the basic unit of access, rather than the intellectual content of the work. As the importance of the unique characteristics of the static physical item declines, the value of the information contained in library catalogs will decline as well.

Problems with the user interface will persist. The greatest constraints on the design of nonspecialist interactive retrieval systems are those imposed by the demands of presenting information to the user. Features or facilities which might seem useful or computationally apt are often impossible to present concisely or comprehensibly to actual users (Walker, 1988; 23).

The current economics of design seems to favor modifications to current systems rather than totally new designs. A time may soon come, however, when the economies and advantages of modifying the existing online systems will disappear. As the current online catalog systems age, there will come a time when the basic assumptions realized in current system designs about economies of scale, economies of processing, and user needs and skills will be so outdated that the systems will be abandoned rather than patched up.

As online catalogs move beyond being just book catalogs to include circulation, acquisitions, serials, and gateways to other databases, the potential for internal political fighting among departments within the organization over design and scope issues increases (Estabrook, 1983, 73). Online catalogs may become targets of hostile takeover attempts from other groups within the institutional environment.

It is difficult to defend the thesis that library users have been instrumental in the development of library technologies (Lee Jones, 1984; 154). Some commentators feel, however, that the needs of the users, not technological innovation or economics, should be the primary force in the future development of online catalogs. The design and management of online catalogs should be influenced primarily by the needs and abilities of the user (Azubuike, 1988; 275). Researchers need to design effective modes of access that can assist the users in the core processes of database searching while accounting for their personal traits, differences in information-seeking styles, and lack of motivation to learn how to use new information technology (Ercegovac, 1989; 26). Users want to feel in control of their searching, and they want to be able to learn and relearn a system easily. These should be the principal items on the design agenda (Arret, 1985; 118). As databases grow in size, early emphasis on high recall will gradually be replaced by emphasis on greater precision during searches of the online catalog (see Lynch, 1989A). One of the main theses of this book has been that most online catalog users always have been more interested in precision than recall.

The creators of online catalog systems need to design intriguing user interfaces which entice and challenge users (Culkin, 1989; 176). Nothing will increase user indifference toward a facility faster than a persistent pattern of the facility's inability or unwillingness to acquire what users need for their work. If libraries come to regard user needs as ephemeral or peripheral, current users can quite easily come to regard libraries as dispensable (Weiskel, 1986; 558).

Libraries of the Future

Remote access to online catalogs may be a significant step toward the obsolescence of the library catalog. As libraries get better at informing users about information held locally by the institution, the value of that information declines.

Do libraries as we now know them have a future? What will libraries of the future look like? Libraries will become distribution points or switches for electronic information, both bibliographic and textual (Brownrigg, 1983; 108). If this is true, libraries will be heavily involved in the transportation of information, which historically has not been one of their functions.

Academic libraries continually worry about obsolescence or replacement by other middlemen in the flow of information. In the future the competition for the execution of the essential functions of the middleman in the flow of information will be intense. The strongest competition, however, may come not from other middlemen, such as private information services, but from current producers and consumers. Academic libraries will be operating in a decentralized environment in which users have simultaneous access to personal, departmental, campus-wide, and national information resources (Arms, 1990C; 335).

Conclusion

We still have much to learn about the process of the development of specific information needs and their satisfaction. Any catalog form (or any information system, for that matter) should determine the structure of that development as little as possible. The system should be as open as possible, yet not be so open, with so many choices, that many users are disinclined to use it.

The online catalog should be more than a database or a gateway to a collection of databases. It should strive to present itself to users as a space or clearing in which the users feel relaxed and confident and free to explore and find the information they need or desire. At the same time, any information system should reveal to the user the accepted social structure for accessing and interpreting scholarly information. This is the paradox of the online catalog: by destroying our old sense of space (through such innovations as remote access and post-coordinated set creation of bibliographic information), the online catalog has opened up the possibility for a new sense of space. The online catalog should be more than a maze or trail of bread crumbs providing structured stimulus and response.

What we may be witnessing is the breakdown of the library as a city-state (each library with its own collection and limited geographical sphere of influence) and the emergence of a fledgling global information economy for academics and scholars, with remote access to online catalogs as a giant first step.

The struggle for control and balance within the academic library, with online catalog design and use as a stark example, is between the mind with its cultural programming and intuitive judgments, and electronic processes with their algorithms (see Beniger, 1986; 61). The challenge to the library and information profession is clear.

Notes

1. This argument may be questionable. Any producer or provider of a service would be overwhelmed if all potential users or consumers suddenly decided to buy the product or utilize the service. The better producers or service centers perform a market analysis to understand who is actually using the product or service.
2. Electronic mail message on the PACS-L Forum, May 7, 1990.

Reference List and Selected Bibliography

Abbott, John, and Jinnie Y. Davis. "Extending Service Beyond the Library Walls: Remote Access to Online Catalogs in Large Academic Libraries." Paper presented as part of conference program on *Remote Access by Users to Library Systems and Services*, moderator, Jinnie Y. Davis. Chicago, IL: American Library Association, 1988.

Adams, Judith A. "The Computer Catalog: A Democratic or Authoritarian Technology?" *Library Journal* 113 (February 1, 1988): 31–36.

Adams, Roy J. *Information Technology & Libraries: A Future for Academic Libraries.* Dover, NH: Croom Helm, 1986.

Aken, Robert A. "Meeting the Patron at the OPAC Crossroads: The Reference Librarian as an Online Consultant." *RQ* 28 (Fall 1988): 42–45.

Alzofon, Sammy R., and Noelle Van Pulis. "Patterns of Searching and Success Rates in an Online Public Access Catalog." *College and Research Libraries* 45 (March 1984): 110–115.

Anderson, Rosemary. "The Online Catalog and the Library Manager." In *The Impact of Online Catalogs*, ed. Joseph R. Matthews, 71–80. New York: Neal-Schuman, 1986.

Arms, Caroline R. "The Technological Context." In *Campus Strategies for Libraries and Electronic Information*, ed. Caroline R. Arms, 11–35. Rockport, MA: Digital Press, 1990A.

————. "Other Projects and Progress." In *Campus Strategies for Libraries and Electronic Information*, ed. Caroline R. Arms, 306–331. Rockport, MA: Digital Press, 1990B.

————. "The Context for the Future." In *Campus Strategies for Libraries and Electronic Information*, ed. Caroline R. Arms, 333–356. Rockport, MA: Digital Press, 1990C.

Arret, Linda. "Can Online Catalogs Be Too Easy?" *American Libraries* 16 (2) (February 1985): 118–120.

Association of Research Libraries. *User Instruction for Online Catalogs in ARL Libraries.* SPEC Kit 93. Washington, DC: Association of Research Libraries, Office of Management Studies, The Systems and Procedures Exchange Center (SPEC), 1983.

Association of Research Libraries. *Online Catalogs.* SPEC Kit 96. Washington, DC: Association of Research Libraries, Office of Management Studies, The Systems and Procedures Exchange Center (SPEC), 1983. ERIC ED 252 208.

Association of Research Libraries. *Remote Access to Online Catalogs.* SPEC Kit 142. Washington, DC: Association of Research Libraries, Office of Management Studies, The Systems and Procedures Exchange Center (SPEC), 1988.

Atherton, Pauline L. *Books Are for Use. Final Report to the Council on Library Resources, Syracuse University, School of Information Studies, Subject Access Project.* Syracuse, NY: Syracuse University, February 1978. ED 156 131. 172 pp.

Aveney, Brian. "Online Catalogs: The Transformation Continues." *Wilson Library Bulletin* 58 (6) (February 1984): 406–410.

Azubuike, Abraham A. "The Computer as Mask: A Problem of Inadequate Human Interaction Examined with Particular Regard to Online Public Access Catalogues." *Journal of Information Science* 14 (5) (1988): 275–283.

Bacon, Glenn C. "Forces Shaping the New Information Paradigm." In *Libraries and Information Science in the Electronic Age*, ed. Hendrick Edelman, 154–165. Philadelphia, PA: ISI Press, 1986.

Bailey, Charles W., Jr. "Public-Access Computer Systems: The Next Generation of Library Automation Systems." *Information Technology and Libraries* 8 (2) (June 1989): 178–185.

_____. "Libraries with Glass Walls." *The Public-Access Computer Systems Review* 1 (2) (1990): 91–93.

Baker, Betsy K. "A Conceptual Framework for Teaching Online Catalog Use." *Journal of Academic Librarianship* 12 (May 1986): 90–96.

Baker, Betsy K., and Brian Nielsen. "Optimizing System Monitoring Facilities for Online Catalog Instruction." In *Conference on Integrated Online Library Systems.* 2nd ed. Canfield, OH: Genaway and Associates, 1984, pp. 127–145.

Baker, Betsy K., and Beth A. Sandore. "The Online Catalog and Instruction: Maintaining the Balance on the Log." In *Conceptual Frameworks for Bibliographic Education*, ed. Mary Reichel and Mary Ann Ramey, 192–206. Littleton, CO: Libraries Unlimited, 1987.

Baldwin, David A., Anne T. Ostrye, and Diana W. Shelton. "The University of Wyoming Catalog Survey." *Technical Services Quarterly* 5 (4) (1988): 15–26.

Bates, Marcia J. "Rethinking Subject Cataloging in the Online Environment." *Library Resources and Technical Services* 33 (4) (October 1989): 400–412.

Bauer, Michael. "The Emerging Role of Workstations in the Library Environment." *Library Hi Tech* 6 (4) (1988): 37–46.

Bechtel, Joan M. "Developing and Using the Online Catalog to Teach Critical Thinking." *Information Technology and Libraries* 7 (1) (March 1988): 30–40.

Becker, Joseph. "Libraries, Society and Technological Change." *Library Trends* 27 (Winter 1979): 409–416.

Beckman, Margaret M. "Online Catalogs and Library Users." *Library Journal* 107 (November 1, 1982): 2043–2047.

Bell, Daniel. *The Coming of Post-Industrial Society: A Venture in Social Forecasting.* New York: Basic Books, 1973.

Beniger, James R. *The Control Revolution: Technological and Economic Origins of the Information Society.* Cambridge, MA: Harvard University Press, 1986.

Blagden, John. "Some Thoughts on Use and Users." *IATUL Quarterly* 2 (September 1988): 125–134.

Borgman, Christine L. "End User Behavior in an Online Information Retrieval System: A Computer Monitoring Study." *Research and Development in IR: Sixth Annual International Association for Computing Machinery (ACM) Special Interest Group in the Information Retrieval (SIGIR) Conference, Bethesda, MD, June 6–8, 1983*, ed. J. J. Kuehn, 17 (4) (1983): 162–176.

_____. "Why are Online Catalogs Hard to Use? Lessons Learned from Information-Retrieval Studies." *Journal of the American Society for Information Science* 37 (November 1986): 387–400.

Borgmann, Albert. *Technology and the Character of Contemporary Life.* Chicago, IL: University of Chicago Press, 1984.

Boss, Richard W. "Current Uses of Automated Systems: A Review and Status Report." In *Changing Technology: Opportunity and Challenge,* ed. Alphonse F. Trezza, 99–102. Boston, MA: G. K. Hall, 1989.

Brindley, Lynne J. "The Future of OPACS: An Academic Library Perspective." In *OPACs and Beyond: Proceedings of a Joint Meeting of the British Library, DBMIST, and OCLC,* 57–66. Dublin, OH: OCLC Online Computer Library Center, 1989.

Broadus, Robert N. "Online Catalogs and Their Users: A Review Article on the CLR Study of Online Catalogs." *College and Research Libraries* 44 (6) (November 1983): 458–467.

Brownrigg, Edwin B., and Clifford A. Lynch. "Online Catalogs: Through a Glass Darkly." *Information Technology and Libraries* 2 (March 1983): 104–115.

Brunning, Dennis R., Helen B. Josephine, and Harvey M. Sager. "New Publics for the Academic Library." In *Building on the First Century: Proceedings of the Fifth National Conference of the Association of College and Research Libraries, Cincinnati, Ohio, April 5–8, 1989,* ed. Janice C. Fennell, 6–8. Chicago, IL: Association of College and Research Libraries, 1989.

Buckland, Michael K. "Combining Electronic Mail with Online Retrieval in a Library Context." *Information Technology and Libraries* 6 (1987): 266–271.

———. "Bibliography, Library Records, and the Redefinition of the Library Catalog." *Library Resources and Technical Services* 32 (4) (October 1988): 299–311.

———. "The Vanishing Library Catalog: Access, Bibliography, and Technology." In *Changing Technology: Opportunity and Challenge,* ed. Alphonse F. Trezza, 87–98. Boston, MA: G. K. Hall, 1989A.

———. "Foundations of Academic Librarianship." *College and Research Libraries* 50 (4) (July 1989B): 389–396.

Byrne, Alex, and Mary Micco. "Improving OPAC Subject Access: The ADFA Experiment." *College and Research Libraries* 29 (September 1988): 432–441.

Carrison, Dale K. "Is 'User Friendly' Really Possible in Library Automation?" In *23rd Clinic on Library Applications of Data Processing (1986),* 45–51. Urbana-Champaign, IL: University of Illinois at Urbana-Champaign, Graduate School of Library and Information Science, 1987.

———. "The Online Catalog: Reference/User Friend or Foe?" In *Changing Technology: Opportunity and Challenge,* ed. Alphonse F. Trezza, 63–74. Boston, MA: G. K. Hall, 1989.

Carson, Sylvia MacKinnon, and Dace I. Freivalds. "MicroLIAS: Beyond the Online Public Access Catalog." *Library Hi Tech* 4 (15) (Fall 1986): 83–90.

Cart, Michael. "Caveats, Qualms, and Quibbles: A Revisionist View of Library Automation." *Library Journal* 112 (February 1, 1987): 38–41.

Chan, Lois Mai. "Library of Congress Class Numbers in Online Catalog Searching." *RQ* 28 (Summer 1989): 530–536.

Clark, Sharon E. "The Online Catalog: Beyond a Local Reference Tool." In *Twenty-Fourth Annual Clinic on Library Applications of Data Processing. Questions and Answers: Strategies for Using the Electronic Reference Collection,* ed. Linda Smith. Urbana-Champaign, IL: University of Illinois at Urbana-Champaign, Graduate School of Library and Information Science, 1989.

Cochrane, Pauline Atherton, and Karen Markey. "Catalog Use Studies—Since the Introduction of Online Interactive Catalogs: Impact on Design for Subject

Access." *Library and Information Science Research* 5 (4) (Winter 1983): 337–363.

Colaianni, Louis Ann. "Evaluating Online Catalogs: The Need for Data." In *The Impact of Online Catalogs*, ed. Joseph R. Matthews, 81–87. New York: Neal-Schuman, 1986.

Corey, James F., Helen H. Spalding, and Jeanmarie Lang Fraser. "Involving Faculty and Students in the Selection of a Catalog Alternative." *Journal of Academic Librarianship* 8 (6) (January 1983): 328–333.

Corsini, Raymond J., ed. *Encyclopedia of Psychology*. 4 vols. New York: John Wiley & Sons, 1984.

Costers, Look, and J. Buys. "The Results of an Experiment with an Online Public Access Catalogue." In *Future of Online Catalogues: Essen Symposium 30 September–3 October 1985*, ed. Ahmed H. Helal and Joachim W. Weiss, 340–358. Essen: Gesamthochschulbibliothek Essen, 1986.

Crawford, Walt. *Patron Access: Issues for Online Catalogs*. Boston, MA: G. K. Hall, 1987.

_____. *Current Technologies in the Library: An Informal Overview*. Boston, MA: G. K. Hall, 1988.

_____. "Public-Access Provocations: An Informal Column." *The Public-Access Computer Systems Review* 1 (1) (January 1990): 48–50.

Cuadra, Carlos A. "The Coming Era of Local Electronic Libraries." In *Libraries and Information Science in the Electronic Age*, ed. Hendrik Edelman, 11–22. Philadelphia, PA: isi Press, 1986.

Culkin, Patricia B. "Rethinking opacs: The Design of Assertive Information Systems." *Information Technology and Libraries* 8 (2) (June 1989): 172–177.

Dale, Doris Cruger. "Subject Access in Online Catalogs: An Overview Bibliography." *Cataloging and Classification Quarterly* 10 (½) (1989): 225–251.

Davis, Scott. "Dial Access Users of Online Catalogs: Responding to the Needs of BI's Newest User Group." *Illinois Libraries* 70 (10) (December 1988): 638–644.

DeBruijn, Debbie, and Arden Matheson. "University of Calgary: Remote Access to On-Line Catalogues." *Canadian Library Journal* 44 (August 1987): 225–228.

De Gennaro, Richard. "Library Automation and Networking: Perspectives on Three Decades." *Library Journal* 108 (April 1, 1983): 629–635.

_____. "Integrated Online Library Systems: Perspectives, Perceptions, and Practicalities." *Library Journal* 110 (February 1, 1985): 37–40.

_____. *Libraries, Technology, and the Information Marketplace: Selected Papers*. Boston, MA: G. K. Hall, 1987.

Dickson, Jean. "An Analysis of User Errors in Searching an Online Catalog." *Cataloging and Classification Quarterly* 4 (3) (Spring 1984): 19–38.

Diskin, Gregory M., and Thomas J. Michalak. "Beyond the Online Catalog: Utilizing the opac for Library Information." *Library Hi Tech* 3 (1) (1985): 7–13.

Dow, Elizabeth H. "The Impact of Home and Office Workstation Use on an Academic Library." Ph.D. diss., University of Pittsburgh, 1988. *DAI* 50 (1) (July 1989): 11A. 117pp.

Drabenstott, Jon, ed. "What Lies Beyond the Online Catalog?" *Library Hi Tech* 12 (1985): 105–114.

_____. "Beyond the Online Catalog: Great Potential and Profound Change." *Library Hi Tech* 6 (1) (1988): 101–111.

Drake, Miriam A. "Electronic Library of the Future, or Visions for the Twenty-First Century Are Okay But What Will We Do for the Rest of the Century?" In

OPACs and Beyond: Proceedings of a Joint Meeting of the British Library, DBMIST, and OCLC, 109–118. Dublin, OH: OCLC Online Computer Library Center, 1989.

————. "Georgia Institute of Technology." In *Campus Strategies for Libraries and Electronic Information,* ed. Caroline Arms, 157–175. Medford, MA: Digital Press, 1990.

Dubois, C. P. R. "Free Text vs. Controlled Vocabulary: A Reassessment." *Online Review* 11 (4) (August 1987): 243–253.

Ercegovac, Zorana. "Augmented Assistance in Online Catalog Subject Searching." *Reference Librarian* 23 (1989): 21–40.

Estabrook, Leigh. "The Human Dimension of the Catalog: Concepts and Constraints in Information Seeking." *Library Resources & Technical Services* 27 (January/March 1983): 68–75.

Farber, Evan Ira. "Catalog Dependency." *Library Journal* 109 (February 15, 1984): 325–328.

Fayen, Emily Gallup. "Microcomputers and Online Catalog: Changing How the Catalog Is Used." ED 281 523. Paper presented at the Annual Meeting of the American Library Association, New York, June 30, 1986.

————. "Loading Local Machine-Readable Data Files: Issues, Problems, and Answers." *Information Technology & Libraries* 8 (2) (June 1989): 132–137.

Ferguson, Douglas K. "Reference and Online Catalogs: Reflections and Possibilities." In *The Impact of Online Catalogs,* ed. Joseph R. Matthews, 25–33. New York: Neal-Schuman, 1986.

Fidel, Raya, and Dagobert Soergel. "Factors Affecting Online Bibliographic Retrieval: A Conceptual Framework for Research." *Journal of the American Society for Information Science* 34 (3) (1983): 163–180.

Freedman, Maurice J. "Must We Limit the Catalog?" *Library Journal* 109 (3) (February 1984): 322–324.

Freedman, Maurice J., and S. Michael Malinconico, eds. *The Nature and Future of the Catalog: Proceedings of the ALA's Information Science and Automation Divisions 1975 and 1977 Institutes on the Catalog.* Phoenix, AZ: Oryx, 1979.

Freeman, David. *Technology and Society: Issues in Assessment, Conflict, and Choice.* Chicago, IL: Rand McNally, 1974.

Freiburger, Gary A. "The Online Catalog: More than a Catalog Online." *Catholic Library World* 55 (5) (December 1983): 213–215.

Freiburger, Gary A., and Marjorie Simon. "Patron Use of an Online Catalog." In *Library and Information Technology Association National Conference: Crossroads,* 106–111. Chicago, IL: American Library Association, 1984.

Freivalds, Dace I., and Sylvia Carson. "Extending the OPAC: Creative Uses of Microcomputers to Enhance Library Services." Paper presented at the Second National Conference of the Library and Information Technology Association, Boston, MA, October 2–6, 1988. ERIC ED 305 091. 29pp.

Frost, Carolyn O. "Subject Searching in an Online Catalog." *Information Technology and Libraries* 6 (March 1987): 60–63.

————. "Title Words as Entry Vocabulary to LCSH: Correlation Between Assigned LCSH Terms and Derived Terms from Titles in Bibliographic Records with Implications for Subject Access in Online Catalogs." *Cataloging and Classification Quarterly* 10 (½) (1989): 165–179.

Gerhan, David R. "LCSH in vivo: Subject Searching Performance and Strategy in the OPAC Era." *Journal of Academic Librarianship* 15 (2) (May 1989): 83–89.

Gerrie, Brenda. *Online Information Systems: Use and Operating Characteristics, Limitations, and Design Alternatives.* Arlington, VA: Information Resources Press, 1983.

Gorman, Michael. "Online Access and Organization and Administration of Libraries." In *Online Catalogs, Online Reference: Converging Trends,* ed. Brian Aveney and Brett Butler, 153–164. Chicago, IL: American Library Association, 1984.

Hancock-Beaulieu, Micheline M. "Online Catalogues: A Case for the User." In *Online Catalog Research: Developments and Directions,* ed. Charles R. Hildreth, 25–46. London: The Library Association, 1989.

Hannabuss, Stuart. "The Importance of User Studies." *Library Review* (Summer 1987): 122–127.

Hardison, O. B., Jr. *Disappearing Through the Skylight: Culture and Technology in the Twentieth Century.* New York: Viking, 1989.

Heidegger, Martin. "The Question Concerning Technology." In *The Question Concerning Technology and Other Essays,* 3–35, trans. William Lovitt. New York: Harper and Row, 1977.

Helal, Ahmed H., and Joachim W. Weiss, eds. *Future of Online Catalogues: Essen Symposium.* Gesamthochschulbibliothek, Essen, 1986.

Henty, Margaret. "The User at the Online Catalogue: A Record of Unsuccessful Keyword Searches." *LASIE* 17 (September/October 1986): 47–52.

Herschman, Judith, Susan Swords Steffen, Gail Persky, Sue Rhee, and James G. Neal. "Tampering with the Online Catalog: A Look at the Issues—A Symposium." *Journal of Academic Librarianship* 12 (6) (January 1987): 340–349.

Hildreth, Charles R. *Online Public Access Catalogs: The User Interface.* Dublin, OH: OCLC, 1982.

_____. "Online Public Access Catalogs." In *Annual Review of Information Science and Technology,* vol. 20. White Plains, NY: Knowledge Industry Publication, 1985A, pp. 233–285.

_____. "Monitoring and Analyzing Online Catalog User Activity." *LS/2000 Communique* 4 (Summer 1985B): 3–6.

_____. "Beyond Boolean: Designing the Next Generation of Online Catalogs." *Library Trends* 35 (Spring 1987): 647–667.

_____. *Intelligent Interfaces and Retrieval Methods for Subject Searching in Bibliographic Retrieval Systems.* Washington, DC: Library of Congress, Cataloging Distribution Service, 1989A.

_____. "Extending the Access and Reference Service Capabilities of the Online Public Access Catalog." In *Questions and Answers: Strategies for Using the Electronic Reference Collection,* ed. Linda C. Smith, 14–33. Papers presented at the 1987 Clinic on Library Applications of Data Processing, April 5–7, 1987. Urbana-Champaign, IL: Graduate School of Library and Information Science, University of Illinois at Urbana-Champaign, 1989B.

_____. *The Online Catalogue: Developments and Directions.* London: The Library Association, 1989C.

Hill, Janet Swan. "Online Classification Number Access: Some Practical Considerations." *Journal of Academic Librarianship* 10 (March 1984): 17–22.

Holley, Robert P. "Classification in the Online Catalog." In *Advance in Library Automation and Networking,* vol. 1, ed. Joe A. Hewitt, 57–88. Greenwich, CT: JAI Press, 1987.

Holloway, Carson. "The Online Catalog: Teaching the User." *RQ* 25 (Winter 1985): 191–914.

Holmes, David, and Derrick Bulger. "A Day in the Life of a Public Terminal—A Transaction Analysis of an Online Catalogue Terminal in a Bilingual Environment." *The Canadian Journal of Information Science* 13 (December 1988): 21–33.

Hood, Webster F. "The Aristotelian Versus the Heideggerian Approach to the Problem of Technology." In *Phlosophy and Technology: Readings in the Philosophical Problems of Technology*, ed. Carl Mitcham and Robert Mackey, 347–363. New York: Free Press, 1983.

Jamieson, Alexis J., and M. Elizabeth Dolan. *University Library Experience with Remote Access to Online Catalogs.* (London, Ontario, Canada: University of Western Ontario), Arlington, VA: ERIC ED 267 805, November 1985. 39 pp.

Jamieson, Alexis J., Elizabeth Dolan and Luc Declerck. "Keyword Searching vs. Authority Control in an Online Catalog." *Journal of Academic Librarianship* 12 (November 1986): 277–283.

Jones, C. Lee. "Library Patrons in an Age of Discontinuity: Artifacts of Technology." *Journal of Academic Librarianship* 10 (July 1984): 151–154.

Jones, Richard. "Improving Okapi: Transaction Log Analysis of Failed Searches in an Online Catalogue." *Vine* 62 (May 1986): 3–13.

Kalin, Sarah G. W. "Remote Access to Online Catalogs: A Public Services Perspective." In *2nd National Conference on Integrated Online Library Systems, September 13–14, 1984*, ed. David C. Genaway, 206–212. Atlanta, GA: Genaway and Associates, 1984.

Kalin, Sally Wayman. "The Invisible Users of Online Catalogs: A Public Services Perspective." *Library Trends* 35 (4) (Spring 1987): 587–595.

Kaske, Neal K. "Studies of Online Catalogs." In *Online Catalogs, Online Reference: Converging Trends*, ed. Brian Aveney and Brett Butler, 20–30. Chicago, IL: American Library Association, 1984.

————. "The Variability and Intensity Over Time of Subject Searching in an Online Public Access Catalog." *Information Technology and Libraries* 7 (September 1988A): 273–287.

————. "A Comparative Study of Subject Searching in an OPAC among Branch Libraries of a University Library System." *Information Technology and Libraries* 7 (4) (December 1988B): 359–372.

Kern-Simirenko, Cheryl. "OPAC User Logs: Implication for Bibliographic Instruction." *Library Hi Tech* 1 (Winter 1983): 27–35.

Kilgour, Frederick G. "Design of Online Catalogs." In *The Nature and Future of the Catalog*, ed. Maurice J. Freedman and S. Michael Malinconico, 34–45. Phoenix, AZ: Oryx Press, 1979.

————. "The Online Catalog Revolution." *Library Journal* 110 (February 15, 1984): 319–321.

————. "Toward 100 Percent Availability." *Library Journal* 114 (19) (November 15, 1989): 50–53.

Kiresen, Evelyn-Margaret M. "Studying Dial-Up Use at UC Berkeley." *DLA Bulletin* 7 (December 1987): 12–14.

Klemperer, Katharina. "New Dimensions for the Online Catalog: The Dartmouth College Library Experience." *Information Technology and Libraries* 8 (2) (June 1989): 138–145.

Knutson, Gunnar. "A Comparison of Online and Card Catalog Accuracy." *Library Resources and Technical Services* 34 (1) (January 1990): 24–35.

Kuhlthau, Carol Collier. "Logitudinal Case Studies of the Information Search Process of Users in Libraries." *Library and Information Science Research* 10 (July 1988): 257–304.

Lacey, Paul A. "Views of a Luddite." *College and Research Libraries* 43 (March 1982): 110–118.

Lane, Liz. "Online Public Access Catalogs: A Selective Annotated Bibliography." In *Library Hi Tech Bibliography*, 99–106. Ann Arbor, MI: Pierian Press, 1986.

Larson, Ray R. *Users Look at Online Catalogs: Part 2: Interacting with Online Catalogs; Final Report to the Council on Library Resources.* Berkeley, CA: University of California, April 1983. ERIC ED 231 401. 105 pp.

Larson, Ray R., and Vicki Graham. "Monitoring and Evaluating MELVYL." *Information Technology and Libraires* 2 (1) (March 1983): 93–104.

Lawry, Martha. "Subject Access in the Online Catalog: Is the Medium Projecting the Correct Message?" *Research Strategies* 4 (Summer 1986): 125–131.

Leder, Drew. "The Rule of the Device: Borgmann's Philosophy of Technology." *Philosophy Today* 32 (Spring 1988): 17–29.

Levinson, Paul. *Mind at Large: Knowing in the Technological Age.* Research in Philosophy and Technology, Supplement 2. Greenwich, CT: JAI Press, 1988.

Lewis, David W. "Research on the Use of Online Catalogs and Its Implications for Library Practice." *Journal of Academic Librarianship* 13 (July 1987): 152–157.

———. "Inventing the Electronic University." *College and Research Libraries* 49 (4) (July 1988): 291–304.

Lipetz, Ben-Ami, and Peter J. Paulson. "A Study of the Impact of Introducing an Online Subject Catalog at the New York State Library." *Library Trends* 35 (4) (Spring 1987): 597–617.

Lipow, Anne Grodzins. "The Online Catalog: Exceeding Our Grasp." *American Libraries* 20 (9) (October 1989): 862–865.

Loder, Michael W. "Remote Searching an Online Catalog Using 'Checkoutable' Microcomputers." *Library Software Review* 7 (1) (January/February 1988): 3–5.

Lunde, Diane B., and Nora S. Copeland. "Online Catalog Use Studies: Part II." In *Library Hi Tech Bibliography, Volume 4*, ed. C. Edward Wall, 99–112. Ann Arbor, MI: Pierian Press, 1989.

Lynch, Clifford A. "Large Database and Multiple Database Problems in Online Catalogs." In *OPACs and Beyond: Proceedings of a Joint Meeting of the British Library, DBMIST, and OCLC*, 51–55. Dublin, OH: OCLC Online Computer Library Center, 1989A.

———. "From Telecommunications to Networking: The MELVYL Online Union Catalog and the Development of Intercampus Networks at the University of California." *Library Hi Tech* 7 (2) (1989B): 61–83.

Lynch, Clifford A., and Michael G. Berger. "The UC MELVYL MEDLINE System: A Pilot Project for Access to Journal Literature through an Online Catalog." *Information Technology and Libraries* 8 (4) (December 1989): 371–383.

Machovec, George S. "Administrative Considerations in Establishing Remote Dial-In Access to an Online Catalog." *Online Libraries and Microcomputers* 6 (4) (April 1988): 1–5.

Magrath, Lynn L. "The Public and the Computer: Reactions to a Second Generation Online Catalog." *Library Trends* 37 (4) (Spring 1989): 532–537.

Mandel, Carol A. "Enriching the Library Catalog Record for Subject Access." *Library Resources and Technical Services* 29 (1) (January/March 1985): 5–15.

Markey, Karen. *Subject Searching in Library Catalogs: Before and After the Introduction of Online Catalogs.* Dublin, OH: OCLC, 1984.

———. "Users and the Online Catalog: Subject Access Problems." In *The Impact of Online Catalogs*, ed. Joseph R. Matthews, 35–69. New York: Neal-Schuman, 1986.

Martin, Lowell Arthur. *Adults and the Pratt Library: A Question of the Quality of Life.* Baltimore, MD: Enoch Pratt Free Library, 1974.

Matthews, Joseph R. *Public Access to Online Catalogs.* 2d ed. New York: Neal-Schuman, 1985.

Matthews, Joseph R., ed. *The Impact of Online Catalogs.* New York: Neal-Schuman, 1986.

Matthews, Joseph R. and Lawrence, Gary S. "Further Analysis of the CLR Online Catalog Project." *Information Technology and Libraries* 3 (4) (December 1984): 354–376.

Matthews, Joseph R., Gary S. Lawrence, and Douglas K. Ferguson, eds. *Using Online Catalogs: A Nationwide Survey: A Report of a Study Sponsored by the Council on Library Resources.* New York: Neal-Schuman, 1983.

McCandless, Patricia, et al. *The Invisible User: User Needs Assessment for Library Public Services.* University of Illinois, final report from the Public services Research Projects. Washington, DC: Association of Research Libraries, Office of Management Studies, 1985. ERIC ED 255 227.

Miksa, Francis L. *Research Patterns and Research Libraries.* Dublin, OH: OCLC, 1987. An OCLC Occasional Paper. Text of an address given at the Fifth Annual Conference of Directors of Research Libraries in OCLC, March 30, 1987.

Mitev, Nathalie N., and E. N. Efthimiadis. *A Classified Bibliography on Online Public Access Catalogues.* London: British Library, 1987.

Molholt, Pat. "On Converging Paths: The Computing Center and the Library." *Journal of Academic Librarianship* 11 (November 1985): 284–288.

————. "Research Issues in Information Access." In *Rethinking the Library in the Information Age*, vol. 2: 93–113. Washington, DC: U.S. Department of Education, Office of Library Programs, 1988.

————. "What Happened to the Merger Debate?" *Journal of Academic Librarianship* 15 (2) (May 1989): 96a–96b. Issue 13 of the center insert, "Libraries and Computing Centers: Issues of Mutual Concern."

Moore, Carole Weiss. "User Reactions to Online Catalogs: An Exploratory Study." *College and Research Libraries* 42 (2) (July 1981): 295–302.

Moore, Mary Jean. "Coming into the Catalog: Remote Access Update." *DLA Bulletin* 8 (4) (Winter 1988): 4–5, 24.

Moran, Thomas P. "An Applied Psychology of the User." *ACM Computing Surveys* 13 (1) (March 1981): 1–11.

Morris, Dilys E. "Electronic Information and Technology: Impact and Potential for Academic Libraries." *College and Research Libraries* 50 (1) (January 1989): 56–64.

Neff, Raymond K. "Merging Libraries and Computer Centers: Manifest Destiny or Manifestly Deranged? An Academic Services Perspective." *EDUCOM Bulletin* 20 (Winter 1985): 8–12, 16.

Nielsen, Brian. "What They Say They Do and What They Do: Assessing Online Catalog Use Instruction through Transaction Monitoring." *Information Technology and Libraries* 5 (March 1986): 28–34.

————. "The Role of the Public Services Librarian: The New Revolution." In *Rethinking the Library in the Information Age*, vol. 2, 179–200. Washington, DC: U.S. Department of Education, Office of Library Programs, 1988.

Nielsen, Brian, and Betsy Baker. "Educating the Online Catalog User: A Model Evaluation Study." *Library Trends* 35 (Spring 1987): 571–585.

Nielsen, Brian, Betsy Baker, and Beth Sandore. "Educating the Online Catalog User: A Model for Instructional Development and Evaluation." Final Report on

CLR Grant No. 2055, January 5, 1985. Bethesda, MD: ERIC Document Reproduction Service, 1986. 196pp. ERIC ED 261 679.

Noble, Grant, and Steve O'Connor. "Attitudes Toward Technology as Predictors of Online Catalog Usage." *College and Research Libraries* 47 (November 1986): 605–610.

Norden, David J., and Gail Herndon Lawrence. "Public Terminal Use in an Online Catalog: Some Preliminary Results." *College and Research Libraries* 42 (2) (July 1981): 308–316.

O'Connor, Stephen V. "Learning a Living: Attitudes Toward, and Acceptance of, On-Line Public Access Catalogues." *Australian Academic and Research Libraries* 155 (September 1984): 143–156.

OPACs and Beyond: Proceedings of a Joint Meeting of the British Library, DBMIST [Direction des Bibliotèques, des Musées et de l'Information Scientifique et Technique], and OCLC. Dublin, OH: OCLC Online Computer Library Center, 1989.

Pease, Sue, and Mary Gouke. "Patterns of Use in an Online Catalog and a Card Catalog." *College and Research Libraries* 43 (July 1982): 279–291.

Penniman, W. David, and W. D. Dominick. "Monitoring and Evaluation of On-Line Information System Usage." *Information Processing and Management* 16 (1980): 17–35.

Peters, Thomas A. "When Smart People Fail: An Analysis of the Transaction Log of an Online Public Access Catalog." *Journal of Academic Librarianship* 15 (5) (November 1989): 267–273.

Peters, Thomas A., and Martin Kurth. "Online Catalog Title Keyword and Controlled Vocabulary Subject Searching During the Same Dial Access Search Session." Poster session presented at the 109th Annual Conference of the American Library Association, Chicago, Il, June 24, 1990.

Pfaffenberger, Bryan. *Democratizing Information: Online Databases and the Rise of End-User Searching.* Boston, MA: G. K. Hall, 1990.

Pitkin, Gary M. "CARL's Latest Project: Access to Articles Through the Online Catalog." *American Libraries* 19 (October 1988): 769–770.

Potter, William Gray. "Readers in Search of Authors: The Changing Face of the Middleman." *Wilson Library Bulletin* 60 (8) (April 1986): 20–23.

Power, Colleen. "Out of the Catalog: The New Renaissance." *Technical Services Quarterly* 1 (1) (Fall 1983): 111–116.

Prabha, Chandra. "Managing Large Retrievals: A Problem of the 1990s?" In *OPACs and Beyond: Proceedings of a Joint Meeting of the British Library, DBMIST, and OCLC,* 33–38. Dublin, Oh: OCLC Online Computer Library Center, 1989.

Quint, Barbara Gilder. "Journal Article Coverage in Online Library Catalogs: The Next Stage for Online Databases?" *Online* 11 (1) (January 1987): 87–90.

Ready, Sandra. "Putting the Online Catalog in Its Place." *Research Strategies* 2 (3) (Summer 1984): 119–127.

Reid, T. R. "Computer Access System Brings the Library Home." *Washington Post,* September 2, 1989, 3.

Rice, James. "End-User Management of Information from Online Search Services and Online Public Access Catalogs." *Microcomputers for Information Management* 4 (4) (December 1987): 303–317.

_____. "The Dream of the Memex." *American Libraries* 19 (January 1988A): 14–17.

_____. "Microcomputer Database Management Systems that Interface with Online Public Access Catalogs." *Reference Services Review* 16 (1–2) (1988B): 57–60.

————. "Managing Bibliographic Information with Personal Desktop Technology." *Academe* 75 (4) (July–August 1989A): 18–21.

————. "MicroLIAS: From the Library to Your Personal Files." *Database* 12 (6) (December 1989B): 77–83.

Riggs, Donald E., and Gordon A. Sabine, eds. *Libraries in the '90s: What the Leaders Expect.* Phoenix, AZ: Oryx Press, 1988.

Rochell, Carleton C. "The Next Decade: Distributed Access to Information." *Library Journal* 112 (February 1, 1987): 42–48.

Roose, Tina. "Computer Databases as 1980s Reference Tools: Still a Long Way to Go." *Library Journal* 113 (September 1, 1988): 144–145.

————. "Online Catalogs: Making Them Better Reference Tools." *Library Journal* 113 (December 1988): 76–77.

Roth, Dana L. "Extending the Online Catalog." In *Questions and Answers: Strategies for Using the Electronic Reference Collection*, ed. Linda C. Smith, 34–37. Urbana-Champaign, IL: Graduate School of Library and Information Science, University of Illinois at Urbana-Champaign, 1989.

Sack, John R. "Open Systems for Open Minds: Building the Library Without Walls." *College and Research Libraries* 47 (November 1986): 535–544.

Saracevic, Tefko. "Cognitive Patterns in Online Searching." In *Information Seeking: Basing Services on Users' Behaviors*, ed. Jana Varlejs, 24–39. Jefferson, NC: McFarland, 1987.

Saracevic, Tefko, and Paul Kantor. "A Study of Information Seeking and Retrieving, II. Users, Questions, and Effectiveness." *Journal of the American Society for Information Science* 39 (May 1988): 177–196.

————. "A Study of Information Seeking and Retrieving, III. Searchers, Searches, and Overlap." *Journal of the American Society for Information Science* 39 (May 1988): 197–216.

Saracevic, Tefko, Paul Kantor, Alice Chamis, and Donna Trivison. *Experiments on the Cognitive Aspects of Information Seeking and Information Retrieving.* Washington, DC: National Technical Information Service, 1986. 577pp. ERIC ED 281 530.

————. "A Study of Information Seeking and Retrieving, I. Background and Methodology." *Journal of the American Society for Information Science* 39 (May 1988): 161–176.

Schuyler, Michael, ed. *Dial In: An Annual Guide to Library Online Public Access Catalogs in North America.* Westport, CT: Meckler, in press.

Sherby, Louise Sharon. "The Design and Implementation of an Online Public Access Catalog in a Large, Multi-Unit Library: A Case Study." Ph.D. diss., Columbia University, 1987.

Sloan, Bernard G. "High Tech/Low Profile: Automation and the Invisible Patron." *Library Journal* 111 (18) (November 1, 1986): LC 4, 6.

Smith, Philip J. "An Analysis of Human Errors in the Use of an Online Library Catalog System." In *IEEE 1985 Proceedings of the International Conference on Cybernetics and Society, Tucson, AZ, November 12–15, 1985*, 273–275. New York: IEEE, 1985.

Steinberg, David, and Paul Metz. "User Response to and Knowledge About an Online Catalog." *College and Research Libraries* 45 (1) (January 1984): 66–70.

Stevens, Norman D. "The Catalog of the Future: A Speculative Essay." *Journal of Library Automation* 13 (2) (June 1980): 88–95.

Stoksik, Pamela. "Random Thoughts on On-Line Catalogues." *Canadian Library Journal* 42 (April 1985): 53.

Stone, Peter. "Remote Access to OPACs and the Use of Electronic Mail in University Libraries: Development in the Use of Joint Academic Network (JANET)." *Vine* 63 (1986): 28–30.

Sullivan, Patricia, and Peggy Seiden. "Educating Online Catalog Users: The Protocol Assessment of Needs." *Library Hi Tech* 3 (2) (1985): 11–19.

Sutton, Brett. "Extending the Online Public Access Catalog into the Microcomputer Environment." *Information Technology and Libraries* 9 (1) (March 1990): 43–52.

Svenonius, Elaine. "Use of Classification in Online Retrieval." *Library Resources and Technical Services* 27 (1) (January/March 1983): 76–80.

Swanson, Don R. "Information Retrieval as a Trial-and-Error Process." *Library Quarterly* 47 (2) (April 1977): 128–148.

_____. "Libraries and the Growth of Knowledge." *Library Quarterly* 49 (1) (January 1979): 3–25.

Tague, Jean M. "Negotiation at the OPAC Interface." In *The Online Catalogue: Developments and Directions*, ed. Charles Hildreth, 47–60. London: Library Association, 1989.

Taylor, Robert Saxton. *Value-Added Processes in Information Systems.* Norwood, NJ: Ablex, 1986.

Tolle, John E. *Current Utilization of Online Catalogs: Transaction Analysis.* Dublin, OH: OCLC, 1983A. OCLC/OPR/RR-83/2.

_____. "Understanding Patrons' Use of Online Catalogs: Transaction Log Analysis of the Search Method." In *Productivity in the Information Age: Proceedings of the 46th ASIS Annual Meeting 1983*, ed. Raymond F. Vondran, Anne Caputo, Carol Wasserman, and Richard A. V. Diener, 167–171. White Plains, NY: Knowledge Industry Publications, 1983B.

_____. "Monitoring Usage of Online Information Systems NLM CATLINE Database." In Barbara Flood, Joane Witiak, and Thomas Hogan, compilers. *1984: Challenges to an Information Society–Proceedings of the 47th ASIS Annual Meeting.* White Plains, NY: Knowledge Industry Publications, 1984.

_____. "Online Search Patterns: NLM CATLINE Database." *Journal of the American Society for Information Science* 36 (March 1985): 82–93.

Tolle, John E., and S. Hah. "Online Search Patterns: NLM CATLINE Database." *Journal of the American Society for Information Science* 36 (2) (1985): 82–93.

Tolle, John E., Patricia Somers, and Christine L. Borgman. "Session 8: User Behavior." *SIGIR Forum* 17 (4) (Summer 1983): 146–176.

Tullis, Thomas S. "An Evaluation of Alphanumeric, Graphic, and Color Information Displays." *Human Factors* 23 (5) (October 1981): 541–550.

Turkel, Sherry. *The Second Self: Computers and the Human Spirit.* New York: Simon and Schuster, 1984.

Tyckoson, David. "The 98% Solution: The Failure of the Catalog and the Role of Electronic Databases." *Technicalities* 9 (2) (February 1989): 8–12.

University of California. *University of California Users Look at MELVYL: Results of a Survey of Users of the University of California Prototype Online Union Catalog; Part 1, Final Report.* Berkeley, CA: Division of Library Automation and Library Studies and Research Division, University of California, 1983. ERIC ED 231 400.

Van Houweling, Douglas E. "The Information Technology Environment of Higher Education." In *Campus of the Future: Conference on Information Resources*, 61–106. Dublin, OH: OCLC, 1987.

Van Pulis, Noelle. *User and Staff Education for the Online Catalog.* June 1985. 19 pp. ERIC ED 257 478.

Van Pulis, Noelle, and Lorene E. Ludy. "Subject Searching in an Online Catalog with Authority Control." *College and Research Libraries* 49 (November 1988): 523–533.

Varlejs, Jana, ed. *Information Seeking: Basing Services on Users' Behaviors.* Jefferson, NC: McFarland, 1987.

Walker, Stephen. "Improving Subject Access Painlessly: Recent Work on the OKAPI Online Catalogue Projects." *Program* 22 (1) (January 1988): 21–31.

Wall, C. Edward. "The Library as Institutional File Server." *Library Hi Tech* 7 (1) (1989): 5.

Walter, Dennis R. "The User at the Online Catalogue: A Record of Unsuccessful Keyword Searches—Another Case Study" *LASIE* 18 (November/December 1987): 74–83.

Walton, Carol, Susan Williamson, and Howard D. White. "Resistance to Online Catalogs: A Comparative Study at Bryn Mawr and Swarthmore Colleges." *Library Resources and Technical Services* 30 (October/December 1986): 388–401.

Weber, David C. "University Libraries and Campus Information Technology Organizations: Who is in Charge Here?" In *Computing, Electronic Publishing and Information Technology: Their Impact on Academic Libraries,* ed. Robin Downes, 5–19. New York: Haworth Press, 1988.

Webster, Frank, and Kevin Robins. *Information Technology: A Luddite Analysis.* Norwood, NJ: Ablex, 1986.

Weiskel, Timothy C. "Libraries as Life-Systems: Information, Entropy, and Coevolution on Campus." *College and Research Libraries* 47 (November 1986): 545–563.

————. "University Libraries, Integrated Scholarly Information Systems (ISIS), and the Changing Character of Academic Research." *Library Hi Tech* 6 (4) (1988): 7–27.

————. "The Electronic Library and the Challenge of Information Planning." *Academe* 75 (4) (July–August 1989): 8–12.

Weller, Ann C. "A Study of Remote Users' Satisfaction with Online Services Before and After Procedural Modifications." *Bulletin of the Medical Library Association* 73 (1985): 352–357.

Whitener, Lynn. "Personal Bibliographic Software for an Online Catalog." *Computers in Libraries* 9 (January 1989): 26–27.

Williams, Martha E. "Transparent Information Systems Through Gateways, Front Ends, Intermediaries, and Interfaces." *Journal of the American Society for Information Science* 37 (1986): 204–214.

Wilson, Patrick. *Second-Hand Knowledge: An Inquiry into Cognitive Authority.* Westport, CT: Greenwood Press, 1983.

————. "The Catalog as Access Mechanism: Background and Concepts." *Library Resources and Technical Services* 27 (1) (January/March 1983): 4–17.

Winner, Langdon. *The Whale and the Reactor: A Search for Limits in an Age of High Technology.* Chicago, IL: University of Chicago Press, 1986.

Woelfl, N. N. "Individual Differences in Online Search Behavior: The Effect of Learning Styles and Cognitive Abilities on Process and Outcome." Ph.D. diss., Case Western University, Cleveland, OH, 1984. *DAI* 46 (1) (July 1985): 7A.

Woodsworth, Anne. "Computing Centers and Libraries as Cohorts: Exploiting Mutual Strengths." In *Computing, Electronic Publishing and Information Technology: Their Impact on Academic Libraries,* ed. Robin Downes, 21–34. New York: Haworth Press, 1988.

Zimmerman, Michael E. *Heidegger's Confrontation with Modernity: Technology, Politics, and Art.* Bloomington, IN: Indiana University Press, 1990.

Index